Mental Time Travel

Life and Mind: Philosophical Issues in Biology and Psychology

Kim Sterelny and Robert A. Wilson, Series Editors

Mental Time Travel

Episodic Memory and Our Knowledge of the Personal Past

Kourken Michaelian

The MIT Press
Cambridge, Massachusetts
London, England

This book was set in Stone Serif Std by Toppan Best-set Premedia Limited. Printed and bound in the United States of America.

Library of Congress Cataloging-in-Publication Data

Michaelian, Kourken, author.
Mental time travel : episodic memory and our knowledge of the personal past / Kourken Michaelian.
Cambridge, MA : MIT Press, [2015] | Series: Life and mind: philosophical issues in biology and psychology | Includes bibliographical references and index.
LCCN 2015038327 | ISBN 9780262034098 (hardcover : alk. paper)
LCSH: Memory (Philosophy) | Episodic memory. | Knowledge, Theory of.
LCC BD181.7 .M53 2015 | DDC 128/.3—dc23 LC record available at
http://lccn.loc.gov/2015038327

10 9 8 7 6 5 4 3 2 1

To Lora and Martin

Out of the same storehouse, with these past impressions, I can construct now this, now that, image of things that I either have experienced or have believed on the basis of experience—and from these I can further construct future actions, events, and hopes; and I can meditate on all these things as if they were present.

—Augustine (398)

Contents

Preface

This book is about the nature of memory and memory knowledge. Though it adopts a firmly interdisciplinary approach and hence is meant to be of interest to both philosophers and psychologists—indeed, it treats the psychology of memory as the appropriate foundation for the philosophy of memory—the questions of the nature of memory and memory knowledge remain recognizably philosophical, if only in their generality. These questions are in fact perfectly traditional in philosophy of mind and epistemology (the theory of knowledge), and the answers developed here build both on psychological research and on philosophical theory. There is, however, less of the latter than might be hoped. It is perhaps rhetorically ill-advised to adopt a pessimistic tone in the preface to a book, but honesty compels a certain degree of pessimism in this case, for, despite the long history of philosophical interest in memory, neither memory nor memory knowledge has enjoyed much prominence in philosophy in recent years.

The current situation in the epistemology of memory is roughly analogous to the situation in the epistemology of testimony as it was prior to the appearance of Coady's landmark study (1992): there is general agreement that memory is of central importance to epistemology, but the number of epistemologists actually specializing in memory knowledge and the overall quantity of work being done in the area remain relatively low. Whereas things have changed dramatically in the epistemology of testimony in recent years, the situation in the epistemology of memory has remained nearly static. The entry in the *Stanford Encyclopedia of Philosophy* on the epistemology of memory, for example, cites a mere five works published since 2000 (Senor 2013), while that on the epistemology of testimony cites too many to count at a glance (Adler 2013). The number of citation-worthy books and articles on the epistemology of memory published during the relevant period is, of course, much larger than this would suggest, but the case is representative of a more general trend. To illustrate, Google Scholar searches for works appearing between 1990 and 2014 using "epistemology of testimony" and "epistemology of memory" as search terms return 893 and 91 results, respectively.

Indeed, from a certain point of view, the current situation in the epistemology of memory may even be worse than the situation in the epistemology of testimony was prior to Coady's book: while epistemologists at that point often simply disregarded testimony, epistemologists today typically acknowledge the centrality of memory in principle, but nevertheless assign it little importance in practice. The relatively high level of activity in the epistemology of testimony may actually provide a partial explanation of the lower level of activity in the epistemology of memory, since testimony and memory are often seen as analogous sources of knowledge (e.g., Burge 1993; Dummett 1994), which can lead to a tendency to assume that views developed in the epistemology of testimony apply, mutatis mutandis, to the epistemology of memory as well. To take just one recent example, eight chapters of Lackey's book are devoted to working out a detailed account of testimonial knowledge, after which a mere appendix is given over to arguing that a specific claim about the nature of testimonial knowledge applies to memory knowledge as well (Lackey 2008). The claim in question is important (see chapter 5 below); nevertheless, the book is symptomatic of a more general tendency in its treatment of the epistemology of memory as a (literal) appendix to the epistemology of testimony.

The relative lack of research on memory in epistemology is no doubt due in part to contingent sociological factors, but it may ultimately be due primarily to the continuing influence of an overly simple model of memory, a model according to which remembering is a process dedicated to preserving beliefs along with their epistemic status. (There are of course epistemologists who reject this view, including—within limits—Lackey.) If the simple model were accurate, there would indeed be relatively little to say about memory knowledge. But it is not. One aim of this book is to demonstrate that, when the simple model—which is both uninformed by and inconsistent with the rich body of theory and data coming from psychology—is replaced by a more adequate model of memory, the importance of the epistemology of memory becomes dramatically more apparent.

In fact, it is only once an empirically adequate answer to the question of the nature of remembering is in place that the difficulty of the question of the nature of memory knowledge becomes clear. The divergence between our simple, intuitive model of memory as a kind of passive internal storage device and the messy reality of constructive, simulational remembering is so great that one natural reaction, once we have grasped its extent, is to conclude that, though we ordinarily take for granted that remembering is a source of knowledge, memory beliefs may simply fail to measure up to the standards for knowledge. In short, in light of the psychology of memory, the possibility that memory can give us knowledge of the past can begin to seem not only mysterious but even unlikely, raising the threat of skepticism about memory knowledge. Responding to this skeptical threat is one key task of the book.

In philosophy of mind, the quantity of research on memory is somewhat larger, probably due to the fact that philosophy of mind tends to receive more direct stimulation from psychology, in which memory has always been a central area of research (Knobe 2015). Nevertheless, there have been relatively few recent attempts to deal systematically with the implications of that research. Sutton's influential book, which builds on connectionist approaches to develop a systematic view of remembering, is now nearly two decades old (Sutton 1998). Bernecker's recent books (2008, 2010) are tightly argued, but by and large do not attempt to take nonphilosophical work into account. There is thus a major gap in the philosophical literature on memory. The present book aims to fill that gap, developing a systematic philosophical view of remembering based on current empirical research.

The lack of prominence enjoyed by memory in recent philosophy of mind may, again, be due in part to purely sociological factors, but the popularity enjoyed by Martin and Deutscher's (1966) causal theory of memory has likely also played a role, leading to a widespread impression that one of the main tasks of the philosophy of memory, namely the so-called analysis of memory—that is, the development of a general theory of remembering—is already largely accomplished. Another key task of this book is to show that, while it has indeed turned out to be surprisingly resilient, current psychological research on constructive memory in general and mental time travel in particular suggests that it is time to move beyond the causal theory.

While there is less recent work on the philosophy of memory than might be hoped, there is also reason for optimism, as there are signs that things may be changing for the better. To the extent that change is afoot, it is driven largely by the increasingly interdisciplinary character of memory research. Memory, of course, remains an extremely active area of research in psychology, and the accelerating pace of research on mental time travel, in particular, is leading some researchers to turn to philosophical work on memory in a search for frameworks capable of making sense of provocative experimental findings; philosophers, in turn, are themselves increasingly aware of mental time travel research. This new interdisciplinary work is discussed throughout the book, which aims, by simultaneously interpreting current (nonphilosophical) research on memory and developing (philosophical) ideas that may be of use in future research, to contribute both to philosophy *of* cognitive science and to philosophy *in* cognitive science (Brook 2009). The book is thus meant, above all, to contribute to the tendency toward increased interdisciplinary interaction in memory research.

Acknowledgments

It would be accurate but misleading to say that I put this book together in about six months of largely solitary work in my office in Ankara. In fact, the book is one outcome of a line of research pursued over the course of several years, during which I was supported by institutions in five countries and colleagues in many more.

I began to work on the epistemology of memory while in the Ph.D. program at the University of Massachusetts, and a number of the ideas presented here originated in that period, during which I was funded by the Social Sciences and Humanities Research Council of Canada. These ideas, which form the basis of chapters 2, 4, and 5, were sharpened by discussion with my thesis committee—Hilary Kornblith, Louise Antony, Charles Clifton, and Jonathan Schaffer—with the members of Hilary's thesis group, and with many of my colleagues in the program, especially Indrani Bhattacharjee and Namjoong Kim, as well as by feedback from Sven Bernecker, Rob Rupert, and John Sutton.

The momentum that my research acquired at UMass was reinforced during my postdoc at the Institut Jean-Nicod, where I was part of a group project funded by the French Agence Nationale de la Recherche and led by Claudine Tiercelin and Joëlle Proust. Our group—including Anne Coubray, Anna Loussouarn, and Conor McHugh—provided an exceptionally dynamic working environment. The same thing goes for the institute as a whole, and my work benefitted especially from discussions with Reinaldo Bernal Velásquez, Fabio Del Prete, Jérôme Dokic, Pierre Jacob, Markus Kneer, Elisabeth Pacherie, and Marina Trakas. Chapter 8 derives from an article written during this period, the argument of which was also improved by comments from a number of audiences, including a seminar at the University of Edinburgh (thanks especially to Andy Clark and Duncan Pritchard); the Justification Revisited conference at the University of Geneva in 2010 (thanks to Pascal Engel); the Aristotelian Society/Mind joint sessions held at University College Dublin in 2010; and the 2010 conference of the Société Française de Psychologie at the Université Charles-de-Gaulle Lille 3. Thanks also to the members of Joëlle's metacognition reading group for detailed feedback and to Chris Lepock and Jennifer Nagel for sharing relevant unpublished work.

Chapter 7 likewise grows out of an article written during this period. My understanding of the impact of communication on memory was improved by feedback from audiences at the 2010 meeting of the European Society for Philosophy and Psychology (thanks especially to my co-symposiasts—Fiona Gabbert, Lorraine Hope, and John Sutton—and to Luca Barlassina); a 2010 meeting of the KnowJust seminar at the Institut Jean-Nicod; the 2010 conference of the Italian Society for Analytic Philosophy at the Università degli Studi di Padova; a 2010 meeting of the Research Colloquium in Philosophy and Cognitive Science at the Ruhr-Universität Bochum (thanks to Anika Fiebich, Albert Newen, and Markus Werning); the 2011 Communication and Cognition conference at the University of Neuchâtel (thanks to Dan Sperber); and a seminar at the University of Illinois Urbana-Champaign (thanks to Rob Cummins). Thanks also to Tim Levine and Hee Sun Park, who provided invaluable advice on my use of their probability model.

Early work on the relationship between source monitoring and process monitoring was presented to audiences at the Copenhagen Conference in Epistemology organized in 2011 by the Social Epistemology Research Group at Copenhagen University (thanks to Kristoffer Ahlstrom, Mikkel Gerkken, Alvin Goldman, Klemens Kappel, and Ronnie de Sousa); the Brains, Minds, and Language workshop at Boğaziçi University in 2012 (thanks to Albert Ali Salah, Mark Steen, and Lucas Thorpe); and a meeting at Lund University in 2012 (thanks to Frank Zenker). Thanks also to Sam Wilkinson for written comments. Chapter 9 itself was produced after I moved to Bilkent University. Versions were presented at the 2012 meeting of the European Epistemology Network in Bologna and Modena (thanks to Carla Bagnoli and Chiara Brozzo); a 2013 meeting of the Cognitive Science Colloquium at Middle East Technical University (thanks to Cem Bozşahin, Annette Hohenberger, and Deniz Zeyrek); and seminars at Cardiff University (thanks to

Alessandra Tanesini), Queen's University Belfast (thanks to Teresa McCormack), and University College Dublin (thanks to Maria Baghramian). This material was further shaped by feedback from Matt Frise, Mine Mısırlısoy, and an audience at the University of Cologne.

An early version of the simulation theory of memory defended in chapter 6 was also presented at Cologne, where I received stimulating comments from Thomas Grundmann, Joachim Horvath, and Jens Kipper. Karen Shanton shared an unpublished paper in which she defends a distinct simulationist approach to memory; thinking about the differences between her approach and my own helped to clarify the latter.

The account of the evolution of simulational memory in chapters 10 and 11 was shaped by discussion with Stan Klein and by feedback from audiences at the 2014 International Symposium on Brain and Cognitive Science in Istanbul and a 2014 meeting of the Cognitive Science Colloquium at Carleton University (thanks to Andy Brook and Dave Matheson).

My departmental colleagues at Bilkent provided a supportive environment while I was working on the book, with István Aranyosi, Lars Vinx, and Bill Wringe, in particular, providing helpful advice. The final stages of the work were completed after I moved to the University of Otago; thanks especially to Alex Miller for ensuring that I made a smooth transition.

Phil Laughlin at MIT Press did an excellent job of shepherding the manuscript through the submission and evaluation process, securing extremely detailed reports from three reviewers. Since the latter revealed themselves to me as Santiago Arango-Muñoz, Felipe De Brigard, and Celia Harris, I can thank them directly for their reports.

Above all, I want to single out two senior colleagues for thanks. First, Hilary Kornblith at UMass: it will be obvious to anyone who knows his work that Hilary's naturalistic approach to epistemology has exerted a strong influence on my own. In addition to owing him a profound intellectual debt, I'm indebted to Hilary for the invaluable practical guidance that he has continued to give freely since my doctorate. Second, John Sutton at Macquarie University: John's influence on the book will likewise be apparent to anyone familiar with his interdisciplinary work on memory. He, too, has given me more support than I can hope to repay, and, in his case as well, I owe not only a deep intellectual but also a deep practical debt. I consider myself exceptionally lucky to be able to count not just one but two such model scholars as mentors.

Finally, thanks to the publishers for permission to reuse material from the following articles:

- Is memory a natural kind? 2011. *Memory Studies* 4(2): 170–189.
- Generative memory. 2011. *Philosophical Psychology* 24(3): 323–342.
- Metacognition and endorsement. 2012. *Mind & Language* 27(3): 284–307.
- The information effect: Constructive memory, testimony, and epistemic luck. 2013. *Synthese* 190(12): 2429–2456.

In line with the conventions governing acknowledgments sections, I note that I may inadvertently have failed to thank certain colleagues for support they gave. In line with some of the themes of the present book, I note that I may inadvertently have thanked certain other colleagues for support they didn't in fact give. I beg forgiveness in both cases.

I   Epistemology and Human Memory

1   Three Questions about Memory

The argument of this book is driven by three core questions:

- What is memory?
- How does memory give us knowledge?
- When and why did memory emerge?

This introductory chapter first provides a brief review of the philosophical and psychological relevance of each of these questions and then sketches the general plan of the book's argument.

1.1   What Is Memory?

The attempt to say what memory *is* amounts, in the first place, to an attempt to give an informative general characterization of remembering—of what it is for someone to remember something. When contemporary philosophers pursue this project, they typically do so by formulating, more or less explicitly, sets of conditions meant to be individually necessary and jointly sufficient for the truth of statements of the form *S remembers x*. Though the book makes use of this sort of analytic methodology in places, it does so primarily as a matter of convenience. Ultimately, the goal is not to develop a theory that can necessarily be adequately expressed in the form of an analysis, but rather to formulate a useful general framework for thinking about human memory, one that draws out and makes explicit the vision of memory implicit in current psychology and that can in turn contribute to interpreting the findings of and suggesting new lines of inquiry for the latter. Consequently, the reasoning employed here is not confined to the a priori "theory → counterexample → revised theory" style of argumentation associated with *S remembers x*-style theories. The goal, in short, is not to develop an account of remembering immune to all possible counter-examples, no matter how far out, but rather to develop an account that captures what is important about *human* remembering, in particular, as it unfolds in the real world.

Interest in the nature of remembering goes back essentially to the dawn of philosophy, and most major philosophers have had something to say about it (Burnham 1888). This is not the place for a comprehensive historical review—an undertaking which would require a book unto itself—but a few highlights will help to orient us. Early on, we find Aristotle remarking that

one cannot remember the future, but of this one has opinion and expectation ... ; nor can one remember the present, but of this there is sensation; for by sensation we cognise neither the future nor the past but only the present. ... Memory is of the past. (Bloch 2007, 25)

Jumping forward in time, we have Hume (1739) arguing for his well-known vivacity criterion for memory, according to which memory has a distinctive kind of content. More recently, Martin and Deutscher (1966) have influentially argued that memory requires a specific kind of causal connection with the past. All three of these views are intuitively plausible, and all have been widely taken up. All three—the view that memory is of the past, the view that memory and imagination are distinguished by their respective contents, and the view that memory necessarily involves a causal connection with the past—are challenged in this book, and, if its argument succeeds, none survives unscathed.

As the examples of Aristotle, Hume, and Martin and Deutscher suggest, what has driven philosophers to develop general theories of remembering is ultimately a question about demarcating memory from related cognitive phenomena: in virtue of what is it the case that a subject on a given occasion counts as remembering *rather than* undergoing some other cognitive process? Aristotle, for example, is concerned with the difference between remembering, on the one hand, and perception and "expectation," on the other, where expectation coincides roughly with what we refer to today as future-oriented mental time travel (Klein 2013a). Typically, the concern has been with the difference between remembering and imagining, where the latter is construed sufficiently broadly to include a range of forms of imagination in addition to future-oriented mental time travel. Hume's vivacity criterion is intended, on one reading, to capture the difference between remembering events and imagining them. And Martin and Deutscher's causal condition is in part a rival attempt to capture that same difference.

Remembering, like imagining (Kind 2013), is a multifarious phenomenon, but this book is concerned specifically with the form of memory that philosophers have referred to as (simply) memory (Earle 1956), memory par excellence (Bergson 1896), true memory (Russell 1921), perceptual memory (Broad 1925; Malcolm 1963), reminiscence (Ryle 1949), retrospective memory (Furlong 1948), event memory (Ayer 1956), recollection (von Leyden 1961), or personal memory (Locke 1971)—to repeat just part of a list compiled by Brewer (1996). In psychology, Tulving has influentially dubbed this form of memory *episodic* (Tulving 1972, 1983), and the term is increasingly catching on in philosophy (Perrin and Rousset 2014). Episodic memory refers, roughly, to the form of memory responsible for allowing us to revisit specific episodes or events from the personal past. It is typically contrasted with semantic memory, which allows us to recall facts without necessarily giving us access to the episodes in which they were learned. Given that we are interested in distinguishing remembering from imagining, and given that we are interested specifically in episodic memory, the question for the theory of remembering becomes: What distinguishes episodic remembering from episodic imagining?

The distinction between episodic imagination and semantic imagination has been referred to in a variety of ways, including imagination versus supposition (Szabó Gendler 2010), perceptual versus propositional imagination (Currie and Ravenscroft 2002), and enactive imagination versus supposition (Goldman 2006). Semantic imagination is, roughly, the form of imagination responsible for our ability to suppose that something is the case (see Byrne 2007); it is analogous to semantic memory, memory for facts. Episodic imagination, in contrast, is the form of imagination responsible for our ability to entertain possible episodes, just as episodic memory is responsible for the ability to revisit past episodes. The distinction between episodic and semantic imagination may be a matter of degrees (Szpunar et al. 2014); imagining generic events, for example, may draw on both episodic and semantic imagination. But our focus here will be on purely episodic forms of imagination.

The question of how remembering is distinguished from imagining derives some of its philosophical relevance from the question of personal identity. Since Locke (1689), episodic memory has figured centrally in accounts of what makes someone count as the same person over time.[1] While personal identity as such is beyond the scope of this book, there is a loose correspondence between the Lockean view that personal identity is determined by memory and the view current in psychology that memory is constitutive of the self (Cosentino 2011; Rubin 1999). More importantly, we will see that the sense of self turns out to be crucial to the ability to reliably remember the past.

The question of the nature of memory derives additional philosophical relevance from its link to the question of the nature of memory knowledge. It is intuitively plausible that, in order for memory to function as a source of knowledge, there must be a difference in kind between remembering and imagining. While the book will argue that memory can in fact provide knowledge of the past even if there is no such difference, the question of the objective difference between memory—viewed as one form of imagination—and *other* forms of imagination continues to be of crucial importance to epistemology, since it is intimately related to the subjective difference or differences on which agents rely to determine whether they are remembering or imagining; hence the question of the nature of remembering remains a necessary prelude to the epistemology of memory.

The philosophical importance of an account of the nature of remembering is relatively uncontroversial. Are philosophical theories of memory likewise relevant to psychology? The answer may depend, to some extent, on the kind of theory at issue, as some philosophical theories are couched in terms that get little empirical traction. This goes, fairly clearly, for the epistemic theory of memory, according to which memory is, roughly, retained knowledge (see, e.g., Holland 1974; Munsat 1967; Zemach 1968). Arguably, it goes as well for recent accounts such as that defended by Martin (2001), according to which remembering is a matter of retaining "acquaintance," or that defended by Byrne (2010), according to which remembering is a matter of preserving "cognitive contact." Such theories, at any rate, will not be discussed in any detail here.

In contrast, other philosophical theories of remembering—including the empiricist theory, the causal theory, and the simulation theory defended in this book—can indeed be brought into contact with the relevant psychology, though it may in some cases take some work to do so. In fact, the simulation theory—according to which there is no essential difference between remembering and imagining, with memory turning out to be simply one form of imagination among others—is intended in part to be a generalization and synthesis of a cluster of views on the nature and function of memory that have emerged recently in psychology in response to the growing recognition that episodic memory is intimately related to a broad range of episodic constructive processes, including future-oriented mental time travel, episodic counterfactual thinking, and mindreading (Szpunar 2010).

Psychologists may, of course, investigate memory without first having fully defined it (Feest 2011), but, as our understanding of memory deepens, it is appropriate to periodically take stock, as the findings that have accumulated may force us to reevaluate our intuitive understanding of memory. The simulation theory is meant to contribute to such a reevaluation. The theory also aims, more broadly, to contribute to reshaping the metaphors that guide both everyday and scientific thinking about memory. Current popular thinking about memory is largely dominated by the metaphor of computer memory (Michaelian 2012). As Draaisma (2000) has shown, while it is natural for us today to conceive of human memory on the model of computer memory, there is, in light of the extraordinary variety of metaphors that have historically been used to describe memory, little reason to suppose that this particular metaphor will be the last. Indeed, in one respect, the computer metaphor is not even particularly novel: human memory has often been compared to new technologies, in particular to forms of external memory or information storage. Thus Plato (in the *Theaetetus*) compared memory to a wax tablet, and it has since been said to be analogous to libraries, archives, photographs, films, holograms, and so on.

These metaphors represent remembering as being essentially a matter of storing and retrieving fixed items of information. But Draaisma reviews another family of memory metaphors, many of them organic rather than technological, including woods, fields, labyrinths, caves, grottoes, mineshafts, the depths of the sea, palaces, abbeys, and theaters, which represent remembering as a complex, effortful, and failure-prone activity. The existence of this second set of metaphors suggests a recognition of the limited utility of a purely storage-and-retrieval conception and the need for a conception which emphasizes remembering as a process in which the agent actively reconstructs the past. Both of these competing conceptions are alive in contemporary psychology, tracing back to foundational work by Ebbinghaus (1885) and Bartlett (1932), respectively.

Ebbinghaus's work, leading to his famous forgetting curve (describing the way in which successful retrieval reduces exponentially as a function of time), focused on the capacity to remember lists of nonsense syllables. This quantity-oriented conception of memory, which views memory as a sort of storehouse into which arbitrary contents can be placed, was crucial to the establishment of experimental psychology and dominated memory research long after Ebbinghaus, for example in the form of the standard list-learning paradigm. In recent years, however, the rival accuracy-oriented conception (Koriat and Goldsmith 1996), which focuses on the correspondence (or noncorrespondence) between memory and reality, has become increasingly influential, due in part to the increasing salience of memory errors and distortions (Brainerd and Reyna 2005). Bartlett's own research focused in part on the influence of schemas in shaping retrieved content, and similar themes have been prominent in recent memory research, for example, in research on the effects of conversation on what is remembered (Stone et al. 2009).

The theory developed here, with its focus on mental time travel as a simulational process, is meant to reinforce the accuracy-oriented conception of memory. Realistically, however, the tension between quantity-oriented and accuracy-oriented approaches is unlikely to be resolved in the near future, for, while it is difficult to incorporate both views within a single model, each captures an important aspect of the workings of memory. Remembering *is* thoroughly constructive, but the simulation theory, in contrast to some Wittgensteinian views (Moyal-Sharrock 2009; Stern 1991), does assign an important role to information storage. Nevertheless, given the current predominance of the computer metaphor in popular discussions of memory, it may be useful to tip the scales in the other direction.

1.2   How Does Memory Give Us Knowledge?

Memory is sometimes listed as a potential "basic" epistemic source alongside other candidate basic sources, including perception, introspection, inference, and communication. There is no uncontroversial list of basic epistemic sources, however, and it is unclear whether memory is basic in an interestingly strict sense.

Relying on Audi's criterion of epistemic basicness, for example, a source is basic if it yields knowledge without dependence on the operation of some other source (Audi 2002). Given that it depends on input from other sources, memory straightforwardly fails to satisfy this criterion. In fact, however, it is unclear whether *any* source satisfies Audi's criterion. Consider perception, our best candidate for a basic epistemic source. Perception appears to be cognitively penetrable, in the sense that top-down expectations influence visual experience (Vetter and Newen 2014). There is increasing evidence for a multisource model of visual perception, according to which visual input provides only part of the content of visual perception, with perceptual representations in effect being simulations driven by a number of factors, including stored information (Intraub 2010). If this model is on the right track, perception is no more independent of memory than memory is of perception. The criterion may thus simply be too strong to be useful, and memory may satisfy a suitably weakened criterion.

But regardless of whether memory is, strictly speaking, epistemically basic, it is uncontroversial that it is basic in the loose sense of being a *core* epistemic source: take memory away, and much—perhaps virtually all—human knowledge goes along with it, including an apparently distinctively human form of knowledge. As many epistemologists have argued, at any given time, most of our beliefs are not occurrent but merely dispositional—that is, on a natural conception of dispositional belief, they are stored in memory.[2] Moreover, an important—and probably distinctively human (Corballis 2011)—form of knowledge depends on memory in an especially strong sense. It is possible for a subject to gain knowledge of his own past without that knowledge amounting to memory knowledge; for example, one typically learns about one's early childhood through testimony from one's family. But a central form of knowledge of one's past—the sort of knowledge that you can have of your own past but not of anyone else's—depends essentially on (episodic) memory.

There is thus a need for an account of how memory functions as an epistemic source and, in particular, of how it functions to give us knowledge of the personal past. Moreover, once the constructive character of memory is taken into account, the threat of skepticism about memory knowledge looms. This is not Russell-style skepticism, based on the observation that, given that there is no logically or metaphysically necessary connection between an apparent memory and the occurrence of the relevant event, the hypothesis that the world came into existence five minutes ago, complete with our apparent memories, cannot be ruled out (Russell 1921). The threat is, rather, from an empirically grounded form of skepticism. Given the constructive character of remembering, opportunities for error and distortion abound. In light of this, it is far from obvious that memory can meet plausible standards for knowledge—not the impossibly high standards of the traditional skeptic but, as Shanton (2011) has pointed out, moderate, well-motivated standards, including reliability.

This book—the basic epistemological claim of which is that, due in part to the adaptive character of the constructive processes involved in remembering, and due in part to the sensitivity of the metacognitive monitoring processes involved in remembering, episodic memory avoids the threat of unreliability—is in part a response to this skeptical threat, with a focus on the standard of reliability. The second part of this epistemological claim, according to which metacognition (the monitoring and control of mental processes; Dunlosky and Metcalfe 2008; Proust 2010) enables remembering subjects to compensate for the uncertainty introduced by the constructive character of remembering in order to minimize unreliability, requires a fair bit of background before it can be meaningfully unpacked. The first part of the claim is somewhat more straightforward. As Schacter once put it, with memorable understatement, "the output of human memory often differs—sometimes rather substantially—from the input" (1995). The claim defended here is that the principles governing constructive processing in remembering tend to result in "retrieved" memories that are accurate despite departing from the relevant stored information, which itself may depart from the information initially encoded, which in turn may depart from the information contained in the original experience of the relevant episode.

One version of the skeptical worry is based on research on the way in which a subject's memories can be shaped and reshaped by interaction with other agents. The focus of the research in question is not on direct interventions in memory (via, for example, pharmacological agents; see Liao and Sandberg 2008) but rather on the routine incorporation, without the agent's awareness, of communicated information into the apparently purely experiential representations produced by reconstructive memory retrieval. Work by Loftus (1996) and others on this sort of incorporation in the context of eyewitness memory led to the notion of the "misinformation effect," in which the incorporation of testimonial information results in inaccurate (or less accurate) memory for experienced events. It might seem obvious that such incorporation can only decrease the accuracy of memory. But the typical experimental setup in this area focuses precisely on providing subjects with misleading post-event information. If it turns out that, in ecological settings, subjects are more likely to receive accurate than inaccurate post-event information, then the incorporation of testimonial information may actually increase the accuracy of retrieved memories, despite resulting in retrieved memories that depart from the experience of events.

The suggestion is, in effect, that there is a sort of "preestablished harmony" between the way in which memory tends to simulate episodes and the shape of the episodes that we actually experience. This suggestion deliberately echoes Kornblith's claim that there is a preestablished harmony between the way in which we tend to perform inductive inferences, which departs dramatically from the canons of good statistical reasoning, and the way in which the properties we project in our inductive inferences are actually grouped in the world (Kornblith 1995). A priori, our tendency to project properties on the basis of extremely small samples—Tversky and Kahneman's "law of small numbers" (1971)—would appear to bode ill for the possibility of knowledge based on inductive inference. But it turns out, Kornblith argues, that this tendency aligns with relevant patterns of properties in the world in such a way that our inductive inferences are nevertheless reliable. Analogously, the constructive, simulational character of our remembering, as opposed to the sort of purely reproductive, computer-style memory that intuition tells us would be preferable, would seem to be bad news for the possibility of memory knowledge. But it turns out, according to the simulation theory, that the relevant constructive processes are engineered in such a way that remembering is nevertheless reliable overall.

The psychological relevance of this account of memory knowledge derives primarily from its emphasis on the mechanisms responsible for ensuring the reliability of potentially unreliable constructive remembering. Such an account may serve as a corrective to the tendency sometimes displayed by psychologists to emphasize errors and distortions due to constructive processes to such an extent that the overall message is that remembering is outright *un*reliable. Critiquing this tendency, Ost and Costall make the reasoning explicit: "remembering is intrinsically reconstruction *and hence* inevitably unreliable" (2002, 246; emphasis added). As Kornblith argues, the initial, pessimistic reaction to findings of apparent inductive irrationality was unwarranted: just as perceptual illusions and errors are studied not because they show that perception is unreliable but rather because they provide, by showing where the mechanisms responsible for the reliability of perception break down, a glimpse of the workings of those mechanisms, inferential errors should be studied because they provide a glimpse of the workings of the mechanisms responsible for the overall reliability of inductive inference. Likewise, the sometimes pessimistic tone of constructive memory research, or at least of commentary on such research, is unwarranted: memory errors and illusions, when all goes well, play a role in memory research analogous to that played by perceptual errors and illusions in perception research, providing a means of investigating the operation of the constructive processes which, under normal conditions, ensure the overall reliability of remembering (Roediger 1996).

1.3   When and Why Did Memory Emerge?

While much of this book is devoted to building a philosophical account of remembering and memory knowledge on the current psychology of constructive memory and mental time travel, the intention is ultimately for that account to feed back into psychology. Hence the book's third question, concerning the evolution of episodic memory, belongs more to psychology than it does to philosophy.

Not long ago, Boyer remarked that there was relatively little work in which a functional, evolutionary perspective on memory is adopted (Boyer 2009). While there were important early exceptions to this generalization (e.g., Anderson 1990; Anderson and Milson 1989), the situation has since changed dramatically, and there is now a fast-developing literature exploring the evolution of memory. The debate over the survival-processing paradigm, which suggests that memory is tuned to remember the kinds of scenarios that tended to be especially survival-relevant in ancestral environments, accounts for a significant fraction of this literature (Nairne and Pandeirada 2008; Schwartz et al. 2014), but it is the debate over the existence of mental time travel in nonhuman animals that is most directly relevant here (Cheke and Clayton 2010). That debate—essentially a debate over *when* episodic memory evolved—turns in part on the interpretation of experimental evidence, but it also turns on a conceptual or definitional matter. If the subjective dimension of human episodic memory—its characteristic phenomenology—is essential to it, then the research that has demonstrated a form of episodic-like memory—memory for specific past episodes—in certain nonhuman species is insufficient to demonstrate that the latter are capable of full-blown episodic memory. According to the simulation theory, the subjective dimension is not, strictly speaking, essential to *memory*, but it is essential to its *reliability*. There is thus good reason to regard nonhuman episodic-like memory, the reliability of which does not depend on such a subjective dimension, as being different in kind from human episodic memory. This insight concerning the necessity of phenomenology for reliability grounds an intervention in the parallel debate over *why* episodic memory evolved. On the view defended here, a capacity for simulational remembering could not have evolved unaccompanied by a capacity for the relevant phenomenology.

1.4 Overview

Part I sets the stage for the rest of the book. Relying on research on the memory systems of the human brain, chapter 2 argues that the deep differences among different kinds of memory militate against any attempt to develop a unified approach to the epistemology of memory as a whole, and makes a case for starting with episodic memory in particular. Chapter 3 sets out the epistemological framework that guides the book's treatment of episodic memory; the framework combines a strong form of naturalism, which urges us to come to grips with empirical research on constructive memory and mental time travel, with a weak form of reliabilism, which suggests a focus on the effects of metacognitive monitoring on the reliability of remembering.

The simulation theory of memory is developed and defended in part II. Chapters 4 and 5 look at research on constructive memory, exploring the prospects for updating the causal theory of memory to enable it to accommodate the constructive character of remembering. Chapter 6 argues that mental time travel research shows that construction in memory is so extensive that it requires abandoning the causal condition entirely. The result is a simulation theory of memory. Whereas the causal theory claims that remembering and imagining are distinguished by the presence, in the case of the former, of an appropriate causal connection with the relevant past episode, the simulation theory claims that there is no intrinsic difference between remembering and imagining—to remember, it turns out, is just to imagine the past.

Part III takes up the question of the reliability of simulational remembering. The goal of this part is not to show *that* remembering is reliable; as epistemologists have often observed, that is not something that could be shown in a noncircular fashion, since any demonstration of the reliability of memory would itself have to rely on memory. Instead, the account is meant to show *how* remembering might achieve reliability despite the opportunities for error and distortion that are inevitably entailed by its simulational character. The argument proceeds in two steps. The first step considers remembering in isolation from other forms of episodic imagination, looking at how it avoids being overwhelmed by error and distortion despite recombining and transformation information so extensively that a "retrieved" memory might end up including little to no information originating in experience of the relevant episode. The claim is that massive error and distortion are avoided due, first, to the reliable character of the constructive processes internal to memory (chapter 7) and, second, to the role of metacognitive monitoring, including source monitoring, in filtering out information originating in unreliable sources (chapter 8). The second step of the argument (chapter 9) deals with a complication that arises when forms of episodic imagination other than episodic memory are taken into account. Episodic remembering would be unreliable were we unable to distinguish it from other forms of episodic imagination. But there is extensive similarity—at the neural, cognitive, and phenomenological levels—between memory and other forms of imagination, raising the question of how we manage to avoid confusing different forms of imagination. The claim defended in this chapter is that agents avoid confusion due to their capacity for a form of metacognition, what we can refer to as "process monitoring," in which the characteristic phenomenology of remembering—consciousness of the self in subjective time—plays an important role.

Part IV turns to the evolution of episodic memory. Chapter 10 surveys the main lines of the debate over the evolution of episodic memory, arguing that, relative to the forms of episodic-like memory that have been demonstrated in animals, human episodic memory has two distinctive features. First (as emphasized in part II), it is one function of a general episodic construction system capable of simulating a wide range of possible past and future episodes. Second (as emphasized in part III), it involves a distinctive form of consciousness of the self in subjective time. Chapter 11 argues that the adaptivity of the first feature is relatively straightforward, and that the first feature explains the second. Existing explanations account for the adaptivity of a capacity to simulate a range of possible episodes, as opposed to simply retrieving information about what happened where and when, as in animal episodic-like memory, but they have a harder time accounting for the characteristic phenomenology of remembering. The claim defended in this chapter is that a general simulational capacity inevitably entails uncertainty about whether simulated episodes actually occurred and that the need for process monitoring suggests that the phenomenology of remembering plays a role in reducing this uncertainty to a manageable level. Finally, chapter 12 brings things to a close, briefly summing up the book's main conclusions.

2 Situating Episodic Memory

In attempting to distinguish among different kinds of memory, philosophers have often relied on intuition or linguistic considerations. The approach taken here departs from this tradition by basing the classification of kinds of memory on research on distinct but interacting memory systems conducted in psychology and neuroscience. This research suggests that, while declarative memory may be a natural kind, memory as a whole—including both declarative and nondeclarative memory—is not. That conclusion, in turn, suggests that it is unlikely to be possible to develop a unified account of remembering and memory knowledge in general. This leaves open the possibility of developing a unified account of *declarative* remembering and memory knowledge, but the unique features of episodic memory suggest that it is likely to be more fruitful to pursue a divide-and-conquer strategy, initially developing separate accounts of episodic and semantic memory and attempting to combine them only at a later stage.

2.1 Is Memory a Natural Kind?

Patricia Churchland once pointed out that we do not know "whether searching for the neural substrate for 'memory' is like looking for the 'principle' that unites jewels, such as amethysts, diamonds, amber, and pearls" (1986, 152)—that is, that we do not know whether memory is a natural kind or, instead, a set of disparate phenomena only superficially similar to one another. The question of whether memory is a natural kind has rarely been posed explicitly, but once we begin to grasp the depth of the differences among the various "kinds of memory,"[1] it becomes clear that, though the view that memory is a natural kind is a plausible default hypothesis, we are by no means entitled to take it for granted.

While this chapter will conclude that memory is not a natural kind, the intent is not to legislate a view of memory for psychology; on the contrary, the aim is to draw out a view already implicit in contemporary psychology. But an answer to the question of whether memory is a natural kind will have practical implications for memory research in psychology, for such an answer will give us an idea of which sorts of empirical approaches are likely to be fruitful. In other words, though the question of whether memory is a natural kind belongs to what we can think of as the metaphysics of memory (Bernecker 2008), it is not of exclusively philosophical interest. A natural kind is one determined by the way properties cluster together in the world, rather than by the concepts we apply to the world. Natural kinds, unlike merely nominal kinds, "carve nature at its joints" (as Plato put it) and are therefore capable of supporting inductions (Quine 1969). If memory is a natural kind, then it will be appropriate to investigate various kinds of memory together, treating them as a coherent whole, for investigation of one kind of memory will often tell us something about features of other kinds of memory. But if memory is not a natural kind, then it will in general not be appropriate to investigate different kinds of memory together, for investigation of one kind of memory will typically not tell us much about the other kinds. In short: if memory turns out not to be a natural kind, then it will not be worthwhile to try to develop a *general* theory of memory.[2]

2.2   The Multiple Memory Systems Hypothesis

In order to determine whether the various kinds of memory make up a single, overarching natural kind, we need to have at least a working list of kinds of memory in hand. Now, of the hundreds of *types* of memory distinguished by psychologists, only a small number have any chance of qualifying as natural kinds (Tulving 2007), and we therefore need a procedure for identifying kinds of memory. A plausible starting point is provided by the multiple memory systems hypothesis, which suggests that we can identify *kinds of memory* by first identifying *memory systems*.

The suggestion may appear to amount to a call to replace one difficult question with another equally difficult one, but the appearance is misleading, for we know a great deal about the memory systems of the brain. To begin with, it is crucial to distinguish the thought that there are different kinds of memory from the view of memory embodied in the multiple memory systems hypothesis, according to which there exist "a number of different learning and memory systems that possess the capabilities of operating independently as well as in conjunction with one another in the production of the large variety of phenomena of learning and memory with which we are already familiar, and an even larger variety of phenomena still to be discovered" (Tulving 1984a, 165). As Schacter and Tulving point out (1994), the concept of a memory system includes the concept of a kind of memory, but the latter does not include the former, and there is an obvious means of reconciling a view of memory as fundamentally unitary with the view that there are multiple kinds of memory: we might simply suppose that different kinds of memory are distinct products of a single memory system. We might, that is, adopt a unitary memory system hypothesis, according to which "a single learning and memory system mediates the behavioral and experiential plasticity of human beings, and other higher animals, and … all phenomena of learning and memory in a species reflect the many ways in which that single system works" (Tulving 1984a, 165).

While the unitary memory system hypothesis was once the default view, that is no longer the case. This is not the place for a review of the process by which researchers have gradually converged on the multiple memory systems hypothesis (see Eichenbaum 2010; Squire 2009). What matters for present purposes is that the hypothesis is now well-established and thus constitutes a legitimate starting point for exploring the metaphysics of memory. Disagreement over the details of the memory systems framework persists—and is taken into account in the discussion below—but there are relatively few today who reject the multiple memory systems hypothesis itself; the distinction between declarative and nondeclarative memory, in particular, is acknowledged essentially universally (Tulving 2000).[3]

2.3   A Standard Taxonomy of Memory Systems

Given the memory systems approach, what kinds of memory must we acknowledge? The basic distinction is between declarative and nondeclarative memory. At the anatomical level, declarative memory depends on the medial temporal lobe, including the hippocampus, and depends on the sensory cortex for retrieval. It involves processes of encoding, storage, and retrieval, and it enables conscious recollection of information. Declarative memory divides into episodic memory, concerned with recalling the events

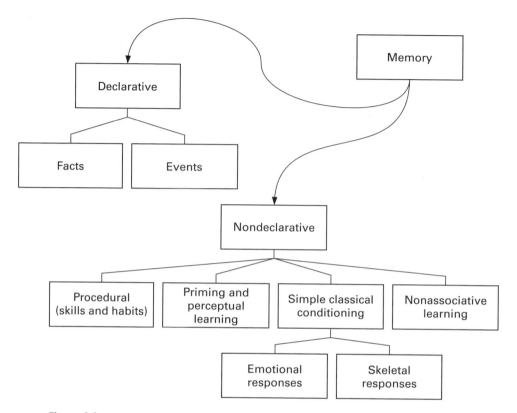

Figure 2.1
Squire's taxonomy of mammalian long-term memory systems. Redrawn from Squire (2004), omitting information about the brain regions implicated in different systems.

of the personal past, and semantic memory, concerned with recalling facts or propositions. Semantic recollection is associated with noetic consciousness: when one remembers a fact, one is normally aware that one is remembering. Episodic recollection, in contrast, is associated with autonoetic consciousness: when one remembers an experienced episode, one is normally aware not only of remembering but also of remembering an event that took place in one's own past (Tulving 2002b). There are differences between the brain regions involved in episodic and semantic memory; these are described as needed below. The phenomenological differences are discussed in detail in later chapters.

Nondeclarative memory refers to a much more varied collection of phenomena. As Schacter and Tulving put it, while declarative memory "refers to a specific memory system with reasonably well-characterized functional and neural properties," nondeclarative memory "is used in a more descriptive sense to refer to a class or collection of memory functions that share certain features in common but also differ from one another in various ways" (Schacter and Tulving 1994, 22). The various systems usually grouped together under the heading of nondeclarative memory are discussed below. Given the memory systems approach to identifying kinds of memory, then, we should aim to account at least for semantic memory, episodic memory, and various forms of nondeclarative memory. Figure 2.1 depicts Squire's taxonomy of memory systems, which captures one influential view of the relationships among these kinds of memory.

2.4   The Trilevel Approach

The question is whether these kinds of memory are, strictly speaking, sub-kinds of a single natural kind, as Squire's taxonomy suggests. In certain other domains, there are established procedures for answering analogous questions about putative natural kinds. Suppose that we want to know, for example, whether the dingo and the domesticated dog, which seem on the face of it to be subkinds of a single kind, are in fact such subkinds. The answer is not self-evident—if it seems to be, we only have to remind ourselves of similar cases (e.g., Churchland's jewel case) in which the "self-evident" turned out to be incorrect. But we can, after sufficient investigation, identify behavioral, morphological, and other properties characteristic of the putative kind (*canis lupus*). And we can identify a set of common genetic and environmental mechanisms responsible for the clustering of those properties. The results of these investigations justify an affirmative answer to the question.[4] This is not to say that it is easy to construct a zoological taxonomy—in fact, there are a great many competing accounts of the nature of species (Wilkins 2011)—but only to point out that, since we have a reasonably well worked-out understanding of the nature of the relevant kinds of kind (species and higher and lower taxa), we have at least an approximate idea of how to go about doing so.

There is no similarly uncontroversial procedure for answering the question of whether memory is a natural kind, but the memory systems approach to identifying kinds of memory suggests one plausible procedure. What we need is a general understanding of the nature of kinds of memory.

The discussion above suggested that memory systems individuate kinds of memory. The discussion to follow will suggest that an understanding of the nature of memory systems can ground an understanding of the nature of kinds of memory. This understanding of the nature of kinds of memory, in turn, can enable us to determine whether any two given kinds of memory are subkinds of a single natural kind.

2.4.1 The Concept of a Memory System

The previous section outlined the basics of current thinking on human memory systems, but said little about the concept of a memory system as such. One way of understanding the concept is via the trilevel hypothesis (Marr 1982), according to which a full description of a cognitive system must cover three levels:

- the computational level—the system must be described in terms of the information-processing task it performs.
- the algorithmic level—the system must be described in terms of the procedure it uses to perform that task.
- the implementational level—the system must be described in terms of the way in which it implements that procedure; that is, in terms of the relevant physical properties and processes of the system.

The concept of a memory system, as it is used in psychology, appears to be precisely a trilevel concept, a concept of a system having reality at—and requiring description at—each of these three levels. Discussing the concept of a memory system, Schacter and Tulving, for example, suggest that "particular memory systems be specified in terms of the nature of their rules of operation, the type of information or contents, and the neural pathways of mechanisms subserving them" (Schacter and Tulving 1994, 31).

2.4.2 Generating the Hierarchy of Kinds of Memory

The suggestion with which we started was that memory systems individuate kinds of memory, allowing us to use the identification of the memory systems of the brain as a means of identifying kinds of memory: in effect, by distinguishing among memory systems, we indirectly distinguish among kinds of memory. But this does not suffice to generate the hierarchy of kinds of memory, for there need not be a one-to-one correspondence between memory systems and kinds of memory: there might be a kind of memory with various subkinds, each of which corresponds to one of the memory systems of the brain, without there being a memory system corresponding to the more general kind.

The trilevel approach to memory systems suggests a simple solution to this problem. First, suppose that, if two memory systems satisfy a single trilevel description, then they are members of a single natural kind. The idea is that the implementational- and algorithmic-level descriptions specify the mechanisms responsible for the clustering of the properties mentioned in the computational-level description. This is sufficient to generate a hierarchy of kinds of memory system, with more general descriptions picking out higher kinds and more specific descriptions picking out lower kinds. Next, replace the claim that *memory systems* individuate kinds of memory with the claim that *kinds* of memory system individuate kinds of memory. This is sufficient to generate the hierarchy of kinds of memory, with higher (more general) kinds of memory being individuated by higher kinds of system and lower (more specific) kinds of memory being individuated by lower kinds of system.

Given this general understanding of the nature of kinds of memory, determining whether two kinds of memory are subkinds of a single natural kind boils down to answering the following three questions:

- Is there an information-processing task common to the relevant memory systems?
- Is there a procedure for performing that task common to the systems?
- Is there an implementation of that procedure common to the systems?

A negative answer to one of the questions implies that the relevant memory systems are not members of a single kind of memory system and therefore that the kinds of memory they individuate are not subkinds of a single kind of memory.

2.5   Declarative Memory

What are the implications of the trilevel approach for the relationship between episodic and semantic memory? There are, as noted above, differences between the episodic and semantic systems, especially at the computational level; only episodic memory necessarily makes reference to the past, and only episodic memory necessarily makes reference to the self.

But it may nevertheless be possible to give a natural general description of an information-processing problem solved by both systems: though, as we will see, it is a mistake to view the function of either episodic or semantic memory as reducing to the simple preservation of information acquired in the past, both forms of memory do presuppose the preservation of information. Since there are strong similarities at the algorithmic and implementational levels, it is reasonably likely that a coherent trilevel description of a kind including both episodic and semantic memory can be given. If so, then, given the proposed criterion, declarative memory will turn out to be a natural kind.

To the extent that the category of declarative memory is projectable (i.e., supports inductive generalizations), this is a desirable result. Giving a precise computational-level description applicable to both episodic and semantic memory would require considerable work, and giving precise algorithmic- and implementational-level descriptions would require carrying out a detailed exploration of similarities and differences between the relevant encoding, storage, and retrieval processes, as well as a detailed exploration of the brain-level mechanisms underwriting them. It may turn out in the end that, due to differences between episodic and semantic memory, declarative memory is not a natural kind. Indeed, as the considerations discussed in section 2.8 below make clear, this is a live possibility. While the trilevel approach does not necessarily imply that declarative memory is not a natural kind, the possibility is consistent with the overall argumentative strategy of the book—in fact, it would reinforce the decision to focus initially on developing separate accounts of episodic and semantic memory.

2.5.1   Functionalism and Multiple Realizability

While the trilevel approach is promising, one might have several worries about it. To begin with, one might object that the approach is incompatible with functionalism (construed, broadly, as the view that what makes a mental state a state of a given type is a matter exclusively of the role that it plays in a larger system) or, more generally, that it is incompatible with the multiple realizability of mental states, arguing that, due to implementational- or algorithmic-level differences among the memory systems of different individuals, the trilevel approach rules out even episodic memory as a natural kind. The requirement of a common implementation and procedure, however, need not be understood in such restrictive terms: the requirement is for significant similarity at the implementational and algorithmic levels, not for perfect similarity. Minor differences among individual systems thus need not imply that they are not members of a common natural kind.

One might object that functionalism, at minimum, suggests that only computational-level similarity between two kinds of memory should be required for them to qualify as subkinds of a single natural kind. The trilevel approach is, of course, not the only possible approach to the nature of kinds of memory. Less restrictive approaches are certainly available, including a computational similarity-only approach, though the psychology tends not to support such purely functional approaches. But note that if the argument of the next section—according to which nondeclarative memory is noncognitive—succeeds, the conclusion that memory is not a natural kind follows even given the less restrictive computational similarity-only approach.

2.5.2 Avoiding Overgeneration

A distinct worry is based on the observation that it is always possible to formulate a more specific or a more general description of a system. In view of this fact, how do we know which descriptions of memory systems to take seriously? There are two opposed dangers here. On the one hand, there is a danger that, because we can always generate a narrower description of a system, we will be forced to acknowledge an endless proliferation of memory systems, in which case we will be forced to acknowledge an endless proliferation of kinds of memory. On the other hand, there is a danger that, because we can easily give a description of a memory system so highly general that the various memory systems of the brain will all automatically satisfy it, the claim that memory is a natural kind will amount to a triviality.

The discussion of nondeclarative memory in the next section responds to the latter danger—in fact, it is not at all clear that we can give a coherent description of a system so general that it is satisfied by both declarative and nondeclarative memory. As far as the former danger goes, Schacter and Tulving (1994) have developed a plausible response to a closely related problem. Responding to charges that the multiple memory systems hypothesis licenses researchers to posit an endless number of systems, they argue that three criteria should be met before a new memory system is posited. The core idea of the first criterion is that we should not individuate the information-processing problem solved by the system too narrowly; this allows us to avoid positing a new memory system for every type of information processed. The second criterion amounts roughly to a statement of the need for a multilevel description of a system (Schacter, Wagner, and Buckner 2000). The third criterion is that we should be able to observe dissociations between the purported systems on a wide range of tasks, since it is relatively easy to produce a dissociation on any single given task (Schacter, Wagner, and Buckner 2000). Only when these three criteria are met, they argue, are we in a position to say that a hypothetical memory system has biological reality. This approach to the problem may strike philosophers as somewhat ad hoc, but it fits well with the practice of empirical memory research and thus with the naturalistic approach to epistemology developed in chapter 3 below.

2.6   Nondeclarative Memory

While declarative memory may or may not be a natural kind, the trilevel approach clearly implies that nondeclarative memory is neither a subkind of a general kind including declarative memory nor itself a natural kind.

Procedural memory—the kind of memory at work when one learns a new behavior or skill—makes up much of nondeclarative memory. As Schacter and Tulving (1994, 26–27) point out, procedural memory "does not store representations of external states of the world, it operates at an automatic rather than consciously controlled level, its output is noncognitive, and it can operate independently of the hippocampal structures." The contrast with other memory systems is vivid. These systems are cognitive, in the sense that "the final productions of all these systems can be, and frequently are, contemplated by the individual introspectively, in conscious awareness. Any conversion of such a product of memory into overt behavior, even symbolic behavior such as speech or writing, represents an optional postretrieval phenomenon, characterized by considerable flexibility regarding the behavioral expression. Such flexibility is absent in nondeclarative forms of memory" (Schacter and Tulving 1994, 26–27). In short, there are deep differences between nondeclarative and declarative memory. At the computational level, declarative memory, but

not nondeclarative memory, is concerned with explicit, consciously accessible representations. At the implementational level, declarative memory,
but not nondeclarative memory, is dependent on the medial temporal lobe,
including the hippocampus. It appears that declarative and nondeclarative
memory are likewise deeply dissimilar at the algorithmic level. Though
researchers sometimes write as if nondeclarative memory involves processes of encoding, storage, and retrieval, Tulving points out that trying to
bring these concepts into play in the context of behavioral skills is "awk-
ward at best and silly at worst" (2000, 38). To cite just one example, consider Cohen and Squire's (1980) assumption that "rule-based information"
is stored in nondeclarative memory, in contrast to storage of "data-based
information" in declarative memory. A reference to storage of rule-based
information in nondeclarative memory is redundant, since an appeal to
changes at the neural level is sufficient to explain the relevant changes in
the organism's behavior. In general, a system need not represent the rules
governing a learned behavior in order for its behavior to be governed by
them; the assumption that rule-based information is stored does no additional explanatory work.

These differences imply that nondeclarative and declarative memory
do not make up a natural kind. Consider, in particular, the computational
question: do they perform a common information-processing task? What
is required here is a coherent general description of an information-processing problem solved in different ways by all nondeclarative and declarative memory systems. The problem is simply that we need not mention
information processing *at all* in order to give a complete description of
nondeclarative memory—nondeclarative remembering is in an important
sense not a kind of cognition. Nondeclarative memory does involve the
modification of the brain of the organism on the basis of its experience.
But, unlike declarative memory, it does not involve the modification of the
brain of the organism as a means of making information available to the
organism in the future.

The point is meant to be a straightforward application of Occam's Razor.
There is no need to posit the storage of information by nondeclarative
memory, for the simple reason that any such stored information would be
causally, and hence explanatorily, inert. In contrast, information stored by
declarative memory is not inert: it is processed in various ways and thereby
affects the behavior of the organism. Declarative memories are available

to consciousness and thus can affect the activities of other cognitive systems. I remember that it has been sunny every day for the past week; I infer that it will be sunny today; I therefore leave home without bringing an umbrella. An appeal to stored information is essential to the explanation of my behavior in this case, for the memory does not cause the behavior directly, but only via an intermediate process of reasoning. Conscious access to stored contents allows them to enter into the causation of behavior in various indirect ways, via reasoning, imagination, and other routes; if the subject were not to have such access, declarative memory would be unable to provide inputs to other cognitive processes. Thus, were we to suppose that declarative memory does not store information, we would be unable to explain certain modifications in the behavior of the organism.

The assumption that information is stored by nondeclarative memory does no such explanatory work. Explanations of modifications of an organism's behavior via nondeclarative learning go through just as well if we do not posit the storage of information by nondeclarative memory, because any such information would never be processed and therefore would be without effect on the behavior of the organism. Appeals to changes at the neural level do all the work done by appeals to neural changes combined with appeals to storage of information. We should therefore say that no information is stored. Notoriously, we are free to treat even simple systems such as thermometers as information processors (Dennett 1987). But parsimony requires that we give the lowest-level explanations of these systems possible. The lowest-level explanation of a thermometer possible confines itself to the physical level, and we should therefore not take the thermometer to be an information processor. Similarly, while it is possible to describe nondeclarative memory as cognitive, parsimony dictates that we refrain from doing so. The lowest-level explanation of nondeclarative memory possible confines itself to the neural level, and we should therefore not take nondeclarative memory to be computational.[5]

2.6.1 Implicit Representation

One might object that, though nondeclarative memory does not involve storage of explicit representations, it might nevertheless involve the sort of implicit representation described by connectionism (Kirsh 1992; Smolensky 1988). Connectionism, however, provides no support for this suggestion, which amounts to another way of invoking the idea of rule-based information. The question of implicit versus explicit representation is a question about how systems represent information *in general* rather than about how they represent rule-based information in particular. A system might represent rule-based information, but it will do so in the same way it represents data-based information. In a connectionist system, both types of information will be represented implicitly, while in a classical system, both types of information will be represented explicitly. But connectionist systems do not implicitly represent the rules governing their behavior: a system represents whatever it represents, and we (from our external perspective) can formulate the rules which govern its operation. The situation is no different than in a classical system: in that case, the system will explicitly represent both rule-based and data-based information, but the rule (formulated by us) describing the role played by the represented rules in the operation of the system is not itself represented by the system. Thus the notion of implicit representation does not provide a means of saving the suggestion that nondeclarative memory involves the representation of rule-based information.

2.6.2 Knowing How

The point that nondeclarative memory is noncognitive (i.e., not concerned with representations that can be evaluated for truth or accuracy) is likely to strike some as surprising and others as obvious. It is surprising to the extent that we are accustomed to thinking of memory as a unified phenomenon. It may start to seem obvious when we note that the distinction between declarative and nondeclarative memory is closely related to the familiar distinction between knowing *that* and knowing *how* (Cohen and Squire 1980), a distinction that philosophers have drawn in recognition of an apparent gap between these two kinds of knowledge. Philosophers are not unanimous on the difference in kind between knowing that and knowing how, but the traditional view is certainly that there is such a difference. The philosophical debate over the relation of knowing how to knowing that has largely been conducted either in an a priori manner (see, for example, Ryle's argument that the "intellectualist legend," according to which performing an action requires contemplating the rule governing the action, leads to a vicious regress; Ryle 1949) or on the basis of linguistic considerations (see, for example, Williamson and Stanley's defense of the view that knowing how is a type of knowing that, which turns on the linguistic forms of knowledge-how and knowledge-that attributions; Williamson and Stanley 2001). The trilevel approach to memory systems provides a novel reason in favor of the traditional view. Coming to know how to do something is sometimes, though not always, purely a matter of nondeclarative learning. Given that nondeclarative memory is noncognitive, then, at least some knowledge-how is noncognitive, and this secures the traditional gap between knowing how and knowing that.

2.7 Toward a New Taxonomy

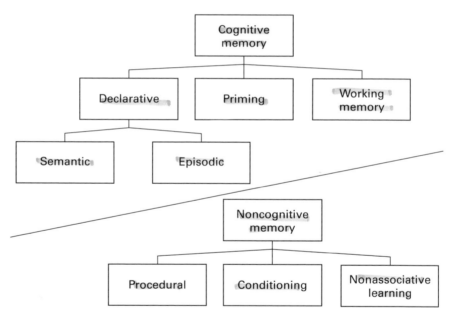

Figure 2.2
A revised taxonomy of memory systems.

The claim that nondeclarative memory is noncognitive is subject to an important qualification. It applies most straightforwardly to procedural memory, as well as conditioning and nonassociative learning. In contrast, priming, which is usually classified as a kind of nondeclarative memory, would seem to be straightforwardly cognitive, since it is a matter of changes in subjects' ability to recognize objects. But priming is precisely the exception that proves the rule. For example, Schacter and Tulving (1994; see also Schacter and Buckner 1998) explicitly group a special "perceptual representation system" responsible for priming with the episodic, semantic, and working memory systems. If something like this approach is right, then priming should not, after all, be classified with procedural memory and other forms of learning usually grouped together under the heading of nondeclarative memory. There is a further question about whether the remaining kinds of nondeclarative memory are subkinds of a single natural kind; that is, whether nondeclarative memory itself is merely a nominal kind. This may well be the case, since nondeclarative memory appears to be a rather heterogeneous collection of phenomena, but pursuing the question in any detail here would take us too far afield.

Working memory, which is normally grouped neither with declarative nor with nondeclarative memory, is also straightforwardly cognitive, as it refers to our capacity to hold information in a conscious workspace. For example, on Baddeley's multicomponent model, working memory includes, in addition to a central executive, a phonological loop capable of maintaining phonological information through active rehearsal as well as a visuospatial sketchpad capable of maintaining visual and spatial information (Baddeley 2012). Thus, while more argument would be required to establish this with confidence, a taxonomy that groups working memory and priming as subkinds of a kind that also includes declarative memory is likely to be more fruitful than the standard taxonomy.

Figure 2.2 sums up the resulting view. The standard taxonomy views declarative and nondeclarative memory as instances of a more general capacity for memory. The revised taxonomy, in contrast, sees memory as fundamentally disunified. Rather than a division between declarative and nondeclarative memory, the basic distinction is now between cognitive and noncognitive forms of memory. Cognitive and noncognitive memory do not represent two forms of "memory," but two fundamentally different types of learning capacity. Cognitive memory groups together not only episodic and semantic memory, which are tentatively assigned to declarative memory as a superordinate kind, but also priming and working memory. Noncognitive memory groups together the remainder of what is normally classified as nondeclarative memory, though it is unclear whether it ultimately constitutes a unified category.

2.7.1 Common Neural Mechanisms

While the revised taxonomy is plausible, the existence of important commonalities between cognitive and noncognitive memory invites a number of objections.

One such objection is that, since common neural mechanisms—namely, modifications of the strength of existing synaptic connections and growth of new synaptic connections (Kandel and Pittenger 1999)—are employed by different memory systems, there is reason to suspect that deep similarities between declarative and nondeclarative memory can be identified at least at the implementational level. However, the use by different memory systems of similar mechanisms at the neural level is not particularly telling; as Weiskrantz puts it, "neurons are neurons and nothing more than neurons. At the level of cellular mechanism there are limited degrees of freedom. It may be, even if there are independent memory systems, that the cellular events used in all are similar or even identical" (1990, 99–100). And given the trilevel approach, of course, even extensive similarity at the implementational level is insufficient to ground the claim that memory is a natural kind. Moreover, while functionalist considerations might support a computational similarity-only approach, it is difficult to see what motivation there might be for adopting an implementational similarity-only approach.

2.7.2 Interacting Systems

A second objection turns on the fact that declarative and nondeclarative memory interact in various ways (Kim and Baxter 2001; McDonald, Devan, and Hong 2004; Poldrack and Packard 2003) in the accomplishment of learning tasks. This interaction confers a degree of plausibility on the idea of a single complex memory system with relatively independent specialized nondeclarative and declarative subsystems, and hence on the claim that nondeclarative and declarative memory are subkinds of a single kind. On closer inspection, however, the fact that memory systems interact provides little support for the unitary memory system hypothesis. The interaction among systems takes the form of relations such as competition, and hence it is arguably not computational—it does not appear that information is passed from nondeclarative memory to declarative memory or vice versa. Nor does the existence of competition among memory systems provide more indirect support for the claim that memory is a natural kind. Poldrack et al. (2001, 549) do, for example, argue that "competition may serve as a mechanism to arbitrate between two fundamentally incompatible requirements of learning: the need for flexibly accessible knowledge ... and the need to learn fast, automatic responses in specific situations," a theme to which we will return in chapter 11. But it would be a mistake to claim that nondeclarative and declarative memory serve a common general function of "learning" and to argue on that basis that they constitute a natural kind. The question of whether learning is a natural kind is not distinct from the question of whether memory is a natural kind. Hence the evidence that memory is not a natural kind is at the same time evidence that learning is not a natural kind.

2.7.3 General Theories of Learning

A final objection is suggested by the existence of general theories of learning. Reinforcement learning theory (Sutton and Barto 1998), in particular, has been applied in the context of multiple memory systems research, and the applicability of a single theory of learning to both declarative and nondeclarative memory may be taken to suggest that memory is after all a natural kind. Reinforcement learning is an approach to the artificial intelligence problem of designing agents that can learn from interactions with their environments. It differs from supervised learning—in which agents are explicitly informed which actions are correct—in that, in reinforcement learning, the agent receives feedback only from the environment and must explore and test different policies in order to discover optimal actions. Crucially, reinforcement learning refers not to a single learning method but rather to a type of learning problem. Significantly different types of learning thus fall under the general heading of reinforcement learning. Daw, Niv, and Dayan have applied reinforcement learning theory to the question of how the brain selects among competing systems for behavioral choice in cases of disagreement among systems. They are concerned in particular with the dorsolateral striatum, which supports "habitual or reflexive control," and with the prefrontal cortex, which supports "more reflective or cognitive action planning" (Daw et al. 2005, 1704). Their account links model-free learning, a method in which an action is simply associated with a value, with the dorsolateral striatum, while model-based learning, a method which involves constructing a model of the environment, is linked with the prefrontal cortex.

While Daw et al. do indeed employ techniques from reinforcement learning theory to describe the behavior of the two systems, the techniques applied differ significantly between the two cases. To describe the system supporting reflective or cognitive action planning (the sort of system at work, for example, when an action associated with a devalued outcome ceases to be performed), they resort to a technique incorporating an explicit model of the environment. To describe the system supporting habitual or reflexive action control (the sort of system at work, for example, when an action associated with a devalued outcome continues to be performed), in contrast, they need not invoke such a model. Thus it appears that there is no common computational-level description of the two systems: while one system influences behavior by relying on information about the environment acquired in the past, the other produces behavior automatically—its selection of an action is *influenced* by its past experience with its environment, but does not involve a *representation* of that environment. Moreover, while the reinforcement learning account is given in terms of computations performed by systems, it is unclear whether the dorsolateral striatal system itself need be given a computational description: while invoking stored information would seem to be indispensable to describe the flexible workings of the prefrontal system, a neural-level description would appear to be sufficient to describe the automatic workings of the dorsolateral system. Thus reinforcement learning gives us little additional reason to suppose that memory is a natural kind.

2.8   Starting with Episodic Memory

If memory is not a natural kind, there is little hope of developing a successful unified account of memory as a whole. This goes for philosophy as much as for psychology. In psychology, Klein (2015) has argued that, given the extensive differences among the various capacities that have been grouped together under the heading of memory, the concept of memory has been stretched to the breaking point. And, while the aims of philosophy are somewhat different, a naturalistically oriented philosophical approach should certainly take the disunity of the concept of memory into account. The remainder of the book will therefore focus exclusively on one specific kind of memory—episodic memory—saying little about other kinds of memory.

2.8.1 Episodic versus Autobiographical Memory

Episodic memory, which gives us knowledge of specific episodes experienced in the past and depends on a dedicated memory system, should be distinguished from autobiographical memory, which is responsible for overall knowledge of one's life history and is usually viewed not as the product of a single memory system but rather as a capacity emerging from the interaction of other, more fundamental capacities, including both episodic and semantic memory—in particular, semantic memory for facts related to the self (Markowitsch and Welzer 2010). On Conway's self-memory system framework, for example, autobiographical memory is a hierarchical combination of general knowledge of the overall structure of one's life, knowledge of periods within that structure, and, finally, "phenomenological records" (Conway 2005). Only the latter, which may represent specific past events, correspond to episodic memory, strictly speaking. Given the systems-based approach to kinds of memory developed here, autobiographical memory is unlikely to qualify as a natural kind, and the task of developing an account of autobiographical memory knowledge is best left until we have adequate accounts of the episodic and semantic memory knowledge on which it depends.

2.8.2 Episodic versus Semantic Memory

Given that the taxonomy developed in this chapter is compatible with the possibility that episodic and semantic memory constitute a natural kind, why not attempt, instead, to develop a unified account of declarative memory as a whole? The reasons for not pursuing such a project here are in part theoretical, in part pragmatic. Theoretically speaking, while it may be legitimate to group episodic and semantic memory together under the heading of declarative memory, there are important differences between them—differences that will be emphasized in subsequent chapters—and declarative memory may, in the end, turn out not to be a natural kind. In addition to differences at the level of the brain bases of the systems, there are differences at the level of both content and phenomenology. As far as content goes, the following chapter will suggest that, while semantic memory is concerned with propositional representations, episodic memory is concerned with representations that have a richer, quasi-perceptual kind of content. This shapes both the theory of episodic remembering developed in part II and the explanation of the reliability of episodic memory developed in part III, and it is unclear to what extent the resulting account is applicable to semantic memory. As far as phenomenology goes, part IV will emphasize that episodic memory is unique among forms of memory in providing the agent with continued access not only to information acquired in the past but also to the circumstances in which information was originally acquired. This feat is possible due to the involvement in episodic memory of a form of consciousness—autonoesis—foreign to semantic memory. Thus it seems advisable to adopt a piecemeal strategy, initially developing separate accounts of episodic and semantic memory and reserving the task of combining them for future research.[6]

Pragmatic considerations, in turn, suggest starting with episodic rather than semantic memory. Epistemologists tend to focus on propositional knowledge, often to the exclusion of other forms of knowledge. In view of the rich variety of forms of knowledge of which we are capable, this is both puzzling and unfortunate. It is especially unfortunate given that our capacity to construct rich episodic representations—not only representations of episodes from the personal past but also representations of episodes that we have not actually experienced—may be one of the capacities most distinctive of the human mind. Hopefully, starting with episodic rather than semantic memory will contribute to correcting this imbalance.

3   Memory Knowledge

While the project of this book, which centers around the reliability of memory, is recognizably epistemological, the argument of the book, with its direct reliance on the psychology of memory, bears relatively little resemblance to standard epistemological approaches to memory. This chapter therefore provides some explicit methodological background for the argument, setting out the brand of naturalism that will be taken for granted in the remainder of the book, arguing that applied epistemological investigations such as that undertaken here are legitimate parts of epistemology, and describing the place of reliability in a pluralistic form of naturalism. It then reviews some important complications that need to be taken into account in applying the concept of reliability to episodic memory.

3.1   Naturalism and Reliabilism

Relying on a rough analogy with ethics, we can view epistemology as dividing into three areas: metaepistemology, first-order epistemology, and applied epistemology. First-order epistemology (the area in which most epistemologists tend to work, most of the time) is in principle devoted to the study of various epistemic phenomena. In practice, it is usually concerned primarily with the nature of the knowledge relation, with what it is for some subject S to know that some proposition P is true. Metaepistemology, in contrast, is concerned with *epistemological* phenomena—epistemological theories, theorists, and theorizing. Of central concern here are, first, questions about the object domain of epistemology (what are the metaphysics of the phenomena studied by epistemologists?) and, second, questions about epistemological method (the epistemology of epistemology: how should epistemologists conduct their investigations of the epistemological object domain?). Controversies over naturalism belong here. Applied epistemology, finally, is devoted to the study of particular epistemic problems and processes—particular ways in which cognitive agents go about building up more or less epistemically adequate representations of the world.

Metaepistemologies and first-order epistemologies are mutually constraining: at minimum, certain metaepistemologies and certain first-order epistemologies are jointly inconsistent. Similarly, first-order epistemologies and applied epistemologies cannot simply be mixed and matched: at minimum, certain first-order epistemologies and certain empirical findings jointly entail certain applied epistemological claims. To the extent that this is a book on epistemology, it is a book on *applied* epistemology, concerned with how episodic memory, in particular, achieves epistemic adequacy to the extent that it does. The applied epistemological argument unfolds against a background of naturalist metaepistemology and reliabilist first-order epistemology. This combination of view is broadly similar to that prominently defended by Kornblith (2003), but differs from the latter both with respect to a number of key issues in metaepistemology and first-order epistemology and in its applied epistemological focus.

As Quine put it in his classic statement of the naturalist program, epistemology, as the naturalist conceives of it, "studies a natural phenomenon, viz., a physical human subject": given naturalism, "epistemology, or something like it, simply falls into place as a chapter of psychology and hence of natural science" (1994, 25). The behaviorist details of Quine's particular brand of naturalism have had little influence on its subsequent development. What naturalists have taken from him, instead, is a pair of more general claims. First, epistemology is—or should be—part of an empirical field. Second, given that epistemology is concerned with how agents acquire knowledge, the relevant empirical fields are psychology and cognitive science more broadly.

These are both methodological claims, saying nothing directly about the appropriate object domain for epistemology. Kornblith's version of naturalism includes, in addition to this methodological commitment, a commitment to a particular metaphysical claim about that object domain: knowledge is, according to him, a natural kind.[1] On this view, the metaphysical claim grounds the methodological claim: knowledge should be studied empirically *because* it is a natural kind and hence a proper object of empirical investigation. While this strategy for grounding the methodological claim has its appeal, it is not unproblematic. Knowledge does not behave much like paradigmatic natural kinds (due in part to the relational character of truth; Pernu 2009). Moreover, the claim that knowledge is a natural kind, even should it turn out to be correct, may be compatible with the denial of the methodological component of naturalism (since it may be possible to investigate natural kinds by a priori means; Kumar 2014; Horvath forthcoming). Taken together, these two problems suggest looking elsewhere for a means of grounding the methodological claim. Fortunately, the metaphysical claim is by no means necessary for the methodological claim, and the latter can be motivated by less controversial arguments, including appeals to the poor track record of purely a priori theorizing relative to the track record of empirical methods, and to the sheer methodological mysteriousness of a priori, intuition-based approaches. Obviously, not all epistemologists have been convinced by these arguments, but the book will nevertheless take methodological naturalism for granted. Explicit methodological debates have their place, but the only real proof of the pudding is in the eating, and the best argument for naturalism is a demonstration that it leads to interesting results.

Rejecting the claim that knowledge is a natural kind does not entail rejecting natural kinds *tout court.* The previous chapter argued that the epistemology of memory ought to respect the boundaries of natural kinds of memory. Taking the claim that episodic memory is a natural kind for granted, subsequent chapters will develop an epistemology of episodic memory that attempts to respect the contours of that kind as they are revealed by empirical investigation.

Turning from metaepistemology to first-order epistemology, the approach employed here follows Kornblith in taking reliabilism—according to which the epistemic status of a belief is determined by the reliability of the process that produced it (Goldman 2012)—as its starting-point but, again, differs from his approach on certain key points. Process reliabilism is clearly *consistent* with methodological naturalism, for the straightforward reason that reliability is—at least in principle—an empirically tractable feature of cognitive processes. But Kornblith argues that reliabilism coheres with naturalism in a stronger sense, maintaining that empirical investigation, primarily work in cognitive ethology (see, e.g., Ristau 2013), reveals that the essence of knowledge is reliably produced true belief; that is, process reliabilism is essentially correct as a theory of knowledge. The framework employed here, in contrast, rejects reliabilism as a theory of knowledge. The problem is not that reliabilism, taken as a theory of knowledge, presupposes metaphysical naturalism; it does not. The problem is rather that there are good reasons for rejecting the attempt to develop a unified theory of knowledge, whether reliabilist or otherwise. This claim is defended below; for now, the point is that, even if we reject the project of developing a unified theory of knowledge, reliability—the standard notion of which is the ratio of true beliefs to total beliefs produced by a process—may remain an important feature of cognitive processes for purposes of epistemic evaluation, even if it is not the only such feature.

Given a robust form of methodological naturalism at the metaepistemological level and a moderate form of reliabilism at the first-order level, applied epistemological questions take center stage. How reliable are our cognitive processes? What factors determine their reliability? This book is concerned with these questions as they apply to episodic memory in particular. Now, as noted above, no noncircular demonstration of the fact *that* memory is reliable can be given—memory is such a fundamental capacity that any attempt to demonstrate its reliability would itself be bound to depend on memory, thus tacitly presupposing what it sets out to show (Alston 1986). Moreover, for reasons given below, what we can say about the *level* of reliability of remembering in general is limited. The primary focus of the book is thus on the question of the *factors* determining the reliability of remembering: assuming that memory is reliable overall, how can its reliability be explained? Crucially, in order to put ourselves into a position to answer this question, naturalism requires us to have in hand an empirically adequate characterization of the *process* of remembering. Hence the development of a theory of remembering takes precedence over the development of an account of memory knowledge—the philosophy of mind precedes the epistemology.

3.1.1 Normativity

One of the main criticisms to which the naturalist program in epistemology has been subjected is that it threatens the normativity of epistemology (see, e.g., Kelly 2003; Maffie 1990; Siegel 1996). Epistemic normativity is a complex and difficult topic, and there is no room to do it justice here; nevertheless, it is worth taking a brief look at two ways in which naturalistic applied epistemological projects such as the one undertaken here can be seen as normative, one way in which they cannot, and why the latter does not amount to a problem for naturalism.

There is a clear sense in which naturalistic applied epistemology can be normative. As noted above, a given first-order epistemology, together with a relevant set of empirical findings, may entail applied epistemological conclusions. The latter, in a straightforward sense, have normative force. To illustrate, suppose that we are interested in the justificatory status of episodic memory beliefs. Suppose, for the sake of simplicity, that we have adopted reliabilism as a theory of epistemic justification. Findings about the reliability or unreliability of episodic remembering may then entail conclusions about the extent and scope of the justification of episodic memory beliefs. Depending on how much normativity we want in epistemology, such applied epistemological evaluations of our cognitive processes may be sufficient to allay worries about the ability of naturalized epistemology to accommodate epistemic normativity. In the view of most of its opponents, however, the problem with naturalized epistemology is that it cannot accommodate certain stronger forms of epistemic normativity.

Some who object to naturalized epistemology worry not about its ability to produce epistemic evaluations, but rather about its ability to provide epistemic guidance. The thought is that psychology, as a purely descriptive field, is in a position only to tell us how we actually *do* go about forming our beliefs, not to tell us anything about how we *should* go about forming our beliefs. An epistemology that reduces itself to a chapter of psychology will, of course, inherit this limitation. While the particular project undertaken here does not have as its aim the provision of epistemic guidance, it is worth noting that nothing prevents closely related naturalistic projects from doing so. As Quine remarked in an oft-quoted passage, on the naturalist view, "normative epistemology is a branch of engineering. It is the technology of truth-seeking, or, in a more cautiously epistemological term, prediction. ...The normative here, as elsewhere in engineering, becomes descriptive when the terminal parameter is expressed" (1986, 665). The suggestion is that naturalized epistemology is normative in the sense that it provides us with guidance about how to go about building up our representations of the world, where the guidance in question is, roughly, hypothetical or conditional in nature. To illustrate, consider the phenomenon of weapon focus in eyewitness memory. (Witnesses to crimes involving weapons tend to focus on the weapons; this later results in impaired memory for other features, such as criminals' faces.) Just as engineering might advise us, for example, to use strong but flexible materials when building a bridge, naturalized epistemology might tell us to avoid relying on eyewitness memory for information about details of crimes involving weapons. The normativity in the engineering case is of an unmysterious kind: what engineering tells us is that, *if* you want to build a bridge that will not collapse the first time a heavy vehicle crosses it, *then* you should use strong but flexible materials. The same thing goes for the normativity in the epistemology case: *if* you want accurate information about the face of the criminal who used the weapon, *then* you should not rely too heavily on eyewitness memory.[2]

While there is nothing puzzling about the ability of naturalized epistemology to provide epistemic guidance, in this sense, there is an important sense in which it is unlikely to be able to fully accommodate epistemic normativity. Though naturalized epistemology can shed light on the norms that we do in fact care about, it appears to be unable to tell us what norms we should care about. Is it reliability that determines the epistemic status of a belief? Coherence? Something else? The list of norms that have been proposed by epistemologists is long, and naturalized epistemology appears to be unable to adjudicate among them. To illustrate, consider recent work on the norms shaping our attitudes toward the trustworthiness of communicated information. When evaluating received information, we are sensitive to a variety of factors, such as the speaker's perceived reliability, expertise, and benevolence (Sperber et al. 2010). A naturalized epistemology can investigate our actual response to these factors; what it cannot tell us is how we ought to respond to them. This is not necessarily a defect of the naturalist approach, however, for the quest for correct epistemic norms itself may rest on a mistake. On the pluralistic view developed below, there is, in the end, no fact of the matter about which norms are correct, about which factors—beyond truth or accuracy—are required for a belief to attain positive epistemic status. To return to Quine's metaphor, normative epistemology is like engineering. Depending on the context, it may be more or less important that a bridge be long-lasting, or resistant to certain environmental conditions, or aesthetically pleasing. There is no fixed standard against which we are required to evaluate it. Analogously, it is up to us to choose the standards relative to which we want to evaluate our beliefs. In many contexts, reliability is paramount. In others, other norms (for example, one or another variety of coherence) may come to the fore.

3.1.2 Pluralism

While *reliability* figures centrally in the account of memory knowledge developed here, the account will not assume that *reliabilism* is adequate as a general theory of knowledge or justification. Two different sorts of problem favor rejecting reliabilism as an adequate general epistemology; the second is at the same time a reason for rejecting the search for a general epistemology itself. First, to the extent that we are committed to reliabilism, a feature of the theory itself suggests that there may be no objective difference between justified and unjustified beliefs. Second, the failure of epistemologists to converge on a unified general epistemology supports the view that reliability is only one member of a larger set of epistemically valuable properties—where epistemically valuable properties are nothing more than properties that we want our beliefs, systems of beliefs, and belief-forming processes to have, insofar as we are concerned with learning about the world—none of which has a reasonable claim to being the sole factor capable of conferring positive epistemic status.

Consider the first problem. As has often been observed, there appears to be no principled way of specifying the precise threshold of reliability that a process must meet in order for the beliefs that it produces to count as justified, and hence—assuming that they are true, and bracketing the question of epistemic luck—to count as knowledgeable. One natural move to make in response to this problem is to go contextualist, letting context determine the degree of reliability required for justification (see, e.g., Green 2014). A contextually variable threshold may or may not be compatible with naturalism, but it is clear that it does not secure the sort of objective distinction between knowledge and mere nonknowledgeable true belief that epistemologists have traditionally sought. Another possible move is to insist that it will prove possible, in the long run, to specify a precise threshold. There is no obvious reason, however, to expect that this will in fact prove possible. A more radical move should therefore be taken seriously: rather than taking the impossibility of specifying a non-vague threshold to constitute a reason for rejecting reliabilism, we might take it to constitute a reason for abandoning the very attempt to theorize knowledge, understood in a strict sense, as a state different in kind from mere true belief.

On this view, though we might conventionally refer to "knowledge," there is in fact no objective difference between knowledge and mere true belief. Subjects have beliefs, and those beliefs can be true or false—there is a difference between believing and failing to believe, between believing accurately and believing inaccurately. And true beliefs can be more or less reliably produced. But it is not as if, once some threshold of reliability is crossed, true beliefs become states of a different sort—*knowledge*, as opposed to *mere true beliefs*. While we may wish, for practical purposes, to specify a degree of reliability that is desirable relative to a given context, such specifications should not be viewed as attempts to mark a real difference between different kinds of true belief (knowledgeable vs. non-knowledgeable). It remains possible to evaluate true beliefs as being epistemically better or worse, since they may be more or less reliably produced, but the differences here will be differences of degree, not differences of kind.

Turning to the second problem, the possibility remains open of insisting that level of reliability determines *degree* of justification; but even this more modest position encounters serious difficulties. Familiar versions of the Gettier problem already show that reliability cannot be the whole story about what determines the epistemic status of a belief, as reliability is insufficient to rule out epistemic luck.[3] The reliabilist might therefore grant that reliability is not sufficient for knowledge, while insisting that justification, in particular, is exhausted by reliability. Even if we set aside epistemic luck, however, what Pritchard (2005) refers to as the "ability intuition" suggests that reliability cannot be the only factor responsible for determining the epistemic status of a subject's beliefs, and that, if reliability is to confer positive epistemic status, it must result from a cognitive achievement on the part of the agent. Consider the case of "Temp." Temp forms his beliefs about the temperature in the room by consulting a thermometer. The thermometer appears to be normal, but in fact it is malfunctioning and randomly indicates different temperatures. However, there is a hidden agent who controls the temperature in the room, adjusting it so that it matches the temperature indicated by the thermometer at any given time. Temp's temperature beliefs are reliably formed, but intuitively he does not *know* the temperature in the room. One natural way of explaining why Temp lacks knowledge is to point to the fact that the reliability of his belief-forming process has nothing to do with his cognitive ability. Or consider the case of "Alvin" (originally from Plantinga 1993; adapted by Pritchard 2010), who has a brain lesion that randomly but reliably causes him to form true beliefs about arithmetical sums. Assuming that Alvin has no understanding of the nature of the lesion, the relevant beliefs intuitively fail to qualify as knowledge, yet reliabilism will count him as having knowledge. Even if, in light of the argument from vagueness, we are no longer aiming at a theory of knowledge as a state distinct from mere true belief, these cases pose a problem, as they suggest that our epistemic evaluations need to take factors other than reliability into account.

Reliabilist responses to cases of this sort are available (e.g., Becker 2013), but betting on the success of one of these would (to put it mildly) be rather risky. This does not, however, imply that we should simply reject reliabilism and adopt another theory of justification, for the fate of reliabilism—a plausible theory of justification which quickly encounters seemingly insurmountable problems—is far from unique. It is no exaggeration to say that *every* major theory of justification or knowledge that has been proposed so far—including versions of foundationalism and coherentism, reliabilism, and virtue epistemology, to list only the most prominent theories—faces a similar fate. Pritchard, for example, takes the ability intuition to be fundamental, and his (anti-luck) virtue epistemology is therefore designed to respect it, but cases can be identified in which the agent's cognitive abilities do not make a significant contribution to the formation of a true belief, but in which this does *not* seem to count against the positive epistemic status of the relevant belief (Lackey 2007b; Michaelian 2014; Vaesen 2011). In short, epistemologists have so far been unable to formulate a theory immune to serious counterexamples. One possible reaction to this track record would be to throw up our hands and give up on the attempt to develop a general epistemology. And in fact something much like this reaction may be appropriate. But throwing up our hands need not amount to an admission that no progress has been made. Nor need it amount to a prediction that no progress is likely to be made.

Consider a (partly fictional) story told by DePaul. After reviewing the history of acrimonious debate over the nature of knowledge and justification in pre- and post-Gettier epistemology, he imagines a happy ending to the story:

Then something started to change. Perhaps it was because no one managed to produce a nice easy definition of knowledge. But for whatever reason, the epistemologists stopped worrying quite so much about knowledge. They started to realize that every one of them (or nearly every one—some poor souls maybe did come up entirely empty-handed) had latched onto something interesting and important and valuable, even if at most one of them had managed to identify what was involved in knowing. They began to think, "Having a proper foundation *and* reliability *and* cohering *and* functioning properly *and even* fulfilling one's epistemic obligations are all valuable and important after all. None of these concepts is perfectly clear; they all require more clarification and explication and analysis. So why fight. There is plenty of work for all of us to do, each on his or her own favorite concept." (DePaul 2001, 171)

A number of years later, we are perhaps entitled to go further than DePaul, to bet explicitly that *none* of the epistemologies that have been proposed so far is correct when taken as a theory of knowledge in the strict sense; none of them is correct because there is no one thing in the world— "justification," or "knowledge," or something else—with respect to which they might be correct.

In other words, the track record of epistemology so far suggests a pluralistic metaepistemology. On this view (cf. Alston 1993), progress has indeed been made in epistemology, just not with respect to the question of the nature of knowledge; we can continue to make progress by continuing to investigate the various epistemically valuable properties that we have been investigating (and more besides), even though none of these may turn out to be necessary or sufficient for knowledge. On a pluralistic and naturalistic approach, any empirically tractable property of beliefs, systems of beliefs, or belief-forming processes that we are inclined to take into account when assessing cognizers' attempts to learn about the world, as well as relationships among these, is a legitimate object of investigation for epistemology. Given this sort of pluralism, the task of first-order epistemology is not to discover *the* correct theory of knowledge, but rather to investigate a range of epistemically valuable properties and their interrelations. "Knowledge," on this view, is a label with no strict conditions of application, an approbative term that we tend to apply to beliefs that have a sufficient number of epistemically valuable properties (to a sufficient extent). Reliability, as a key truth-linked property, remains an appropriate object of sustained epistemological investigation, but it is only one member of a larger set of epistemically valuable properties. In line with this view, "knowledge" should be understood, in the investigation of episodic memory knowledge to follow, as a term of convenience.

DePaul is ultimately interested in monism and pluralism about epistemic value, and, in particular, in the monistic view that truth is the only thing of epistemic value. Regardless of whether this specific form of veritistic epistemic value monism is correct, it is uncontroversial that truth (more broadly, accuracy) is epistemically valuable (Ahlstrom-Vij 2013), and the value of truth explains why we value truth-linked (accuracy-linked) properties such as reliability. But reliability is not the only such property. Goldman (1992), for instance, has emphasized additional properties, including power and speed. Though they take a back seat to reliability, both of these properties are taken into account below. And, though the argument to follow will not be concerned with the ability intuition, it will also take the anti-luck condition defended by Pritchard (2005) into account.

It may be objected that pluralism entails epistemological relativism and that relativism, in turn, is a deeply unappealing view. Suppose, for example, that we want to evaluate a given belief-forming process in terms of its reliability. What can we legitimately say to persuade someone who refuses to recognize the importance of reliability, preferring to employ, say, some purely aesthetic standard of evaluation? Given relativism, one norm would seem to be as good as the other. In responding to this objection, it is important to distinguish between more and less extreme forms of relativism. The worry is that, if there are no objectively correct epistemic norms, then one who endorses a given set of norms is not in a position to maintain that those who endorse rival norms are mistaken, in which case an "anything goes" attitude would be appropriate. Now, on the pluralistic view, it is indeed the case that an evaluator who cares about, say, coherence rather than reliability is not making a mistake but simply endorsing a different, equally legitimate epistemic norm. But this does not mean that anything goes. There are limits on what may count as a legitimate standard of evaluation, limits imposed by the nature of the epistemic itself. As Quine put it, normative epistemology is the technology of *truth*-seeking. A norm is legitimate, as an *epistemic* norm, to the extent that it is concerned with allowing us to attain true beliefs or, more generally, accurate representations, and likewise to avoid false beliefs and inaccurate representations. On this sort of moderate pluralism, a broad range of norms will turn out to be legitimate, but there are limits. Purely aesthetic norms, for example, are illegitimate, as are any norms that are demonstrably not truth-linked.

3.2 The Reliability of Episodic Memory

With this background in place, the remainder of this chapter looks at the implications of the naturalist-reliabilist framework for episodic memory knowledge, beginning with the generality problem and then considering how the notions of belief, truth, and reliability itself apply to episodic memory.

3.2.1 The Generality Problem and Memory

Any view that assigns a central role to reliability will inherit certain problems from reliabilism, chief among them the generality problem—the problem of determining the belief-forming process type the reliability of which is relevant to the epistemic assessment of a given belief (Conee and Feldman 1998; Feldman 1985; Pollock 1984). Any given belief-forming process token falls under indefinitely many process types. I form a belief about what I did last April by relying on memory, episodic memory, episodic memory in a cognitively normal adult, episodic memory in a cognitively normal adult wearing a white shirt on a Friday morning, and so on. The reliability of these process types inevitably varies. How are we to determine which level of reliability affects the epistemic standing of my belief?

Opponents and proponents of reliabilism alike sometimes assume both that the generality problem requires a solution which is specific to epistemology, in the sense that it does not just import some pre-existing method of singling out processes from another field, and that it requires a solution which is fully general, in the sense that it provides a formula for singling out a unique process as relevant in any given case. Given a commitment to naturalism, however, neither assumption is justified. As far as the first assumption goes, we are free to say simply that belief-forming processes are to be individuated in epistemology in the way in which cognitive processes are individuated in cognitive science in general. As a chapter of psychology or cognitive science, epistemology is concerned with natural kinds of belief-forming processes, and these can be individuated using the methods employed in other branches of cognitive science. Individuating cognitive processes is often a messy affair, and there need be no one-size-fits-all formula for doing so. As the previous chapter demonstrated, we can make considerable progress on individuating memory processes by relying carefully on memory systems research. Subsequent chapters will show that relying on mental time travel research allows us to delineate the episodic memory process with a reasonable degree of clarity. Both bodies of research, of course, themselves rely on converging evidence from multiple experimental paradigms, as well as a range of theoretical considerations.

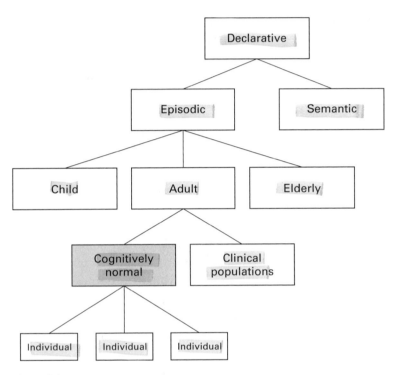

Figure 3.1
Episodic memory and the generality problem.

Turning to the second assumption, suppose that we arrive at an adequate general account of the process of episodic remembering. Such an account will allow us to rule out such unnatural processes as "episodic memory in a cognitively normal adult wearing a white shirt on a Friday morning." Are we then in a position to say that the generality problem is solved, as far as episodic memory knowledge is concerned? Yes and no. On the one hand, we have only a partial solution to the problem. As we saw above, natural kinds are arranged in a hierarchical manner, ranging from more general to more specific. If the analysis so far is right, episodic memory may be, along with declarative memory, a subkind of the more general kind declarative memory. But there are important variations in the operation of episodic memory in different populations. For instance, children lack the capacity for full-blown episodic memory—and mental time travel more generally (Russell, Alexis, and Clayton 2010)—before a certain age, and once they do develop the capacity, their episodic remembering may initially be particularly susceptible to certain kinds of distortion. Similarly, there are age-related changes in mental time travel in adults after a certain age, with older adults generating fewer episodic details (Addis, Roberts, and Schacter 2011; Gaesser et al. 2011). To make matters worse, just as there are important variations in the operation of episodic memory between populations, there are important variations between individuals.[4] Thus we might end up with something like the (incomplete) hierarchical picture given in figure 3.1. So, while the naturalist approach gives us a means of ruling out unnatural kinds, we are still in need of a justification for locating our investigation at one node in the hierarchy of natural kinds—say, cognitively normal adults in general—rather than another.

On the other hand, this partial solution is all that is required. Suppose that we are interested in investigating the reliability of episodic remembering. Which node should we select? Should we, for example, take very young children or older adults into account? Given that we are dealing with a hierarchy of natural kinds, there is no principled reason for choosing one node rather than another as fixing the reliability of episodic remembering. We may in certain contexts be interested in the workings of episodic memory on average, across all subjects capable of it, ignoring developmental and other differences. In other contexts, we may be interested in a more specific population (for example, older adults) or even, in the limiting case, in a specific subject (for example, a patient with an unusual memory impairment). Just as we are free, within the limits set by truth-relevance, to choose the standards (reliability, coherence, etc.) by which we assess a cognitive process, we are free, within the limits set by the hierarchy of kinds found in nature, to choose how widely or narrowly to individuate the process. The focus in this book is on episodic remembering in cognitively normal adults, but investigations of the reliability of remembering at other levels or in other populations are equally legitimate.

The foregoing responds to the generality problem as it applies to a general inquiry into the epistemology of episodic memory, but it does not provide a means of determining which process type is relevant when evaluating the epistemic status of a given belief. Consider again my belief about what I did last April; which level of reliability, among those associated with the potentially relevant processes, determines its epistemic status? The pluralistic framework sketched above suggests the following view. Epistemologists usually presuppose that there must be a determinate fact of the matter about the epistemic status of a given belief. But this assumption is not compulsory. Indeed, if we are free to individuate belief-forming processes more or less narrowly, and if there is no privileged, uniquely correct standard of epistemic evaluation, it is clear that there is no determinate fact of the matter about the epistemic status of specific beliefs. In short, epistemic evaluation is always relative both to the norms that we choose to apply *and* to a way of individuating processes.

3.2.2   Metamemory and Belief

The focus in epistemology is usually on justification, warrant, or other such factors; that is, the focus is usually on "epistemizing" factors (Alston 1978), factors responsible for conferring positive epistemic status on true beliefs, and less often on belief and truth themselves. But there are difficulties involved in applying the notions of belief and truth to episodic memory, and the remainder of this section looks at how the concepts of belief, truth, and (consequently) reliability apply to episodic memory.

Epistemologists sometimes say, in an offhand way, that memory stores beliefs (e.g., Goldman 1986). While this may be acceptable shorthand for certain purposes, it suggests far too simple a picture of the relationship between memory and belief. As subsequent chapters will demonstrate, even to the extent that it is legitimate to view memory in terms of storage, it is not *beliefs* that are stored, but rather *contents* that, depending on the outcome of the agent's metacognitive monitoring of his memory, might or might not end up being accepted when retrieved. In other words, in advance of retrieval, the agent does not have a determinate attitude toward a given stored content. The point is not that memory stores beliefs that are merely dispositional, in the sense that it stores contents that the subject is inclined to endorse, thereby forming an occurrent belief, upon retrieval. The subject's dispositions themselves vary depending on the course of the retrieval process and the subject's metacognitive monitoring of it, and it therefore cannot be said even that memory stores dispositional beliefs. As Koriat and Adiv (2012) emphasize, there is evidence for a model of belief formation—they focus specifically on social beliefs, but the model is likely to generalize—on which beliefs are constructed online via a sampling procedure in which subjects access a variety of cues from memory and select the answer best supported by the accessed cues. According to this model, the attitude that the subject ends up adopting toward a given content is not determined by a stable disposition but rather by a range of contingent, contextually variable factors. Moreover, the subject's level of confidence in a given belief is itself determined by metacognitive monitoring of the construction process. To give just one vivid illustration, a subject's attitude toward a given proposition is affected not only by his evidence for and against it but also by criteria such as fluency, where fluency can be increased or decreased by contingent factors such as the mere repetition of a statement or the ease of readability of the font in which it is written (Reber and Unkelbach 2010).

3.2.3 Episodic Content and Truth

Setting aside the question of what is stored, the applicability of the notion of belief to episodic memory also depends on the applicability of the notion of truth. While semantic remembering produces propositional contents which are then, depending on the outcome of metacognitive monitoring, endorsed (or rejected) by the agent, at which point it becomes meaningful to say that the agent believes (or disbelieves) the relevant proposition, episodic remembering produces not propositional contents but rather contents of a sort such that the agent's attitude toward them cannot easily be assimilated to simple (dis)belief. The goal here is not to give a detailed theory of episodic memory content. Given the tight link between episodic content and perceptual content, and given ongoing debate over the nature of perceptual content, this would take us too far afield. But a brief description of some key features of episodic memory content is in order.

While the nature of the link between perceptual content and memory content is unclear, it is clear that they differ in interesting ways, with the consequence that episodic remembering cannot be viewed simply as a matter of reproducing perceptual content. Going back to Locke (1689), who argued that memory enables the mind "to revive Perceptions, which it has once had, with this additional perception annexed to them, that it has had them before," many views have located the difference between perceptual and memory content in their respective temporal dimensions, holding, roughly, that whereas perception presents a scene as occurring now, memory presents a scene as having occurred in the past. Byrne (2010), for example, argues that memory content includes the information that the represented event is located in the past. McCormack and Hoerl (1999) argue that it includes a representation of the agent's temporal perspective with respect to the event in question. Fernández (2008) argues that it includes a representation of the causal connection between a past event and the larger memory representation itself. And Searle (1983) goes so far as to argue that the content of an episodic memory represents an event, the relevant past experience as caused by the event, and the present memory itself as caused by the past experience. Martin (2001) and Recanati (2007) endorse similar views. The view developed here, in contrast, will assign the temporal aspect of episodic memory to the phenomenology of remembering rather than to its content. But even on such a view, there are important differences between perceptual content and memory content, stemming from the constructive character of remembering. Perception itself may be a constructive process, but the construction involved in remembering is, as we will see, dramatically more extensive.

Regardless of whether we locate the temporal aspect of episodic memory in content or in phenomenology, the key point, for present purposes, is that episodic remembering, along with other episodic constructive processes, produces representations that are like perceptual representations in having sensory rather than propositional content. Episodic content need not be purely sensory; it may have propositional aspects, especially given the involvement of semantic memory in mental time travel (Klein 2013a; Martin-Ordas, Atance, and Louw 2012). But it consists at least in part of sensory content, and sensory content is nonpropositional, in the sense that it cannot be evaluated for truth and falsity in a binary manner. Unlike the propositional contents delivered by semantic memory, which can be evaluated as simply true or false, the richer representations delivered by episodic memory can be *more or less* accurate—accurate in some respects and inaccurate in others. For example, when I remember my lunch with a visiting German colleague last month, my memory may be accurate with respect to the appearance of my colleague's face but inaccurate with respect to the clothing that he was wearing, or accurate with respect to the gist of the news he gave me about mutual acquaintances in Germany but inaccurate with respect to specific phrases he used, and so on (see, e.g., Neisser 1981).

This characteristic of episodic content has two important consequences. First, strictly speaking, a graded notion of accuracy is needed when assessing the reliability of episodic memory. Second, the standard, binary notion of belief as an all-or-nothing state—either an agent endorses a proposition or he does not—is not straightforwardly applicable to episodic memory. We have already seen that memory stores not beliefs but contents and that an agent's confidence in a retrieved content varies according to his metacognitive assessment of the retrieval process. The present point is distinct: when it comes to episodic representations in particular, all-or-nothing belief is not straightforwardly applicable because the agent may have differing levels of confidence with respect to different aspects of a given retrieved episodic representation. Returning to the example given above, I may be highly confident that my memory for my colleague's face is accurate, less confident in my memory for what he was wearing, and so on.

3.2.4   The Concept of Reliability

These consequences threaten to turn assessing the reliability of episodic memory into an extremely delicate matter. Fortunately, things are not quite as bad as they seem. Despite the second consequence (concerning all-or-nothing belief), there is clearly a sense in which an agent can accept or reject an episodic representation as a whole. Indeed, in many cases, we find episodic memories so compelling that we have difficulty accepting that they are not wholly accurate even when presented with decisive evidence that they are inaccurate in certain respects (Payne et al. 1997). Evaluations of specific components of an episodic representation thus can give rise to overall endorsement or rejection of the representation as a whole. Thus, when assessing the overall reliability of episodic memory, we may concern ourselves with the attitudes that are produced by metacognitive monitoring, and these are binary (endorse/reject), keeping in mind that this is not the whole story about reliability.[5] Returning to the first consequence (graded accuracy), however, since the accuracy of the contents of the relevant attitudes cannot themselves be assessed in a binary manner (true/false), we do require a concept of reliability that takes graded accuracy into account, in contrast to the standard concept of reliability as the ratio of true beliefs to total beliefs produced by the process. One natural solution to this problem is to consider the average accuracy of those episodic representations that are endorsed by the agent.

Of course, given that we do not actually have a measure of the accuracy of episodic representations, this solution is merely conceptual. But it is adequate for present purposes. The goal here is not the hopeless one of coming up with a measure of the reliability of memory, but rather investigating the factors that enable memory to achieve an acceptable level of reliability. Moreover, the argument is largely concerned not with the reliability of the attitudes resulting from endorsing episodic memory representations as wholes but rather with the reliability of beliefs resulting from endorsing specific aspects of retrieved episodic memory representations. Chapter 7, for example, is concerned with the incorporation of testimonial information into retrieved episodic memory representations, and, while the effects of this process on the reliability of the resulting episodic memory representations as wholes will be discussed, the focus will be on its effects on the beliefs resulting from endorsement of the relevant aspects of the resulting representations. For the most part, then, as long as we keep the necessary caveats in mind, the argument can make do with the standard notion of reliability.

A final remark on reliability: The focus on the reliability of memory should not be taken to suggest that remembering functions exclusively to produce accurate representations of past experience. Reliability is context-relative in two distinct senses. First, the reliability of memory depends on how we as observers individuate the process of remembering, which is in part a matter of which contexts we take into account. This is the sort of context-relativity at issue in the generality problem and discussed above. Second, the reliability of memory varies according to the subject's context and goals, with accuracy sometimes taking a back seat to social and identity-related factors (Alea and Bluck 2003; Harris, Rasmussen, and Berntsen 2014; Pillemer 2003). This second sort of context-relativity is acknowledged in the argument that follows, with chapter 7, for example, looking at social influences on memory. The evolutionary perspective developed in part IV, however, will ultimately suggest that there are limits on the level of unreliability to which these other factors can give rise.

II Episodic Memory as Mental Time Travel

Part II deals with the book's first main question: what is the nature of episodic memory? The answer defended here—an account of remembering as imagining or simulating the past—builds on existing work in philosophy and psychology but goes beyond available accounts in both disciplines. The current psychological literature contains a number of competing approaches that have in common the basic claim that episodic remembering is a constructive process intimately related to future-oriented mental time travel and to a broader range of forms of episodic imagination. The argument builds on these approaches to develop an explicit account of episodic memory as a form of episodic imagination. The simulation theory of memory implies that memory does not have a privileged status relative to other forms of imagination: episodic memory is distinguished from other forms of episodic imagination only by its specific temporal orientation.

At the same time, the argument draws out the implications of research on constructive memory and mental time travel for extant philosophical theories of remembering. The causal theory, according to which remembering crucially involves an appropriate causal connection with the agent's past experience of the relevant episode, is arguably the most influential of these theories. It is relatively straightforward matter to establish that the constructive character of remembering, which may introduce a significant gap between the content of a retrieved memory and the content of the subject's earlier experience, necessitates modifications to the causal theory. The current argument goes beyond this relatively modest point to argue that treating remembering as imagining the past requires abandoning the requirement of a causal connection altogether, replacing the causal theory with a *purely* simulational theory of remembering.

4 The Commonsense Conception

What does common sense tell us about the nature of remembering? We could do worse than to start with Reid, the great philosophical partisan of common sense, who argued:

Things remembered must be things formerly perceived or known. I remember the transit of Venus over the sun in the year 1769. I must therefore have perceived it at the time it happened, otherwise I could not now remember it. Our first acquaintance with any object of thought cannot be by remembrance. Memory can only produce a continuance or renewal of a former acquaintance with the thing remembered. (Reid 1785, 305)

In one respect, Reid's view accords well with our common sense: we ordinarily take it for granted that remembering is, roughly, a matter of reproducing an earlier thought or experience. But this way of putting things suggests that remembering involves an internal *representation*—in the case of episodic memory, a representation of a past event, entertained by the subject at the current point in time, standing in some sort of correspondence with a representation of the same event entertained by the subject at an earlier point in time—and in this respect Reid departs from current common sense, as he himself favored a form of direct realism. As he put it, "upon the strictest attention, memory appears to me to have things that are past, and not present ideas, for its object" (1764, 46). The dispute between direct and indirect (or representative) realism, according to which memory puts us in contact with the past only via the intermediary of an internal representation, is discussed below. For now, the point is simply that our commonsense conception of remembering, contra Reid, seems best cashed out in terms of the preservation or reproduction of internal representations of experienced events.

While philosophers often take this preservative conception more or less for granted, it is difficult to reconcile with the constructive view of remembering that predominates in psychology. The constructive view is compatible with the involvement of internal representations in remembering, but it denies that remembering is a matter of simply preserving representations. In his foundational statement of the constructive view, for example, Bartlett argued:

> It is with memory as it is with the stroke in a skilled game. We may fancy that we are repeating a series of movements learned a long time before from a text-book or from a teacher. But motion study shows that in fact we build up the stroke afresh on a basis of the immediately preceding balance of postures and the momentary needs of the game. Every time we make it, it has its own characteristics. (Bartlett 1932, 204)

The view that remembering is not a matter of *reproducing* but rather a matter of *recreating* a representation of an episode has been abundantly confirmed by subsequent empirical work. This chapter and the next will argue that the recreative character of remembering requires us to abandon the idea that "things remembered must be things formerly perceived or known." Things remembered need not be things formerly perceived or known, in the sense that remembering can—without ceasing to qualify as genuine remembering, in a full, strict sense—give us access to a past episode that goes beyond the access we had at the time at which it occurred. Fundamentally, on this view, remembering is generative, not preservative: it is not a matter of preserving a representation but rather of constructing, on the basis of stored information originating in a variety of different sources, as well as information available in the subject's current environment, a *new* representation of a past episode. In short, remembering is a matter of imagining or simulating the past. Episodic simulation may in some cases eventuate in a representation that comes close to reproducing a previous representation of the target episode, but its function is not reproduction. In most cases, there are important differences between the representation produced by remembering and the agent's original experience of the event. In principle, there may even be cases in which the agent remembers an event that he did not originally experience.

This chapter and the next take us partway toward the simulation theory of memory. Beginning by explicitly spelling out the commitments of the commonsense conception of remembering, this chapter shows how the causal theory—arguably the most successful philosophical theory of remembering to date—is motivated by the inability of the commonsense conception to distinguish between remembering and imagining. Chapter 5 then argues that the constructive character of remembering at minimum requires a significant update to the causal theory. Turning to recent work on mental time travel, chapter 6 takes us the rest of the way to the simulation theory, arguing that even the updated version of the causal theory fails to fully accommodate constructive remembering, and that doing justice to the latter requires abandoning the requirement of a causal connection entirely. If the simulation theory is right, it turns out that the very search for criteria sufficient for distinguishing between remembering and imagining is mistaken.

Before proceeding, a note on the dialectic: the early stages of the argument appeal to our intuitions about whether certain cases qualify as cases of genuine remembering. Given the naturalist framework, such appeals can only be provisional at best, and later stages will in fact conclude that our intuitions about many of these cases are mistaken, in the sense that, while they provide insight into our ordinary concept of remembering, that concept itself fails to correspond to the nature of the process of remembering. One might therefore wonder whether, once we have given up on trying to satisfy the relevant intuitions, one of the theories which had previously been abandoned on the ground that it failed to conform to them might not end up being a feasible theory of memory after all. This is possible in principle, but it will turn out not to be the case.

4.1   The Experience Condition

Ordinarily, we take it for granted that a person cannot remember an event that he did not personally experience. This assumption is captured by the experience condition, according to which, if S remembers an episode e, then

- S experienced e.[1]

That we take the experience condition for granted is reflected in the ease with which we grasp the distinction between episodic and semantic memory. One may semantically remember *that* a certain event occurred, regardless of whether one experienced it. I (semantically) remember that my great-grandfather traveled from what was then the Ottoman empire to the United States when he was a child. In contrast, we suppose, it is only possible to episodically remember a given event if one experienced it when it occurred. I am unable to (episodically) remember my great-grandfather's voyage, but I am able to (episodically) remember my own (much less dramatic) voyage from France to Turkey several years ago because I experienced the latter but not the former event.[2]

Two features of the experience condition will be important in what follows. First, it implies that if a subject is involved in an event without experiencing it—for example, because he was unconscious at the time—then he cannot later remember it. Beyond this, the relevant notion of experience is flexible. In particular, it applies both to experience of external events and to experience of internal, mental events. Thus one can remember not only events which one observed via one's senses, but also episodes in one's mental life such as thoughts and daydreams. This straightforward point will turn out to have important epistemological consequences. Second, the condition should be interpreted as saying merely that the subject experienced the relevant episode, not that his experience of the episode exhausts the content of his memory of it; the reason for interpreting the condition in this way will be made clear below.

4.2   The Current Representation Condition

Assuming that we are concerned with occurrent remembering, remembering implies that the subject now entertains a representation of the relevant episode. In other words, if S remembers e, then

- S now has a representation R of e.

On the face of it, the current representation condition appears to be incompatible with direct realism. Given that many philosophers have favored direct realism (in addition to Reid, see Bergson 1896, Russell 1912, and, more recently, Bernecker 2008), it is worth looking at this matter more closely.

4.2.1   Direct Realism

While direct realism about memory has found its defenders, the view is subject to a number of powerful objections. Some of these are analogous to objections to direct realism about perception, while others pertain specifically to direct realism about the objects of memory. The cotemporality objection belongs to the latter category. According to this objection, remembering cannot be a matter of direct awareness of past events, simply because past events do not exist at the time at which we are aware of them (Furlong 1951). Bernecker (2008) argues that this objection can be avoided by rejecting presentism, the view that past events do not exist. While this is technically correct, rejecting presentism is a high price to pay for preserving direct realism, simply because eternalism—the denial of presentism; that is, the view that past events continue to exist—is not a particularly plausible view. Despite its intuitive implausibility, of course, it might turn out to be correct, but adopting such a bold ontological view simply in order to avoid an objection to a specific theory of remembering seems unacceptably ad hoc.

Direct realists must also respond to an argument from illusion (Furlong 1953) which runs in parallel to the standard argument from illusion in the philosophy of perception. The argument from illusion against direct realism about perception appeals to perceptual illusions and other sorts of perceptual error to motivate the claim that perceiving does not put the subject in direct contact with the events he perceives. Analogously, the argument from illusion against direct realism about memory appeals to memory illusions and errors to motivate the claim that remembering does not put the subject in direct contact with the things he remembers. To illustrate, compare the blind spot illusion, in which the visual system fills in a visual region from which no information is received by assuming that it is similar to the surrounding region, to the sort of memory illusion at work in the Deese-Roediger-McDermott (DRM) paradigm, in which subjects are induced to remember nonpresented lure words (e.g., *doctor*) when asked to recall a series of thematically related presented words (*hospital, nurse, sick, medicine* ...) (Deese 1959; Roediger and McDermott 1995). Bernecker argues that the direct realist can resist the argument from illusion by adopting a form of disjunctivism about memory analogous to disjunctivism about perception—that is, by maintaining that genuine and illusory memory are states of different kinds, with the subject being in direct contact with a past episode in the case of genuine remembering, but in contact with an internal representation in the case of illusory remembering. Again, while this is technically correct, adopting disjunctivism is a high price to pay for preserving direct realism. Disjunctivism about memory, like disjunctivism about perception, portrays a unified phenomenon as something fundamentally disunified. While disjunctivism may be coherent as an account of our concept of remembering (Debus 2008), it thus has little appeal as part of an account of remembering as a psychologically real process. Accurate and illusory memories are products of one and the same cognitive process; while the process produces an inaccurate representation in the latter case, it nevertheless remains the same process that is at work in the former case.

4.2.2 Indirect Realism

In light of these problems, indirect realism appears to be the more promising alternative. But it, too, is subject to objections. The most serious of these, as Sutton (2012) points out, turns on the observation that remembering does not typically seem to involve awareness of internal representations from which past episodes are then inferred; that is, that remembering is phenomenologically direct.

Now, while it may be the case that remembering is *typically* phenomenologically direct, it is nevertheless clear that it is *sometimes* phenomenologically indirect. Later chapters will discuss forms of metamemory including source monitoring, a metacognitive monitoring process in which the subject attempts to determine the origins of memories in sources such as experience, imagination, and communication by relying on features of their contents. Source monitoring is typically unconscious, in the sense that the subject is unaware of the unfolding of the metacognitive monitoring process; the source monitoring framework is thus compatible with the phenomenological directness of remembering. However, source monitoring on occasion takes on a conscious form, with the subject actively attempting to determine the origin of remembered information; in such cases, remembering is phenomenologically indirect, as the subject consciously contemplates a retrieved memory representation. Conscious source monitoring, along with other forms of conscious metamemory, supports the mediation of remembering by internal representations. The involvement of unconscious source monitoring in retrieval suggests that remembering is mediated by internal representations even when it is phenomenologically direct.

4.2.3 A Compromise View

The phenomenology of remembering may thus simply turn out to be a poor guide to the metaphysics of the process. The phenomenological directness of remembering in typical cases notwithstanding, the role of metamemory suggests a moderate form of indirect realism, according to which representations can mediate our contact with the past without remembering necessarily involving awareness of the representations themselves (Sutton 2012). Interestingly, this form of indirect realism is sufficiently moderate that it may be acceptable even to direct realists. Bernecker (2008), for example, secures the compatibility of the causal theory of remembering—which, as we will see, claims that remembering essentially involves memory traces, which amount to internal representations—with direct realism by granting that memory traces play a role in putting us in contact with the past even if we are not aware of them: it is in virtue of *having* an appropriate representation that one is in contact with the relevant past event, but remembering the past event does not require that one be *aware of* the representation itself. This moderate form of direct realism appears to be more or less equivalent to the moderate form of indirect realism described by Sutton, and at this point any remaining disagreement between the two views may be merely verbal.

4.3   The Previous Representation Condition

Intuitively, it is not enough, if a subject is to be said to remember a past event, for him to satisfy the experience condition and the current representation condition—that is, to have experienced the event and to now represent it; he must, roughly speaking, have committed a representation of the event to memory after his initial experience of it. In other words, if S remembers e, then

- S previously had a representation R' of e.

A previous representation condition along these lines is needed to rule out cases in which the subject experiences an event (thus satisfying the experience condition), forms no memory of it, but then later entertains a representation of it (satisfying the current representation condition). Such cases are not merely hypothetical; most of our experiences fail to lead to the formation of memories, and we are capable of thinking about past events even when they are not remembered. For example, I know that I gave a lecture on the Gettier problem last month, but, perhaps because it was uneventful and because I have given similar lectures many times before, I retained no memory of the episode. Nevertheless, I am able to generate a detailed mental image of it, drawing on memories of previous lectures on the same topic, knowledge of the students enrolled in the course, my own views about the Gettier problem, my familiarity with the layout of the relevant classroom, and so on. Unless we require satisfaction of a previous representation condition, we will have to say that I remember the lecture, which, intuitively, I do not.

4.4   The Appropriate Connection Condition

The previous representation condition refers not to the agent's original experience of the event but to an initial *memory* representation.[3] Hence we require a condition describing the relationship between the original experience and the memory representation:

- there is an appropriate connection between R' and S's experience of e.

The appropriate connection condition is intended to capture the idea that the stored representation of the episode must originate in the subject's experience of the episode in the right way. A variant of the preceding example can be used to illustrate the need for the condition. Suppose, as before, that I gave a lecture on the Gettier problem last month but formed no memory of the event. Suppose that, last week, I imagined the lecture and formed a memory representation of the imagined lecture. Suppose, finally, that today I retrieved this stored representation. In this scenario, the experience condition, the current representation condition, and the previous representation condition are satisfied, but intuitively I do not remember the lecture because no appropriate connection obtains between my previous representation of the lecture and my original experience of it.

In order to give the appropriate connection condition any real content, something obviously needs to be said about what sort of connection between memory representations and experiences is "appropriate." The idea cannot be that the representation is simply a copy of the experience, since even the commonsense conception allows that a certain amount of processing might intervene between these two stages in the memory process. For example, a subject may see a fluttering red, blue, and orange rectangle and, after performing certain inferences based on contextual information— perhaps he has just flown into Zvartnots airport—end up storing a representation of the Armenian flag flying. This stored representation, in turn, may later serve as the basis for his remembering the Armenian flag flying.

The commonsense conception of appropriate connections between experiences and memory representations thus builds in a certain degree of flexibility. (This is why, as noted above, the experience condition should not be interpreted too strictly.) The question then becomes: *how much* difference between the original experience of the episode and the stored representation is permissible? Intuitively, the answer is "not very much"—the addition of some minimal conceptual content, as in the example above, may be permissible, but not much more. As we will see below, we in fact need to permit much more extensive differences, so we may set this point aside for now.

4.5   The Content-Matching Condition

The commonsense conception of remembering allows for some difference between the subject's experience of an event and his initial memory representation of it, but it allows for little difference between the latter representation and the retrieved representation of the event. The conditions discussed so far, however—the experience condition, the current representation condition, the previous representation condition, and the appropriate connection condition—allow that the particular way the subject now represents an episode may deviate dramatically from the way he previously represented it. To illustrate, suppose that I take a colleague visiting Paris for the first time to see the Panthéon and retain only an image of him posing for a snapshot in front of the building. Later, when I "remember" the scene, I have a detailed image of the building as a whole (which I have seen on many other occasions) with crowds of tourists swarming around it (which I have also often seen). Does this count as a genuine memory? Intuitively, if the divergence between the content originally stored and the retrieved content is too great, I am not remembering, even if the retrieved content happens to be accurate with respect to the relevant event.

In order to capture the idea that, in order for genuine remembering to occur, there must be a close fit between the subject's current representation and his previous representation, we may assume that

- the content of R is the same as or a subset of that of R'.

This content-matching condition does not require that the content of the current representation be *identical* to that of the previous representation. Ordinarily, we allow that the content of a retrieved memory might be significantly less detailed than that of the representation initially stored, due to intervening forgetting. So, for example, it is compatible with my remembering the episode that I initially stored a detailed representation of the full scene in front of the Panthéon but now can recall only the sight of my colleague in front of the building. In other words, the content of the retrieved representation may be a subset of that of the representation stored earlier. But it must not be a superset of that of the previous representation; nor is mere intersection sufficient. The content of the current representation, in short, must not go beyond that of the previous representation.

The current representation condition, the previous representation condition, and the content-matching condition constitute the core of preservationism, the view that remembering is essentially a matter of preserving content originally produced by another cognitive process. Preservationism is widespread in philosophy; indeed, more than eight decades after Bartlett (1932), it arguably continues to be the default view. While there have been a number of recent challenges to the view that memory is essentially preservative, these have been limited in scope. Lackey (2005) argues that remembering can generate epistemic justification but assumes that it cannot generate new content. Bernecker (2008; 2010) argues that remembering is compatible with limited modification of content but assumes that it cannot generate fundamentally new content. Preservationism and the alternative generationist view are discussed in more detail below.

4.6   The Factivity Condition

In epistemology, knowledge is usually said to be factive, meaning that if S knows that P, it is true that P. This claim has occasionally been challenged (e.g., Hazlett 2010), but it is relatively uncontroversial that our concept of knowledge implies that one cannot know what is false. Memory is likewise often said to be factive, in the sense that if S remembers that P, it is true that P. This view, too, has been challenged, but it seems clear that, though it may not imply that one must *know* if one remembers (Bernecker 2007), our concept of memory does imply that one cannot remember what is false. Since episodic remembering does not produce propositional contents but rather representations of events, the notion of factivity needs to be loosened slightly if it is to get a grip here. Saying that episodic memory is factive amounts, roughly, to the claim that, if S remembers e, then

- *e* occurred.

Stronger and weaker readings of this episodic factivity condition are available. On a strong reading, the condition says that the episode occurred just as the current representation *R* represents it as having occurred. On a weaker reading, the condition merely says that the episode occurred, remaining silent about whether it had precisely the features *R* represents it as having had. Given that a certain amount of inaccuracy with respect to the details of an episode is compatible with remembering the episode itself, the strong reading is too strong. The weak reading, however, may be too weak, since presumably if a representation of an episode is *too* inaccurate, the subject no longer counts as remembering it. What seems to be needed, then, is an intermediate interpretation of the factivity condition.

Even assuming that a suitable intermediate interpretation can be spelled out, however, it should not be included in a general theory of remembering, for it threatens to lead us back to a view akin to disjunctivism. Consider a pair of simple cases. In the first, the subject satisfies whatever conditions he needs to satisfy in order to count as remembering, including factivity. In the second, he satisfies all conditions other than factivity, perhaps because he originally succumbed to an illusion and misperceived the relevant event. Given that we build factivity into our account of remembering, we are bound to say that he remembers in the first case but not in the second. Intuitively, this conclusion may sound right—in ordinary contexts, we do not tend to say that one can *remember* an event that did not in fact occur, any more than we say that one can perceive an object that is not there. But the conclusion comes at a high price. The only difference between the two cases, we may suppose, is the accuracy of the subject's current representation, and this is purely a matter of a relation between the representation and past events. In other words, it is entirely external to the subject's cognitive processes and states. Psychologically speaking, everything is the same—it is not as if there is one kind of remembering responsible for producing accurate memories and another responsible for producing inaccurate memories. If our ultimate goal were to describe the ordinary concept of remembering (or the conditions under which we are ordinarily prepared to say that a given subject remembers), this would not be an issue. But the factivity condition has no place in the naturalistic project of describing memory as a psychologically real process (cf. Hopkins 2014). Hence, while factivity is undoubtedly part of our commonsense conception of remembering, it will not be discussed further here. Since factivity is entirely an external, relational matter, however, we can reincorporate it into the account of remembering at any point. Those not convinced by the foregoing considerations are thus free to insist on factivity, though they should bear in mind that the resulting concept of remembering will not correspond to a real cognitive process—a natural kind.[4]

4.7   Distinguishing between Memory and Imagination

Setting aside factivity, the commonsense conception says that, if S remembers e, then

- S experienced e
- S now has a representation R of e
- S previously had a representation R' of e
- there is an appropriate connection between R' and S's experience of e
- the content of R is the same as or a subset of that of R'.

While versions of these conditions are incorporated, more or less explicitly, in most available theories of remembering, they do not by themselves provide a satisfying account of remembering, as they fail to distinguish between cases of (what we would ordinarily count as) remembering and certain cases of (what we would ordinarily count as) imagining.

Consider a simple case involving forgetting. Suppose that a subject experiences an episode (thus satisfying the experience condition) and forms a short-term memory representation of it in the usual way (satisfying the previous representation and appropriate connection conditions). Suppose further that, as time goes by, he completely forgets the episode. Later, someone reminds him of the episode and, drawing on this information as well as on his knowledge of episodes of the relevant general type, he forms a detailed mental representation of it (satisfying the current representation condition). Suppose, finally, that the content of his current representation happens to correspond closely to the content of his previous representation (so that he satisfies the content-matching condition). Intuitively, the subject is merely imagining the episode, not remembering it, but the conditions considered so far do not mark this distinction.

Such cases are not merely hypothetical. Many cases involving childhood amnesia, for example, satisfy this description (Perner and Ruffman 1995). A criterion designed to discriminate between *remembering the past* and *imagining the past* therefore seems to be needed. The following section looks at two such criteria: a formal (Flage 1985), epistemic (Noxon 1976), or constitutive criterion (McDonough 2002), namely, degree of flexibility; and what has been referred to as a phenomenal criterion, namely, vivacity (Bernecker 2008)—discussed by Hume in the context of his empiricist account of memory. As the aims of the current project are not historical, the focus in both cases is on the adequacy of the criteria, not on textual faithfulness.[5] But while the focus here is not on interpreting Hume, it is important to note that, when Hume proposes his criteria, he might be responding to either of two questions about memory and imagination, questions which are sometimes run together but which should be kept apart.

McDonough gives a clear statement of the difference between them:

How are ideas of memory distinguished from ideas of imagination? [The question is] ambiguous. It might ask either (a) What constitutes the difference between an idea of memory and an idea of imagination? or (b) What are the marks which we, in practice, use to distinguish (what we take to be) ideas of memory from (what we take to be) ideas of imagination? (McDonough 2002, 73)

In this part of the book, the focus is on question (a), that is, on the objective difference between remembering and imagining. In the following part, the focus will shift to question (b), that is, to the subjective difference or differences on which subjects rely to discriminate between remembering and imagining. Because the two questions are distinct, our answers to them need not coincide. In order for a criterion to mark the objective difference between remembering and imagining, it must be applicable in every case; that is, it must refer to a feature shared by all cases of remembering and no case of imagining, or vice versa. In order for a criterion to serve as a subjective marker of the difference between remembering and imagining, in contrast, it need not apply in every case, simply because our capacity to distinguish remembering from imagining is imperfect. Hence criteria that are unacceptable in the context of the theory of remembering may nevertheless play a role in an account of memory knowledge.

4.7.1 Degree of Flexibility

Hume argues that remembering is distinguished from imagining by its preservative character, with memory preserving "the original form, in which its objects were presented," while imagination "is not restrain'd to the same order and form with the original impressions" (1739, 24–25), that is, that remembering and imagining are distinguished by the latter's greater degree of flexibility. As Pears (1990) points out, Hume himself already recognized that degree of flexibility is not a criterion that the subject himself might use to determine whether he is remembering or imagining, as there is no way of comparing a current representation to an earlier representation. In part III, we will see that degree of flexibility might nevertheless play a role in enabling the subject to distinguish between remembering and imagining. In the current context, however, we are concerned with degree of flexibility not as a criterion by means of which a subject might distinguish remembering from imagining, but rather as a condition that a process itself needs to satisfy in order to qualify as remembering, and, while it is not implausible that remembering is *on average* characterized by a lower level of flexibility than imagining, it is clear that the correlation between low flexibility and remembering is imperfect. First, remembering may sometimes in fact involve a great deal of flexibility. As Bernecker (2008) points out, for example, we are not constrained to remember the components of an episode in the order in which they occurred. More generally, as the discussion below will show, remembering is in an important sense a highly flexible process, in which information is transformed and recombined to produce a representation of the target episode. Second, while it may appear that remembering is nevertheless highly constrained relative to imagination, since it has a specific target (a given past episode), many forms of episodic imagination (for example, attempts to imagine counterfactual episodes) are similarly constrained. For this reason as well, degree of flexibility does not suffice to distinguish remembering from imagining.

4.7.2 Level of Detail

The phenomenal criterion—"vivacity"—faces a similar fate. As Pears (1990) remarks, there is an ambiguity in Hume's discussion of vivacity. In some places, as when he says that memory "paints its objects in more distinct colours, than any which are employ'd by [imagination]" (1739, 24), he seems to be thinking of vivacity as a *pictorial* property—that is, as a feature of the representation produced by remembering. In others, as when he says that when we remember an event, "the idea of it flow in upon the mind in a forcible manner" (1739, 24), he seems to be thinking of vivacity as what Pears refers to as a *behavioral* property—as a feature of the process of remembering itself.

If, on the one hand, we take vivacity in the pictorial sense, Hume's suggestion seems to be that remembering is distinguished from imagining by the fact that the representations produced by remembering are characterized by a level of detail greater than that of representations produced by imagining. For reasons discussed in part III, the vivacity criterion, so understood, cannot provide a complete account of how subjects themselves distinguish between remembering and imagining, but it may nevertheless play a limited role in such an account. In contrast, it is clear that vivacity should not be built into the theory of remembering as a condition that must be satisfied if the subject is to count as remembering rather than imagining— as an account of what makes "the difference betwixt [memory] and the imagination" (Hume 1739, 24). Representations produced by remembering may be more detailed *on average* than representations produced by imagining. Even this is not clear, but it is clear that the correlation between greater detail and remembering is imperfect at best. To see this, we need only to compare a case in which a subject imagines a counterfactual scene in great detail to a case in which he remembers a scene but is unable to recall it in much detail. I can construct a fairly detailed representation of a counterfactual experience of proctoring an exam, drawing on my knowledge of the layout of a familiar classroom, students who have recently taken my courses, and well-remembered past episodes of proctoring. In contrast, my ability to recall the details of a given exam that I actually proctored, say, five years ago, may be quite limited.

If, on the other hand, we take vivacity in the behavioral sense, everyday experience suffices to confirm that in many cases remembered episodes do not "flow in upon the mind" in a more forcible manner than do imagined episodes. We need only consider phenomena such as intrusive sexual fantasies or intrusive thoughts during mourning for a loved one and compare the ease with which we imagine in such cases to the difficulty of recalling dimly remembered episodes to see that vivacity in this second sense does not reliably distinguish between remembering and imagining.

The empiricist theory thus appears not to provide an adequate means of distinguishing between remembering and imagining. The following chapter therefore turns to the causal theory, considering, first, whether it provides an intuitively satisfactory distinction between remembering and imagining and, second, whether it can be reconciled with the constructive character of memory.

5 The Causal Theory

5.1 The Causal Condition

While the empiricist theory is unable to distinguish between remembering and imagining, many have taken the causal theory to do a better job. Martin and Deutscher argue that any theory which, like the empiricist theory, does not view the existence of a causal connection between the subject's previous representation and his current representation as a necessary condition for remembering is bound to be inadequate.[1] Consider the following case.

A man whom we shall call Kent is in a car accident and sees particular details of it, because of his special position. Later on, Kent is involved in another accident in which he gets a severe blow on his head as a result of which he forgets a certain section of his own history, including the first accident. ... Some time after this second accident, a popular and rather irresponsible hypnotist gives a show. He hypnotizes a large number of people, and suggests to them that they will believe that they had been in a car accident at a certain time and place. ... Kent is one of the group which is hypnotized. The suggestion works and so, after the act is over, Kent satisfies [conditions analogous to the current representation condition and the previous representation condition]. (Martin and Deutscher 1966, 174)

There is nothing that prevents Kent from satisfying the appropriate connection condition and the content-matching conditions as well; if he does, the commonsense conception will classify him as remembering. Similarly, there is nothing that prevents him from satisfying conditions such as level of detail or degree of flexibility, in which case the empiricist theory will likewise classify him as remembering. Intuitively, however, Kent clearly does not remember the accident.

This is not meant to be a case of Freudian "repressed memory": there is no causal connection whatsoever between Kent's earlier representation of the accident to his current representation of it. Martin and Deutscher's core claim is that what is missing here is precisely such a causal connection: what prevents Kent from remembering is the lack of a causal chain connecting the earlier representation to the current representation. In other words, the suggestion is that we incorporate something like the following condition into the theory of remembering:[2]

- there is a causal connection between R and R'.

5.2   The Memory Trace Condition

Inclusion of such a condition gives us a simple causal theory of memory, but a plausible version of the theory requires some additional ingredients. As Martin and Deutscher recognize, it is not enough to require simply that there be some causal connection or other between the subject's previous representation and his current representation, for many causal chains are not of the right sort to underwrite remembering—they are (as we now say) deviant. Consider the following case:

[Kent] told his friend Gray what he saw of an accident in which he was involved. Kent has a second accident in which he gets a blow on the head which destroys all memory of a period in his past, including the time at which the first accident occurred. When Gray finds that Kent can no longer remember the first accident, he tells him those details which Kent had told Gray in the period between the first and second accidents. After a little while Kent forgets that anyone has told him about the first accident, but still remembers what he was told by Gray. (Martin and Deutscher 1966, 180)

In this scenario, since there is a causal connection between Kent's current representation and his previous representation of the accident, albeit a somewhat roundabout causal connection, the causal condition is satisfied. But intuitively, of course, Kent does not remember the accident.

In order to rule out such roundabout connections, Martin and Deutscher in effect suggest adding the requirement that the relevant causal connection go via a memory trace:

- the causal connection between R and R' goes via a memory trace.

The trace connecting the current representation R to the previous representation R' may provisionally be viewed as a stored copy of R' itself. However, as the discussion of the consolidation process below will show, this is an oversimplification: roughly speaking, the initial representation R' maps on to a short-term, malleable memory representation, while the stored trace maps on to a long-term, stable memory representation resulting from consolidation.

The memory trace condition, by itself, is insufficient to deal with the case of Kent and Gray, but before considering additional complications, it is worth pausing to consider several worries about the very notion of a memory trace.[3] If the notion itself is, as some have argued, neither scientifically nor philosophically respectable, there is little point in developing the causal theory any further, as no version of the theory is able to make do without traces. Moreover, while chapter 6 will argue that we should abandon the causal theory in favor of a simulation theory of remembering, the simulation theory likewise invokes traces, so objections to this aspect of the causal theory apply equally to the simulation theory.

5.2.1 Traces in Philosophy and Psychology

On one standard metaphilosophical view, philosophy is in the business of analyzing concepts or language use. A philosophical account of remembering, on this view, should be an analysis of the concept of memory, or perhaps of the language we use to talk about memory. Assuming such a view, some (e.g., Locke 1971) have argued that a philosophical theory of remembering should not invoke traces, since traces concern the mechanisms by which memory is realized and since such mechanisms belong to the domain of psychology, rather than philosophy. Responding to this objection, Sutton (1998) has pointed out that we are not entitled to assume that the nature of remembering can be understood independently of the relevant mechanisms. Granted the form of naturalism assumed here, which rejects the project of linguistic or conceptual analysis, we can go further: the aim is not to analyze "what memory is in itself," but rather to understand the nature of specifically human memory. Given such a naturalistic project, the difference between the philosophical theory of remembering and psychological accounts becomes one of degree, not of kind, and we are therefore free to invoke traces in the philosophical theory.

A distinct methodological objection seeks not to protect philosophy from psychological incursions, but rather to protect psychology from philosophical incursions. The argument here is that the philosophical theory of remembering should not dictate to empirical science what it "must" discover about the workings of memory, and that assuming that traces are essential to remembering would run precisely that risk (Zemach 1983). In response, some have proposed a purely "logical" notion of memory traces (Rosen 1975), the idea being that we can be confident that remembering must involve traces of *some* sort and that the philosophical theory of remembering need not be more specific than that. Unless we are prepared to endorse Russellian direct "mnemic causation" (Russell 1921) across the temporal gap between an episode and an occasion of remembering the episode—a form of causation which is, at best, utterly mysterious—it does indeed seem a safe bet that remembering must involve traces of some sort. However, given that we base our conception of traces on what current psychology itself tells us about the way in which content is stored (and transformed) in remembering, we are free to go beyond the bare logical notion without running any real risk of dictating to empirical science.

5.2.2   Local versus Distributed Traces

A different sort of objection claims that either common sense or science reveals that it is an empirical mistake to posit traces. Wittgenstein's remark "If I say, rightly, 'I remember it,' the *most different* things can happen, and even merely this: that I say it," (1974, 42) is often cited in the context of the commonsense version of the objection. As Sutton points out, the fact that we may truly say "I remember" in a variety of contexts simply tells us nothing about whether remembering involves traces. "Scientific" versions of the objection, on the other hand, typically presuppose what Sutton refers to as a localist conception of traces, which sees a trace as "an entity permanently and passively stored at a fixed memory address" (1998, 286), pointing out that there is no scientific evidence for traces, so conceived. It has indeed long been known that the localist conception of traces is empirically untenable (Lashley 1950). However, it is both compatible with the spirit of the causal theory (though Martin and Deutscher themselves do refer to traces as "structural analogues" of experience) and consistent with contemporary psychology to view traces along the alternative lines suggested by Sutton. The model here is the form of distributed storage described by connectionism. In connectionist networks, "storage of a trace of the episode or event … occurs through the modification of the strengths of the connections among the units" (McClelland 1995). On this view, a trace is not a discrete thing in the brain, but rather a modification of existing patterns of connectivity in the brain.[4] Such a distributed conception of traces fits well with the current, constructive view of memory.

5.3   The Continuous Connection Condition

Returning to the case of Kent and Gray, while the trace is destroyed by the time the putative remembering occurs, the causal connection between Kent's initial representation and his retrieved representation does initially pass through a trace. Hence the fact that a causal connection goes via a memory trace is not sufficient to guarantee that it is nondeviant. In order to avoid this sort of problem, Martin and Deutscher suggest a condition that amounts to a requirement of *continuous* causal connection.[5]

The continuous connection condition is not meant to suggest that remembering is incompatible with the existence of a period during which the subject was unable to recall the relevant episode. Thus it is consistent, for example, with research suggesting that even discontinuous memories of childhood sexual abuse can turn out to be genuine (Geraerts et al. 2007). The requirement is not that the subject must have been able to retrieve the trace at all points between the time of the experience and the time of retrieval, but only that the trace must have been continuously stored between the time of the experience and the time of retrieval. Continuous storage is compatible with the existence of periods during which the subject is unable to retrieve the trace, and such periods presumably account for discontinuous but genuine memories of childhood sexual abuse.

Adding the continuous connection condition, along with Martin and Deutscher's other conditions, to the commonsense conception produces a theory according to which S remembers e when, and only when,

- S experienced e
- S now has a representation R of e
- S previously had a representation R' of e
- there is an appropriate connection between R' and S's experience of e
- the content of R is the same as or a subset of that of R'
- there is a causal connection between R and R'
- the causal connection between R and R' goes via a memory trace
- the trace exists continuously in the period between the occurrence of R' and the occurrence of R, and it is causally active in the production of R.

Assuming that we interpret the appropriate connection condition in causal terms, the causal theory distinguishes remembering from imagining by requiring a continuous causal connection running from the subject's original experience of the relevant event to his retrieved representation of the event.

While the theory does a good job of accounting for our intuitions about a broad range of cases, those intuitions themselves may not be a reliable guide to the nature of remembering. The remainder of this chapter shows that taking the constructive nature of remembering seriously requires several significant modifications to the causal theory. The following chapter, however, will argue that even the resulting causal theory of constructive memory is inadequate.

5.4 Properly Functioning Memory Systems

Objecting to the causal theory, Zemach asks us to consider the following scenario: "A past experience of mine, *e*, produced a physical memory trace in my brain. I do not remember *e* at all, but, owning an autocerebroscope, I can inspect the anatomy of my brain. What I do then is *read* the said trace from time to time, much as I read inscriptions in my diary" (1983, 37–38). The thought is, of course, that the mere involvement of a memory trace is no guarantee of remembering.

While the details of Zemach's case are fanciful, and while it presupposes a localist conception of traces, the case nevertheless illustrates the point that there are multiple ways in which a trace might be doing causal work at the time of (apparent) remembering. Consider a case in which a subject has suffered severe damage to the brain regions that support episodic memory processes. Damage to these regions may result in a range of memory distortions. These include forms of confabulation, many interesting cases of which have been studied by Dalla Barba. Patient SD, for example, had suffered severe head trauma. When asked what he had done the day before, he replied: "Yesterday I won a running race and I was awarded with a piece of meat which was put on my right knee" (Dalla Barba 1993). Needless to say, this report was inaccurate. Nevertheless, in an important sense, SD was not just making an event up: he had in fact been an enthusiastic runner, and he had in fact fallen and injured his knee during one race. Thus, as Dalla Barba and Boissé observe, SD's report, while bizarre, includes genuine "autobiographical elements put together in an inappropriate semantic structure" (2009, 97). A malfunctioning episodic memory system, rather than simply failing to produce a memory representation, may draw on available traces in an attempt to produce a representation of a target event. Such a system will often produce inaccurate representations of events, as in this example, but there is nothing that would prevent it from occasionally producing accurate representations. (Suppose that, by chance, SD *had* won a race the day before and been rewarded with a piece of meat on his right knee.)

As it stands, the causal theory implies that, on such occasions, the subject remembers. Of course, there may be cases of subjects with malfunctioning memory systems that occasionally happen to function properly, and, in cases of that sort, it would be correct to say that the relevant subjects occasionally manage to remember. But in the case at hand, we are not dealing with a subject with a malfunctioning system that occasionally happens to function properly, but rather with a subject with a malfunctioning system that, by chance, occasionally happens to produce an accurate representation. In order to deal with this difficulty, we may incorporate the following condition into the causal theory.

- the causal connection between R and R' goes via a properly functioning memory system.

To fully explore the notion of a properly functioning episodic memory system would require a great deal of space. Functional perspectives on memory are considered in the following chapter and, in more detail, in part IV, but the notion of proper function intended here is a broadly evolutionary one (Millikan 1984). For now, the essential point is that assuming that remembering presupposes causation via a properly functioning memory system allows the causal theory to avoid classifying cases of confabulation (along with more fanciful cases, such as that described by Zemach) as cases in which the subject remembers.

5.5 Content Similarity

Confabulation provides a first illustration of the constructive character of remembering, but it should be taken to suggest neither that remembering in agents with properly functioning memory systems is not constructive nor that constructive remembering inevitably gives rise to inaccurate memories. This section deals with the latter point, which requires weakening the content-matching condition; the next two sections explore the implications of the former point.

The need to weaken the content-matching condition can be seen by considering the ways in which content is transformed even in mundane, unproblematic cases of remembering. Bernecker appeals to a range of ways in which content is modified to argue for a principle of content similarity according to which "the informational content stored in traces may stay the same or decrease (to a certain degree); but it may not increase" (2008, 155). This covers phenomena such as tense adjustment, which is at work when we go from "Murat *is* fasting for Ramadan" to "Murat *was* fasting for Ramadan"; as well as universal instantiation and existential generalization, at work when we go from "*everyone* fasted for Ramadan" to "*Murat* fasted for Ramadan" and from "*Murat* fasted for Ramadan" to "*someone* fasted for Ramadan"; and a number of other cases. What these relatively minor transformations of content have in common is that they do not involve the addition of content going beyond the content of the subject's earlier representation. Hence they suggest the following replacement for the content-matching condition.

- *R* does not contain information not implied by that contained in *R'*.

Articulating the difference between the original content-matching condition and this weaker content similarity condition in precise terms would require us to have a detailed account of the informational content of representations in hand. Roughly, though, the difference is that, whereas the only modifications permitted by the content-matching condition amount to mere *deletions* of aspects of a representation, the content similarity condition allows for *replacement* of aspects of the representation, as long as they do not introduce information not already implicitly contained in it.

5.6 Constructive Memory

While the content similarity condition is a step in the right direction, it is only a first step, for the basic lesson of constructive memory research is that remembering *does* in fact routinely involve modifications that introduce information not even implicitly contained in the earlier representation.

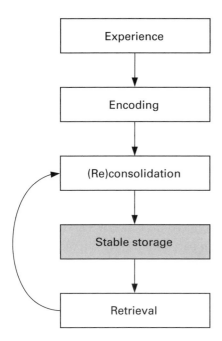

Figure 5.1
Stages of the memory process. Content can be transformed or generated at any stage other than stable storage.

Figure 5.1 depicts the basic stages of the memory process. Mapping this vocabulary onto that used in the discussion so far, *encoding* is the process that takes us from the subject's original experience of an episode to an initial, labile short-term memory representation; *consolidation* is the process that takes us from the short-term representation to a stable long-term representation—that is, the memory trace; *storage* refers to the period after consolidation, during which the trace is more or less inert; and *retrieval* refers to the process giving rise to the subject's current representation. After retrieval, a process of *reconsolidation* occurs during which the representation is again labile.

These processes are described in more detail below. There is disagreement over exactly how to distinguish among them and even, in some cases, about whether it is necessary to posit them at all. For example, Anastasio et al. (2012), on the basis of an updated version of McClelland, McNaughton, and O'Reilly's connectionist model (1995), argue that consolidation should be viewed as a permanent, ongoing process, with stable memory itself being susceptible to changes, though these occur much more slowly than in short-term memory. On this view, to the extent that it is legitimate to speak of stably stored memory traces, even stored traces can be modified. Nevertheless, the vocabulary of encoding, consolidation, storage, and retrieval provides a useful means of organizing discussion of the constructive character of remembering, and the possibility that representations never achieve fully stable storage only reinforces the view defended here.

There is no uncontroversial general definition of the sense in which memory is constructive. One obvious suggestion is that construction in memory is a matter of the generation of new content, in the sense at issue in the debate over preservationism introduced in section 4.5 above. Given that memory is viewed as constructive in part because it is "supplemental," in the sense that "some of the changes that occur between study and test involve 'memory' for information that was not contained in the input" (Koriat, Goldsmith, and Pansky 2000, 485), the suggestion is not implausible. But, while generation of new content will indeed be of central interest here—it is this aspect of construction that ultimately requires a more dramatic departure from the content-matching condition—simply identifying construction with content generation would disregard a number of phenomena usually regarded as exemplifying the constructive character of memory.

The suggestion can nevertheless be used to illustrate an important ambiguity in the concept of construction. Content generation can occur at various points. To begin with, content other than that provided by the original experience might be incorporated into the initial, short-term memory representation produced by encoding, and content other than that provided by the stored memory trace might be incorporated into the representation resulting from retrieval. Koriat et al. (2000), following Alba and Hasher (1983), suggest referring to relevant processes occurring at encoding as *construction* and to relevant processes occurring at retrieval as *reconstruction*. As we will see, however, the generation of new content can also occur during the consolidation process responsible for shaping the long-term, stable memory trace, and it is natural to include such processes under the heading of construction. This ambiguity—construction during encoding (and consolidation) versus reconstruction during retrieval—is familiar to psychologists; it is less so to philosophers, and so worth emphasizing here. As long as we are in the grip of a picture on which the memory trace is a faithful record of experience, we will be inclined to suppose that remembering must be a matter of retrieving a trace unaltered. But if we grant that the trace itself is constructed, it should begin to seem much less obvious that remembering should be a matter of retrieving it unaltered: if there is nothing lost by construction at one stage, there need be nothing lost by reconstruction at the other; indeed, if there is something gained by construction at one stage, there may also be something gained by reconstruction at the other.

Alba and Hasher provide a useful general framework for distinguishing among dimensions of construction in memory.[6] They describe four ways in which memory might be constructive. In *selection*, only certain aspects of an experience are selected for encoding. In *abstraction*, the meaning of an experience is abstracted from its surface features. In *interpretation*, the encoded representation is shaped by the subject's relevant prior knowledge. And in *integration*, a coherent representation is formed from the products of the selection, abstraction, and interpretation processes. While these processes are described with respect to encoding, they may continue during the consolidation process. Finally, in *reconstruction*, the stored representation, along with whatever information is available from other sources— representations of other events, semantic information, and information available in the context of retrieval—is used to generate a representation of the target episode. Given that the stored representation contains limited information about the original experience, and given that it may already include information not present in the experience itself, the representation output by reconstructive retrieval may in principle deviate significantly from the subject's original experience of the target episode.

Interpretation makes additional content available, but selection and abstraction both *reduce* the quantity of information incorporated into the memory representation. In integration, the simplified content and the newly available content are incorporated into a single memory representation. Hence construction cannot simply be identified with content generation. Nevertheless, in what follows, the question of content generation will be particularly important. The content-matching condition already accommodates selection, and moving to the weaker content similarity condition makes room for abstraction. Accommodating interpretation, integration, and reconstruction, in contrast, will require an alternative to the content-matching condition considerably weaker than the content similarity condition, as a review of some representative examples of construction and reconstruction during encoding, consolidation, and retrieval will demonstrate.

5.6.1   Encoding

False recognition—at work in the DRM paradigm mentioned above, in which subjects who study words related to a nonpresented theme word later "recognize" the theme word as having been presented—provides an illustration of selection and abstraction during encoding. Brainerd and Reyna's (2002) fuzzy trace theory grounds one plausible explanation of the DRM effect. According to fuzzy trace theory, both verbatim traces (records of individual items) and gist traces (records of the theme common to the individual items) are formed during encoding; since gist traces are more readily accessible, subjects are led to falsely recognize nonpresented theme words (Koriat et al. 2000). Boundary extension, in which subjects remember seeing more of a scene than they actually saw (Intraub, Bender, and Mangels 1992), provides a revealing illustration of the role of interpretation. According to one explanation of this effect, it is a consequence of the fact that information about the likely layout of a scene is automatically retrieved and then incorporated into the memory of the scene (Koriat et al. 2000; Schacter, Norman, and Koutstaal 1998). Finally, the superportrait phenomenon, in which caricatures are recognized faster and more accurately than faithful portraits, provides an illustration of integration. According to Rhodes (1997), faster recognition of caricatures is likely the consequence of the fact that the relevant representations are highly schematic, in that they emphasize the distinctive properties of the things represented (Koriat et al. 2000).

We could extend this list of examples of construction during encoding almost indefinitely. There are ongoing debates about how to explain some of these phenomena, but there is no significant debate over *whether* encoding is constructive. Some of the construction occurring at encoding, moreover, clearly involves content generation. Boundary extension, for example, does not occur because the subject first forms a belief to the effect that the scene before his eyes appears to have such-and-such a layout and then infers that the scene must extend in certain ways. Rather, the representation of the scene is modified automatically as a memory for the scene is formed. The modification proceeds in stages, with early stages reflecting the operation of perceptual schemas and later stages apparently involving normalization in memory (Intraub et al. 1992).

As encoding is the process taking us from the original experience of the episode to an initial, short-term memory representation, its generative character pertains to the appropriate connection condition, as opposed to the content-matching condition (or the content similarity condition). Content generation is consistent with the letter of the appropriate connection condition, but it is incompatible with our intuitive understanding of what constitutes an appropriate connection, as it implies that we may literally remember more than we experienced—in the case of boundary extension, for example, that we may remember more of a scene than we saw. Content generation at encoding thus requires considerably expanding our conception of permissible divergences between what the subject experienced and what he remembers.

5.6.2 Consolidation and Reconsolidation

It is natural to suppose that—even if construction occurs at encoding—a memory representation, once formed, will remain stable until retrieved (ignoring forgetting over time).[7] In fact, a process of consolidation, during which the memory trace is not fully stabilized, intervenes between encoding and stable storage (Lorenzini et al. 1999). If this process, which unfolds over a period of many years, is interrupted, unconsolidated memories can be partly or entirely lost. This is why, for example, amnesia often involves loss of memory for an extended period preceding the damage giving rise to it. Even once consolidation has run its course, memories are not permanently fixed. This is due not only to the possibility of reconstruction at retrieval but also to the occurrence of *re*consolidation. When retrieved, memories again become susceptible to modification, and a period of reconsolidation is required before they can be said simply to be stored again (Sara 2000). As Dudai puts it, "it is not the time since encoding that determines the susceptibility of a trace to interventions, but rather the functional state of the trace: An active (retrieved) trace can be truncated, but also augmented; an inactive (stored) trace is immune to such manipulation" (2004, 68–69).

5.6.3 Retrieval

Remembering, as Schacter and Addis emphasize, "is not a literal reproduction of the past, but rather is a constructive process in which bits and pieces of information from various sources are pulled together" (2007a, 773). As noted above, just as perceptual illusions can be studied to reveal the normally invisible constructive workings of the perceptual system, memory distortions can be studied to reveal the normally invisible reconstructive workings of the memory system. False recognition arising from misleading post-event suggestions (Zaragoza and Mitchell 1996), for example, might occur because thinking inaccurately about an event can create a representation of the event that cannot easily be distinguished from a representation of the event actually witnessed (Schacter et al. 1998). Misleading retrieval cues can be incorporated into retrieved memories to produce false beliefs, as when students with high GPAs overestimate their marks for classes for which they received low marks (Bahrick, Hall, and Berger 1996; Schacter et al. 1998). Related phenomena include the retrospective bias and the "knew it all along" effect (Schacter et al. 1998): in the former, recall is distorted to render memory consistent with present beliefs (Levine 1997); in the latter, subjects adjust their memories of earlier probability estimates in light of their current knowledge of the occurrence or nonoccurrence of the relevant events (Fischhoff and Beyth 1975). Additional clues to the nature of reconstruction come from observations of various biases in spatial memory (Koriat et al. 2000): e.g., landmarks produce asymmetric distance estimates, suggesting that spatial information is subject to interpretation according to the demands of the context of retrieval (Mcnamara and Diwadkar 1997). Perhaps the most dramatic example of reconstruction is provided by cases of confabulation in which subjects are led to recall entirely fictional events in great detail (Hyman, Husband, and Billings 1995; Hyman and Pentland 1996): merely imagining a fictional event increases the probability that the subject will later remember it as having occurred (Schacter et al. 1998).

The source-monitoring framework (Johnson, Hashtroudi, and Lindsay 1993; Mitchell and Johnson 2000) provides plausible explanations of confabulation and a number of other memory distortions. In confabulation, for example, the subject may mistake internally generated information for information originating in experience. Source monitoring will be discussed in detail below, but note that a crucial element of this explanation is the claim that retrieval involves reconstruction and, in particular, that it involves generation of new content. Nor is the source-monitoring framework unique in this respect: any account of retrieval that takes seriously the claim that memory distortions reveal the normal workings of memory will grant that retrieval involves reconstruction and, moreover, that it involves generation of new content. When all goes well, there is a close match between the retrieved memory (including the newly generated content) and the initial representation; the content generation involved in retrieval is thus normally invisible. But under certain circumstances (when memory is distorted), the retrieved memory will fail to match the initial representation in virtue of incorporating inappropriate newly generated content. The point is that the same reconstructive processes are at work in both cases: reconstruction in general—and content generation in particular—is not the exception but the rule.

5.7 Approximate Content Similarity

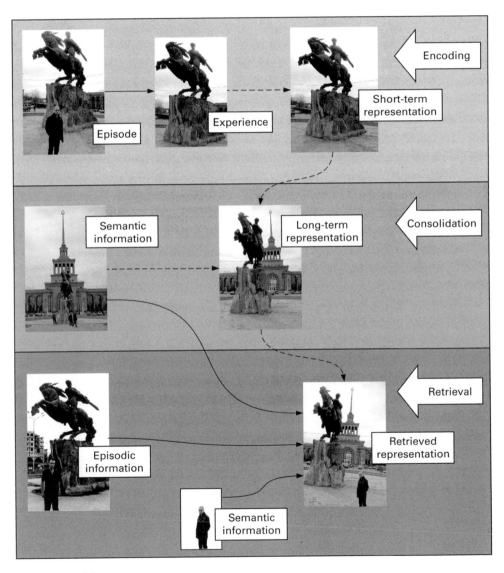

Figure 5.2
A simple example of content generation in remembering. (For the dashed lines, see chapter 6.)

The original content-matching condition permitted the introduction of no new content in remembering. The weaker content similarity condition permits only the introduction of content already implicitly contained in the earlier representation. What the research reviewed above tells us, however, is that significant new content may be introduced during encoding, consolidation, retrieval, and reconsolidation. How much new content is consistent with remembering? One natural view is captured by the following *approximate* content similarity condition:

- the content of R does not go too far beyond that of the trace; the content of the trace does not go too far beyond that of R'.

As we saw above, the appropriate connection condition must be interpreted along similar lines: what it is for a connection between an experience of an episode and the agent's initial memory representation R' of the episode to be appropriate is, in part, for the content of R' not to go too far beyond that of the experience.

Consider the simple case of content generation illustrated in figure 5.2. I visually experience a scene consisting of a statue in front of a train station. I see only part of the statue and take in little of the train station behind it; obviously, I do not see myself in the scene. The encoding process may involve extrapolating unseen components of the scene, and consolidation may involve integrating information previously stored in memory, such as the appearance of the train station, into the representation of the episode. Retrieval may likewise draw on previously stored information, such as a representation of a related episode or information about my own appearance. The result is a representation of the scene which includes information differing significantly from—and going significantly beyond—that contained in my original experience of the episode. This representation may nevertheless be fairly accurate with respect to the episode.

Supposing that it is, do I remember the episode? We should resist the urge to answer that, obviously, I do not, for that would rule out many perfectly ordinary cases of remembering. As noted above, constructive memory research often focuses on cases in which constructive remembering goes wrong; that is, on cases in which there is a mismatch between the retrieved representation and the original episode. While this is methodologically useful, there is a danger that it will lead us to assume that construction typically results in such mismatches—in short, to assume that construction means unreliability and hence that "memories" produced by

constructive remembering are not genuine memories at all. But construction need not result in mismatches. Indeed, while there is no reason to
expect retrieved episodic memory representations to be perfectly accurate
in all details, there are, as we will see in subsequent chapters, good reasons
to suppose that constructive remembering is typically reasonably accurate
overall. Assuming the reliability of constructive remembering, we should
not say that I do not remember the scene because the retrieved representation does not correspond to my original experience of it, and in particular
because it includes more information than my original experience. Instead,
we should say that I remember aspects of the scene that I did not originally
experience. This may sound almost paradoxical, but only as long as we are
in the grip of the naïve, commonsense conception of memory.

Given that remembering is compatible with content generation, why
suggest that there are limits on how much content generation is compatible
with remembering? Intuitively, if the content of a "retrieved" representation goes too far beyond that of the subject's experience of the relevant
episode, he can no longer said to be remembering. Suppose that the subject dimly sees just a small fragment of a scene but ends up inferring and
"remembering" a far larger portion of it in great detail. At some point, we
want to say, he is no longer remembering but imagining. Hence the apparent need for something like the approximate content similarity condition.
As it stands, of course, the approximate content similarity condition, along
with the appropriate connection condition, imports a certain amount of
vagueness into the theory. How much similarity is required? Which dimensions of similarity are relevant? This vagueness may or may not be a toler-
able defect, but, as both conditions will eventually be abandoned, we need
not explore the prospects for establishing a precise cut-off point between
remembering and imagining here.

5.8   A Causal Theory of Constructive Memory

Replacing the content-matching condition with the approximate content
similarity condition and building in the requirement of a properly functioning memory system produces a version of the causal theory according
to which S remembers e if, and only if,

- S experienced e
- S now has a representation R of e

- S previously had a representation R' of e
- there is an appropriate connection between R' and S's experience of e
- there is a causal connection between R and R'
- the causal connection between R and R' goes via a memory trace
- the trace exists continuously in the period between the occurrence of R' and the occurrence of R, and it is causally active in the production of R
- the causal connection between R and R' goes via a properly functioning memory system
- the content of R does not go too far beyond that of the trace; the content of the trace does not go too far beyond that of R'.

Before turning to the epistemological implications of this updated version of the causal theory, it is worth pausing to contrast it with several broadly similar theories.

5.8.1 Remembering and Updating

While the notion of a properly functioning memory system will play an important role in the argument to follow, the updated version of the causal theory goes beyond available theories primarily in terms of its tolerance of divergences between the contents of experience and the contents of retrieved memories—that is, in terms of the extent to which it views memory as a generative source of content or information. As we saw above, for example, Bernecker's version of the causal theory grants that remembering is compatible with certain minor modifications of content, but it rules out modifications that generate information not included at least implicitly in the agent's experience. On this theory, memory can perhaps be said to be generative in a weak sense, since it acknowledges that the content produced by remembering need not be literally the same as the content of experience, but it is incompatible with a view of remembering as generative in any more robust sense.

5.8.2 Remembering and Pastness

The causal theory of constructive memory likewise differs significantly from accounts, such as those discussed in chapter 3, that view episodic memory as generative to the extent that it produces representations that refer explicitly to the past. While he views semantic memory as purely preservative, for example, Dokic (2001) argues that episodic memory is not purely preservative (cf. Fernández forthcoming). His focus, however, is on one very specific kind of content generation. In order to account for the fact that episodic memory provides the subject with a reason to believe that the representations it provides originate in the subject's past experience of the relevant events, unlike semantic memory, which can at most provide the subject with a reason to believe that an event occurred, Dokic proposes an account of episodic memory on which "the fact that [it comes directly from the subject's own experience] is presented in the memory experience itself" (2001, 228). On this account, episodic memory is generative of a specific sort of content, but the account does not cover the sort of generation of content which is covered by the causal theory of constructive memory— generation of additional information about the target episode itself.

5.8.3 Remembering and Acceptance

Finally, the new causal theory differs from Matthen's recent account (2010). Matthen is not concerned with the nature of the causal connection required for remembering, the question of how much generation of content is compatible with remembering, or the problem of how the reliability of memory is ensured despite its constructive character. Instead, his focus is epistemological: how can memory justify a belief, given that it does not simply preserve content? The context is Burge's discussion of the "acceptance principle," according to which a "person is entitled to accept as true something that is presented as true [including by memory] and is intelligible to him, unless there are stronger reasons not to do so" (Burge 1993, 467); Burge's defense of the principle, which will be discussed in more detail in chapter 7, assumes that there is a purely preservative form of memory. Since Matthen argues, in the course of dealing with this question, that what is preserved in memory is "a trace from which it is possible to reconstruct an image or belief," and since his discussion makes clear that he acknowledges that the trace can differ from the experience from which it stems, his account appears to be compatible with the causal theory of constructive memory.

5.9 The Epistemology of Constructive Memory

The causal theory of constructive memory represents a compromise between the commonsense view, according to which memory is purely preservative, and the more thoroughly constructive view, emerging from mental time travel research, which will be described in the following chapter. But while it may be an unstable halfway point along the road to the simulation theory, it does enable us to draw out the implications of the constructive character of memory for the ongoing debate between preservationists and generationists in the epistemology of memory.

5.9.1 Preservationism

The question at issue in this debate is whether memory is a generative *epistemic* source. Roughly speaking: can memory generate new justification? According to the default preservationist view—Lackey (2005) cites Audi (1995), Dummett (1994), Plantinga (1993), and Owens (2002), for example, as endorsing some form of preservationism—the answer is negative: since memory is a merely preservative *doxastic* source (i.e., since it is capable only of preserving beliefs), the level of justification of the output of memory cannot exceed the level of justification of its input.

A recent exchange between Lackey (2005) and Senor (2007) encapsulates the main themes of the debate. But there is a danger, in working through the exchange, of failing to notice that there is in fact a substantial area of agreement between them. While Lackey claims to argue against preservationism, Senor to argue for preservationism, they are in fact in agreement on what is best viewed as a moderate form of generationism. This point of agreement, however, is undermined by the causal theory of constructive memory.

5.9.2 Moderate Generationism

Lackey challenges preservationism on the basis of three arguments—two turning on the way in which a belief's relationship to defeaters (i.e., propositions that undermine its justification) can change while it is stored in memory and one turning on memory's capacity to generate new beliefs. The first of Lackey's arguments concerns normative defeaters (defeaters that the subject ought to believe), while the second concerns doxastic defeaters (defeaters that the subject does in fact believe). There are subtle differences between the normative defeaters argument and the doxastic defeaters argument, but these need not concern us here. The two arguments share a common basic structure: a subject's relation to defeaters for a belief can change over time while the belief remains stored in memory; in particular, if there were defeaters for the belief at the time at which it was committed to memory, these may no longer apply—they may themselves be defeated—when it is retrieved, so a belief that was unjustified when initially formed may, when retrieved from memory, be justified.

Senor points out that the defeaters arguments overlook the distinction between prima facie justification (the kind of justification sufficient to confer ultima facie justification in the absence of defeat) and ultima facie justification (all-things-considered justification, the kind of justification sufficient to turn true belief into knowledge). Since preservationism is most naturally understood as a thesis about prima facie justification, this effectively undermines the defeaters arguments, which show only that memory can generate ultima facie justification, not that it can generate prima facie justification. In less technical terms, the problem with the defeaters arguments is that they do not show that memory is actually capable of *generating* anything, merely that memory is capable of preserving a belief while the world changes around it in epistemically relevant ways.

Lackey (2007a) has conceded the point, appealing to her belief-generation argument to undermine preservationism. The gist of that argument is as follows: a subject might acquire some information without forming the corresponding belief; if he comes to believe the information in question when he later retrieves it, and if the overall belief forming process is reliable, the resulting belief will be justified; memory, therefore, can generate justification.[8] Senor accepts that memory can be generative in this sense. In short, the opponents are in agreement on a moderate form of generationism, according to which memory can generate (prima facie) justification by generating belief.

5.9.3 Radical Generationism

An implicit presupposition of the debate between Lackey and Senor is that memory does not generate new content. (Lackey emphasizes, for example, that no new content is generated in her belief-generation case.) Denying this presupposition results in a more radical form of generationism, according to which memory can generate justification both by generating a new belief with a pre-existing content and by generating a new belief along with its very content. If the causal theory of constructive memory (or the simulation theory developed in the next chapter) is right, we must indeed deny the presupposition. The work on constructive memory reviewed above (and the work on mental time travel reviewed below) shows that remembering involves the generation not just of new *beliefs* but of new *content*. If content generation in remembering is reliable, then we must endorse radical generationism. Translating into pluralistic terms: insofar as we are concerned with reliability, memory can produce epistemically adequate beliefs despite generating not only beliefs but even their contents.

As epistemologists tend to gravitate toward preservationism or, at best, toward moderate generationism, the importance of this conclusion should not be underestimated. If it is right, then memory must, contra epistemological dogma, be grouped with sources such as perception, sources capable of providing us with fundamentally new knowledge. Radical generationism follows from the constructive character of memory, however, only given that memory is reliable despite its constructive character, and this may be doubted. The focus in what follows will therefore be on assuaging doubts about the reliability of constructive memory.

6   The Simulation Theory

The previous chapter argued that the causal theory requires significant modifications if it is to have a chance of accommodating the constructive character of memory, in virtue of which the content of the representations produced by retrieval may deviate significantly from the content of the corresponding experiences, and outlined an updated version of the causal theory designed to take this point into account while respecting as much of the commonsense conception as possible. The current chapter, however, argues that the constructive character of remembering ultimately requires us to abandon the causal condition itself, along with most of the rest of the causal theory and the commonsense conception on which it is built. What we are left with, in the end, is a view of remembering as simulating or imagining episodes from the personal past. According to the simulation theory of memory defended here, the only factor that distinguishes remembering an episode from *merely* imagining it is that the relevant representation is produced by a properly functioning episodic construction system (a notion which replaces the notion of a dedicated episodic memory system with which we have been working so far) which aims to simulate an episode from the personal past.

6.1   The Changing Concept of Episodic Memory

The discussion to this point has treated episodic memory simply as memory for specific past episodes. This corresponds to Tulving's early, influential definition, which described episodic memory essentially as a specialized system responsible for storing and retrieving representations of experienced events (Tulving 1972). The definition favored by Tulving has shifted over time, and his current, equally influential definition describes episodic memory as a function of a system responsible for "mental time travel" into *both* past and future (Tulving 2001). The details of Tulving's more recent defini-tion, and the controversy between those who have adopted something like it and those who continue to work with something closer to the original definition, will be discussed in detail in part IV. For now, the point to note is simply that episodic memory is currently viewed, by most psychologists working in the area, as one instance of a more general capacity allowing the agent both to re-experience past episodes and to "pre-experience" possible future episodes.[1] In retrospect, the shift to viewing remembering the past as being intimately linked to imagining the future may appear unsurprising. After all, as Hesslow remarks, "there is no clear distinction between imagery and recall of memory. ... If I imagine that I am walking around a familiar city, I am also recalling memories of the city. Even when we are imagining things that we have never experienced, we are using remembered experi-ences as building blocks" (2012, 75–76). Hindsight is 20/20, of course, but the shift involved a radical reconceptualization of memory and occurred only as a result of converging evidence from a number of sources.[2]

The ability to remember the past had already been tentatively linked to the ability to imagine the future in early work by Tulving (1985), which showed that amnesic patients, unable to remember past episodes, were like-wise impaired with respect to their capacity to imagine future episodes. The link between remembering the past and imagining the future was reinforced as imaging research began to show that similar brain regions were involved in both processes (Okuda et al. 2003) and as studies establishing the link in normal (nonamnesic) individuals began to appear (D'Argembeau and Van der Linden 2004, 2006; Spreng and Levine 2006). As the link became more firmly established, a variety of concepts intended to describe future-oriented mental time travel emerged, including prospection (Buckner and Carroll 2007; Gilbert and Wilson 2007), episodic foresight (Sudden-dorf 2010; Suddendorf and Corballis 1997), and episodic future thinking (Atance and O'Neill 2001, 2005). While they differed in their details, these proliferating concepts served to emphasize the growing consensus that remembering the past is one instance of a more general capacity for mental time travel, a capacity which can be directed both at the personal past and the personal future.

As additional imaging studies explored the neural underpinnings of this capacity (Addis, Wong, and Schacter 2007; Szpunar, Watson, and

McDermott 2007), remembering the past was increasingly linked not only to imagining the future but to a broader range of forms of episodic imagination as well (Buckner and Carroll 2007; Hassabis, Kumaran, and Maguire 2007b; Hassabis and Maguire 2007, 2009; Schacter and Addis 2007a, 2007b; Schacter et al. 2007), all of which appear to depend on the brain's default network, a network of regions including but not limited to the hippocampus. For example, there is a growing body of research investigating episodic counterfactual thought, the capacity to imagine alternatives to past experiences (De Brigard, Szpunar, and Schacter 2013; De Brigard and Giovanello 2012; De Brigard et al. 2013; Moulton and Kosslyn 2009; Schacter et al. 2015; Van Hoeck et al. 2010, 2013). The basic lesson of this research is that the capacity to imagine episodes that did not occur, or to imagine alternative outcomes for episodes that did occur, is, like imagining the future, a product of the same system that allows us to remember past episodes. The standard view, in short, is increasingly that episodic memory is one function of a more general episodic construction system, a process not different in kind from imagining a range of nonactual episodes. We are now a long way from Tulving's early definition of episodic memory in terms of storage and retrieval of information about past episodes. By the same token, we are a long way from any philosophical theory that views episodic memory as a matter of simply preserving a connection to past experiences.

6.2 Remembering as Mental Time Travel

As Manning, Cassel, and Cassel (2013) point out, the view that remembering the past and imagining the future share a common basis goes back at least to Augustine, who remarked that "out of the same storehouse, with these past impressions, I can construct now this, now that, image of things that I either have experienced or have believed on the basis of experience—and from these I can further construct future actions, events, and hopes; and I can meditate on all these things as if they were present" (398). Recent research has put this view on a firm empirical footing, and a number of theoretical frameworks have been proposed to characterize the relationship between remembering the past, imagining the future, and other episodic constructive processes in both functional and anatomical terms. Focusing on their functional claims, this section looks at two such frameworks, the constructive episodic simulation approach and the scene construction approach. There are important differences between the two approaches, but what matters, in the current context, is not their points of disagreement, but rather their agreement on the point that episodic remembering must be characterized in terms that render it impossible to draw a firm distinction between remembering and imagining the past.[3]

6.2.1 Constructive Episodic Simulation

In anatomical terms, while the scene construction approach focuses specifically on the hippocampus, the constructive episodic simulation approach (Schacter 2012; Schacter et al. 2007, 2008, 2011) focuses on the default network (Buckner, Andrews-Hanna, and Schacter 2008; Schacter et al. 2007) as a whole, including structures beyond the hippocampus and the medial temporal lobe. As noted above, the default network appears to underwrite both episodic memory and a number of other forms of episodic construction, including imagination of future episodes.[4] Schacter and colleagues appeal to this fact to respond to an important challenge posed by the constructive character of remembering—that of explaining why remembering should involve the transformation and recombination of information originating in various sources, as opposed to the simple storage of information deriving from experience. The insight driving their approach is that "since the future is not an exact repetition of the past, simulation of future episodes may require a system that can draw on the past in a manner that flexibly extracts and recombines elements of previous experiences—a constructive rather than a reproductive system" (Schacter and Addis 2007a, 773). Imagination of future events of necessity draws on a system capable of flexibly transforming and recombining stored information originating in a variety of sources. Hence, if the system responsible for imagining future events is likewise responsible for remembering past events, it is unsurprising that memory of past events should likewise have a flexible, simulational character.

This claim, in turn, raises the question of why remembering should depend on the same system as imagining. Why not, for example, have one system dedicated to retrieving stored representations of past experiences unaltered, and another dedicated to flexibly modifying such information so as to produce representations of possible future events? One possible reason for relying on a single system for remembering the past and imagining the future is that it is more efficient to do so, especially given that perfectly accurate recall is seldom necessary—if simulational remembering produces sufficiently accurate representations of past episodes sufficiently often, the cost imposed by frequent minor inaccuracies and even occasional wild inaccuracies may be less than the gain achieved by relying on a single system. A distinct but compatible explanation is that the simulational character of human episodic remembering is a contingent outcome of the particular evolutionary history of remembering, in which the capacity to imagine the future may have emerged *prior* to the capacity to remember the past; this explanation is discussed further in part IV.

Regardless of how we answer this question, the constructive episodic simulation approach implies that episodic memory inevitably involves what Schacter has referred to as "adaptive constructive processes," processes which are necessary for the functioning of memory—or of cognition more generally—but which, due to their constructive character, inevitably give rise to distortions, errors, and illusions (Schacter 2012).[5] For example, Schacter and Addis review research suggesting that false recognition is a characteristic by-product of a properly functioning memory system, with patients suffering from amnesia and dementia due to damage to the hippocampus and related medial temporal lobe structures actually being *less* prone to false recognition than healthy controls (Ciaramelli et al. 2006). This surprising finding can be explained by pointing out that the extraction of the gist of an episode (Brainerd and Reyna 2005) is adaptive insofar as it permits useful generalization and abstraction, thus enabling the cognizer to extract common features of episodes.[6] Regardless of the details of particular adaptive constructive processes, the episodic constructive simulation approach implies that, given the way remembering the past is related to imagining the future, remembering is bound to have an imaginative character; representations of past episodes are produced by the same sort of imaginative or simulational process that is responsible for producing representations of future episodes. Remembering, in short, is itself a matter of simulating.

6.2.2 Scene Construction

Despite important points of disagreement with the constructive episodic simulation approach, the scene construction approach (Hassabis and Maguire 2007, 2009; Maguire and Mullally 2013; Mullally and Maguire 2014) has similar implications. The focus of the scene construction approach is both narrower and broader than that of the constructive episodic simulation approach: it is narrower in the sense that, at the level of anatomy, it concerns the hippocampus in particular, rather than the default network as a whole; it is broader in the sense that, at the level of function, it emphasizes that the hippocampus plays a crucial role not only in remembering the past and imagining the future but also in a number of other episodic constructive processes, including imagining fictitious experiences (Hassabis et al. 2007b), spatial navigation (Spiers and Maguire 2006), and possibly mindwandering and dreaming. As we saw above, it is now well-established that damage to the hippocampus impairs both the ability to remember the past and the ability to imagine the future. While this fact lends support to the view that the function of the hippocampus is bound up with the core capacity common to remembering the past and imagining the future— namely, an ability to grasp the subjective time in which the episodes making up one's life are situated—Maguire and Mullally (2013) contend that such a view cannot explain why hippocampal damage likewise impairs the ability to imagine *atemporal* scenes (Hassabis et al. 2007b; Mullally et al. 2012). They therefore favor the alternative hypothesis that the basic function of the hippocampus is what they refer to as scene construction: "The hippocampus facilitates the construction of atemporal scenes allowing the event details of episodic memories and imagined future experiences to be martialed, bound and played out in a coherent spatial context" (Maguire and Mullally 2013, 1181); the other regions activated during mental time travel, meanwhile, are responsible for its properly temporal aspects.[7]

For present purposes, we need not choose between the constructive episodic simulation approach and the scene construction approach. The former starts from the commonalities between remembering the past and imagining the future and arrives at a picture of a cognitive system, subserved by the default network as a whole, responsible for simulating past and future events. The latter starts from the commonalities among a somewhat broader range of episodic constructive processes and arrives at a picture of a capacity, subserved by the hippocampus, responsible for simulating possible scenes. Thus, while there are differences between the approaches at the anatomical level, they are in broad agreement with respect to their functional characterizations of episodic memory, both viewing episodic memory as a function of a more general episodic construction system responsible for simulating a range of possible episodes.

6.3   Remembering as Simulating the Past

Though it is natural to view episodic and semantic memory as being parallel memory systems, differentiated by the fact that each is devoted to
storing a different type of information, current empirical frameworks favor
a rather different picture. While we may still speak of encoding, consolidation, storage, and retrieval in episodic memory, remembering is not a matter
of encoding, consolidating, storing, and retrieving discrete representations
of discrete episodes. In the previous chapter, we saw that these processes
involve selection, abstraction, interpretation, integration, and reconstruction, all of which may introduce significant modifications to remembered
information. The lesson of mental time travel research is that construction and reconstruction do not simply introduce modifications in representations that are nonetheless essentially preserved. The episodic memory
system is in reality a general episodic construction system, designed to
draw on information originating in past experience to simulate possible
episodes. Obviously, when the target of the system is, for example, a future
episode, simulation cannot amount to reproducing a previous experience
of the episode; instead, simulation is a matter of drawing on a range of past
experiences to produce a novel representation of the target episode. What
must be appreciated is that remembering is not different in kind from other
episodic constructive processes. While simulation of a given past episode
presumably *often* draws on information originating in the agent's experience of that particular episode, it will rarely draw *exclusively* on such information, and in principle it need not draw on such information *at all*.

6.3.1   Nonexperiential Information

In his foundational work on the constructive character of memory, Bartlett
emphasized that information not originating in the subject's experience of
the remembered episode routinely plays a role in remembering:

Remembering appears to be far more decisively an affair of construction rather than
one of mere reproduction. The difference between the two cases ... seems to be that
in remembering a man constructs on the basis of one "schema," whereas in what
is commonly called imagining he more or less freely builds together events, inci-
dents, and experiences that have gone to the making of several different "schemata"
which, for the purposes of automatic reaction, are not normally in connexion with
one another. Even this difference is largely only a general one, for as has been shown
again and again, condensation, elaboration and invention are common features of

ordinary remembering, and these all very often involve the mingling of materials belonging originally to different "schemata." (Bartlett 1932, 205)

Bartlett's insight is that, while remembering an experienced episode may draw on a representation originating in the subject's experience of the episode, in contrast to imagining a nonexperienced episode, which necessarily draws on representations originating in the subject's experience of other episodes, remembering, like imagining, may also draw on representations originating in the subject's experience of episodes other than the episode in question. This insight is consistent with the causal theory of constructive memory described in the previous chapter. What the mental time travel framework suggests is that neither Bartlett nor the causal theory of constructive memory goes quite far enough. At least in this passage, Bartlett appears to assume that, while remembering may draw on information originating in experience of episodes other than the remembered episode, it always draws on at least *some* information originating in experience of the remembered episode. This assumption, which is likewise built into the causal theory of constructive memory, now appears to be unjustified.

In many cases, of course, the most efficient way of simulating a given experienced episode will be to draw at least in part on information originating in experience of that episode. In some cases, however, information originating in experience of the episode may be more difficult to retrieve than relevant information originating in experience of other episodes. And in some cases, information originating in experience of the episode may be inaccessible or entirely unavailable, while relevant information originating in experience of other episodes remains accessible. The mental time travel framework suggests that, in such cases, remembering may proceed without reliance on information originating in experience of the episode; it suggests, in other words, a pure simulation theory of remembering, on which there is no difference in kind between remembering the past and imagining it.

6.3.2   Properly Functioning Episodic Construction Systems

If remembering is just imagining the past, little of the causal theory, or the commonsense conception of memory on which it is based, survives. It may appear, in fact, that of the conditions making up the theory, only the current representation condition need be retained; that is, that to remember is nothing more than to entertain a representation of a past episode. On

closer examination, however, a condition similar to the properly functioning episodic memory system condition built into the causal theory of constructive memory is required as well—it is an oversimplification, though
only a slight oversimplification, to say that remembering just is imagining
the past.

As it stands, the condition requires that the causal chain connecting
the subject's current representation to his previous representation go via
a properly functioning episodic memory system. Given that a pure simulation theory will discard the causal condition, the reference to causal
chains becomes irrelevant. And given that the notion of a dedicated episodic memory system needs to be replaced with the notion of a broader episodic construction system, what we need is a condition along the following
lines:

- R is produced by a properly functioning episodic construction system
  which aims to produce a representation of an episode belonging to S's
  personal past.

While we are no longer attempting to capture the traditional distinction
between remembering the past and imagining it, a condition of this sort is
required to distinguish between remembering the personal past, on the one
hand, and, on the other hand, both other forms of episodic imagination—
including other forms of past-directed episodic imagination—and certain
forms of defective simulation of the past, which we can refer to as *merely
imagining the past*. Both sorts of cases are discussed below, but before the
discussion can proceed, we need to clarify two key notions invoked in the
condition: that of an episodic construction system and that of the personal
past itself.

6.4 The Episodic Construction System

The concept of an episodic construction system is meant to be neutral
among competing views of the nature of the system responsible for mental
time travel and other forms of episodic imagination. It is neutral in two
senses. First, while we may assume that the relevant system is capable of
simulating not only past episodes but also a range of other episodes (future
episodes, counterfactual past episodes, and so on), the concept does not
take a firm stand on exactly which episodic constructive processes are

executed by the system or whether any of these is more central to the function of the system than the others. Second, while we can take it for granted that the hippocampus plays a core role in the system and that other areas of the default network contribute, the concept also does not take a stand on the implementational-level details of the system. The neutrality of the concept is intended to ensure its compatibility—and hence the compatibility of the simulation theory—with the constructive episodic simulation approach, the scene construction approach, and other approaches to mental time travel that have been proposed in the literature. At the same time, the concept is meant to be sufficiently determinate to capture the common core of these approaches, the claim that episodic remembering is not the product of a dedicated episodic memory system, but rather one product of a system responsible for episodic imagination more generally.

The concept of an episodic construction system itself should be unproblematic, but the notion of the system's "aiming to" produce a representation of an episode from the subject's personal past, or any other kind of episode for that matter, may strike some as odd. The apparent oddity is inevitable, as talk of the system's aiming at producing a representation of an episode from the subject's personal past is meant to cover both cases of voluntary simulation, in which the agent initiates an attempt to simulate the episode, and cases of involuntary or spontaneous simulation, in which a cue triggers the process without the agent himself being responsible for initiating it. A background assumption here is that, even in cases of involuntary simulation, there is a fact of the matter about what kind of episode—whether from the actual past, the counterfactual past, the possible future, and so on—the system is "trying" to simulate; the assumption is grounded in the claim, to which we will return below, that an episodic construction system that did not differentiate between past and future, actual and counterfactual, likely could not have evolved. The proper function of the episodic construction system, which can likewise be understood in evolutionary terms (Millikan 1984), is explored in detail in part IV.

6.5   The Personal Past

Granted that we can make sense of the notion of an episodic construction system's attempting to simulate a given kind of episode, what is it for a system to attempt to simulate an episode from the *personal past*, in particular?

The notion of the personal past is usually not given an explicit definition in the psychological literature. One natural definition says that an episode belongs to a subject's personal past just in case he experienced it, but there is reason to resist this definition. On the one hand, if we adopt a broad notion of experience, it may be possible for a subject to experience events that it makes little sense to include in his personal past. For example, one might experience an event via a live video feed without the event in question (as opposed to the event of watching of the video feed) belonging in any meaningful sense to one's personal past. On the other hand, if we adopt a narrow notion of experience, it may be possible for a subject not to experience events that should be included in his personal past. For example, at a sufficiently young age, one may lack the conceptual capacities necessary for experiencing certain events in one's life in a full sense—one might be involved in an event, and one might have an experience, without having an experience of the event, but it might nevertheless make sense to include the event in one's personal past.[8]

Rather than defining the notion of the personal past in terms of experience, it therefore seems preferable to fall back on our intuitive sense of what it is for a subject to be involved in an event. A subject's personal past can then be viewed as an ordered sequence of episodes in which the subject was involved. Both the notion of an ordered sequence of episodes and the notion of an episode itself should be understood here in a loose sense. The episodes making up a subject's past cannot be ordered by a simple earlier-than/later-than relation, as some episodes may overlap with others or include others as proper parts. And given the sorts of episodes that we remember and imagine, episodes themselves may include temporally disjoint components.[9]

6.6   Remembering and Merely Imagining the Past

The simulation theory says that S remembers an episode e just in case

- S now has a representation R of e
- R is produced by a properly functioning episodic construction system which aims to produce a representation of an episode belonging to S's personal past.

This theory is far weaker than most available accounts, in the sense that it counts as cases of genuine memory many cases that other theories would classify as instances of mere imagination, but it does discriminate between genuinely remembering the past and certain kinds of mere imagination.

First, remembering is not the only form of past-directed episodic imagination. Consider episodic counterfactual thought, in which the subject imagines alternatives to past episodes. The notion of the personal past, as employed in the simulation theory, refers to the *actual* personal past, and the theory thus discriminates between memory and episodic counterfactual thought by the requirement that the episodic construction system must aim at simulating an episode from the personal past. This implication of the simulation theory is consistent with the finding that distinct subsystems of the default network are involved in episodic remembering and episodic counterfactual thinking (Addis et al. 2009), as well as with the finding that there are phenomenological differences between these two episodic constructive processes (De Brigard and Giovanello 2012). Similarly, one may also imagine past episodes in which one was not even counterfactually involved; such forms of imagination are distinguished from memory by the fact that the episodic construction system does not attempt to simulate an episode belonging to the subject's *own* personal past.

Second, the theory discriminates between remembering the past and the sort of mere imagining of the past that can occur due to a malfunctioning episodic construction system. Consider again the case of patient SD, described in the previous chapter. When attempting to describe the events of the previous day, SD drew on information originating in his past experience, though not his experience of the previous day. This information was integrated into a representation of the previous day's events that was both implausible and inaccurate. While SD does attempt to represent an episode from the personal past, he should not be classified as remembering, for to do so would be to ignore a difference in kind between the cognitive process responsible for producing his representation and the cognitive process at work when a healthy subject remembers. The difference in question is not that his representation is inaccurate, for a healthy subject might also represent the past inaccurately. Neither is it that the confabulating subject draws on information not originating in the target episode, for the healthy subject might draw on such information as well. Nor is it that he draws on no information originating in the target episode, for, if the simulation theory is right, remembering is compatible with this possibility as well. The difference lies, rather, in the way in which the patient's episodic construction system simulates the target episode. In the healthy subject, the system recombines information, whether or not it originates in the target episode, following procedures designed to enable it to produce a representation of the episode which is (within certain limits) accurate. In the confabulating subject, in contrast, the system malfunctions, following procedures which tend to produce inaccurate representations. This gives us a second sense in which remembering can be distinguished from merely imagining the past: the relevant representation is produced by an episodic construction system which aims to produce a representation of an episode from the subject's personal past, but the system is malfunctioning. If by chance SD really had won a race the day before and been rewarded with a piece of meat on his right knee, he would—assuming that his memory system had not undergone an instantaneous, miraculous recovery—still not count as remembering, since any correspondence between his representation and the relevant episode would be a matter of chance.

The simulation theory thus respects our intuitions about the distinction between memory and imagination in some cases. But not in all. Consider again the two examples from Martin and Deutscher discussed above. In the first, Kent experiences an event at a certain place and time, loses his memory of it, and is later hypnotized in such a manner that he takes himself to have experienced an event of the relevant kind at the relevant place and time. In the second case, Kent experiences an event at a certain place and time, loses his memory of it, is later told about the event, forgets having been told, and eventually, on the basis of the testimonial information he received, takes himself to have experienced an event of the relevant kind at the relevant place and time. Both Martin and Deutscher's original causal theory of memory and the updated causal theory of constructive memory imply that Kent remembers in neither case—in the former, because there is no causal chain connecting the putative memory and the event; in the latter, because, while there is a causal chain, it is deviant. The simulation theory, in contrast, implies that Kent remembers in the second case but not the first. Given the way the hypnotist case is described, we may assume that the hypnosis interferes with the normal workings of Kent's episodic construction system. If so, the apparent memory, while accurate, is only coincidentally so, as it is not the output of a properly functioning episodic construction system. Given the way the testimony case is described, on the other hand, we may assume that nothing is amiss with Kent's episodic construction system at the time at which the putative remembering occurs. If so, the correspondence between the apparent memory and the accident is not a coincidence, as properly functioning episodic construction systems are designed to draw on testimonial information in order to simulate past events.

The admittedly counterintuitive possibility of remembering on the basis of testimonial or other nonexperiential information will be discussed in detail in chapter 7. For now, note that the simulation theory also gives us a third sense in which a subject can be said to merely imagine. A properly functioning episodic construction system might attempt to simulate an episode not belonging to the subject's personal past, but the subject himself might nevertheless take the simulated episode to belong to his personal past. In such cases, while nothing goes wrong with the operation of the episodic construction system itself, there is a sense in which the subject can be said to merely imagine. Schacter (1996) uses an anecdote involving US president Ronald Reagan to make a related point. Reagan, it seems, told a tragic story of heroism involving a World War II bomber pilot, as if recounting his own experience of the episode. Eventually, it emerged that what Reagan was "remembering" was in fact a scene from a popular film. One possibility is that Reagan's episodic construction system was malfunctioning; in that case, he was merely imagining, in the sense given above. Another possibility is that Reagan mistakenly took himself to be remembering something that he had experienced, as opposed to something he had seen in a film, or that he mistakenly took himself to be remembering, when in fact he was engaged in another sort of episodic imagination entirely; in either case, he was, in a distinct sense, merely imagining. Cases of this sort will be discussed in detail in chapters 8 and 9.

6.7 Beyond the Causal Theory

These ways of merely imagining the past aside, the simulation theory simply equates remembering with imagining the past. It thus departs significantly from the causal theory of constructive memory, which itself already departs significantly from the commonsense conception of remembering and the classical causal theory.

Consider the relationship between the subject's retrieved memory representation, his initial memory representation, and his original experience of the relevant episode. The commonsense conception and the causal theory allow for minor transformations of content between the experience and the initial encoding of a memory representation (due to a conservative interpretation of the appropriate connection condition). Between encoding and retrieval, they allow only for transformations that reduce content (due to the content matching condition). The causal theory of constructive memory, in contrast, allows for more extensive transformations of content between experience and encoding (due to a more liberal interpretation of the appropriate connection condition). It also allows for extensive transformations of content between encoding and retrieval, including transformations that introduce new content (due to the approximate content similarity condition).

The causal theory of constructive memory nevertheless assumes that remembering necessarily involves preservation of *some* content between experience and retrieval. On the simulation theory, in contrast, neither the appropriate connection condition nor the approximate content similarity condition need be satisfied, since the subject need not have encoded an initial memory representation at all (i.e., because the previous representation condition need not be satisfied). Moreover, even in cases where an initial, short-term memory representation is encoded, the simulation theory does not assume that this will eventuate in the consolidation of a long-term memory trace. Hence the requirement of an unbroken causal chain, captured by the experience condition, the causal condition, the continuous connection condition, and the memory trace condition, need not be satisfied.

The simulation theory thus supports radical generationism even more emphatically than does the causal theory of constructive memory. Consider again the simple case of content generation illustrated in figure 5.2. The simulation theory implies that the connections represented by the dashed lines are optional. In many cases, remembering no doubt involves the sort of continuous causal connection described by the classical causal theory, and at least the sort of approximate content similarity described by the causal theory of constructive memory. But it need not. What it is for a subject to remember, according to the simulation theory, is for him to imagine an episode belonging to his personal past. And imagining need not draw on stored information ultimately originating in experience of the relevant episode. I might see the statue in front of the train station and, for one reason or another, end up not encoding even a short-term representation of the scene. Or I might encode a short-term representation but end up not consolidating a long-term representation. In neither case need the absence of stored information deriving from my experience of the episode prevent me from remembering it. If sufficient information originating in other sources—for example, stored representations of similar episodes, or semantic knowledge of the layout of the relevant area—is available, my episodic construction system may produce a representation of the episode when I later attempt to remember it. When this occurs, the simulation theory implies, I remember the episode, just as much as I do when part or even all of the content of the retrieved representation originates in my experience of the episode.

If an unbroken causal chain between the event and the "retrieved" memory is not required for remembering, what determines which event a given memory is a memory *of*? I remember walking home from my office on a hot day. I have done so many times, and nothing in the content of the memory singles out a specific episode. On the causal theory, if I am genuinely remembering, there must be an unbroken causal chain stretching from the retrieval of the memory back to a given episode. While information originating in other experiences of similar episodes might end up being incorporated into the retrieved memory, this chain would appear to enable us, in principle, to single the relevant episode out as the episode that I remember. On the simulation theory, no such procedure is available. Where there is a causal chain, the simulation theorist is in principle free to say that it plays a role in grounding the reference of the memory, but, since this strategy is inapplicable in cases where there is no causal chain, it would lead to an unappealingly disjunctive overall account of reference. It thus seems preferable to say that whatever mechanism determines reference in cases where there is no causal chain is also at work in cases where there is a causal chain. The obvious mechanism to which we might appeal is intention—either the intention of the subject himself or the "intention" of his episodic construction system. In light of the possibility that the subject might misclassify another form of episodic imagination as memory, the latter option is preferable. Again, while it might seem odd to think of the episodic construction system as intending to simulate a determinate episode from the past, this can be understood as shorthand for talk of the system responding to given retrieval cues provided by either the agent or his environment (e.g., "how did I get home yesterday?"). Admittedly, where the cue is indeterminate ("think of a time you walked home from work"), the reference of the retrieved memory may itself be indeterminate. But an analogous problem arises for the causal theory as well, since in cases in which remembering draws on information originating in more than one experience, there may be unbroken causal chains between the retrieved representation and multiple episodes.

6.8   Related Approaches

The simulation theory represents a significant departure from the causal theory, but the recent philosophical literature contains a number of proposals sharing its general spirit. While there are important differences between the simulation theory defended here and these other views, the growing tendency to view remembering in simulational or imaginative terms reinforces the claim that it is time to move beyond the causal theory.

6.8.1   Remembering and Imagining

One apparently similar approach that turns out to bear only a superficial resemblance to the simulation theory is that defended by Hopkins (forthcoming), who argues that episodic remembering is a kind of imagining—specifically, imagination "controlled by the past." Hopkins' account does link remembering to imagining more closely than has been standard, but, given how he defines what it is for imagination to be controlled by the past, the account ultimately turns out to be a version of the causal theory, since it requires that the subject's current representation derives from his original experience of the relevant episode. The account is therefore subject to the same limitations as the classical causal theory and the causal theory of constructive memory, in that it ignores the possibility that remembering can occur absent a causal connection between the current representation and the original experience of the episode. The same thing goes for the sequence analysis of memory defended by Cheng and Werning (forthcoming), which combines a simulational view with the requirement of an unbroken causal chain.

6.8.2   Remembering and Mindreading

Perrin (2011) has likewise argued for an explicitly simulational approach. Basing his approach less on psychological research than on conceptual considerations, he argues that a theory of episodic memory corresponding to the simulation theory of mindreading—where mindreading refers to the process of inferring the mental states of another subject—is preferable to an approach corresponding to the theory theory of mindreading (see, e.g., Perner 1993 for one such approach), since the latter implies that the form of self-consciousness involved in episodic memory necessarily involves a concept of oneself. The worry here is that viewing episodic memory as depending on a capacity to attribute the origin of remembered content to one's past self overintellectualizes memory. Drawing on Perry's (2002) notion of agent-relative knowledge, Perrin develops a notion of remembering as simulating the past in which the self is involved without being represented—just as one is the "background" of one's own perceptions (Perry 1985), one is the background of one's own memories. While Perrin's approach agrees with the simulation theory in not building a representation of the self into the content of episodic memory, it differs in denying that the attribution of the origin of a memory to one's own past experience is the output of an inferential process—as we will see in the following chapter, such attributions are indeed produced by inference-like (albeit normally unconscious) processes.

Episodic memory has similarly been compared to mindreading by Shanton and Goldman (2010), who argue for their simulationist approach in part on the basis of the same mental time travel research that grounds the simulation theory developed here.[10] On Goldman's account of mindreading (2006), mindreading involves a form of episodic imagination: starting from whatever background information one has about the target subject, one inhibits one's own mental states and attempts to imagine or simulate the subject's mental state; this simulated mental state can then be fed into task-specific mechanisms to produce further mental states which can be attributed to the target subject. Taking the simulation theory of mindreading for granted, Shanton and Goldman essentially argue that episodic remembering amounts to reading one's own past self's mind: one begins by retrieving whatever relevant information is available and, inhibiting one's current mental states, attempts to simulate one's own past mental state; this simulated mental state can then be fed into task-specific mechanisms to produce further mental states which can be attributed to one's past self.

While Shanton and Goldman's account is in tune with the account developed here, it differs from the latter in two key respects. First, Shanton

and Goldman treat the mindreading capacity as fundamental, with episodic memory being derivative. On the simulation theory, in contrast, what
is fundamental is a general capacity for episodic construction; this capacity
can be directed at one's own past or future (as in mental time travel), the
mental states of another subject (as in mindreading), and a variety of other
targets, such as counterfactual and fictitious episodes. To the extent that
one form of episodic construction is more basic than the others, chapter 11
will argue that it is likely future-oriented mental time travel, not mindreading. Second, Shanton and Goldman treat episodic memory as being a matter of simulating one's past *mental states*, in particular. On the simulation
theory, in contrast, episodic memory enables us to simulate past *episodes* in
general. This represents a fundamental advantage of the present simulation
theory, for, while episodic memory is sometimes a matter of remembering
past mental states, one often remembers events as such (see, e.g., Hoerl and
McCormack 2001). Consider again the example described in figure 5.2. I
may remember the events involved in my visit to the statue without remembering my own thoughts or feelings on that occasion. Arguably, I need not
even remember *seeing* the statue, as I may adopt an observer perspective on
the scene.[11] This suggests that, while we presumably do sometimes read our
own past selves' minds, it is unlikely that remembering reduces to reading
one's own past self's mind.

6.8.3 Remembering and Episodic Counterfactual Thought

To the extent that it is concerned with the simulation of events as opposed
to mental states, the approach developed by De Brigard (2014a; 2014b),
which focuses on characterizing the function of memory rather than developing an account of the nature of the process of remembering, is closer
to being compatible with the simulation theory defended here. There are,
however, two important differences between De Brigard's approach and the
simulation theory. First, while he views both remembering and episodic
counterfactual thinking as instances of the more general category of episodic hypothetical thinking, in line with the present treatment of them as
forms of episodic imagination, De Brigard views episodic counterfactual
thinking as primary and is therefore relatively pessimistic about the overall
reliability of remembering. In contrast, the simulation theory is, for reasons developed in part III, relatively optimistic with respect to reliability.
Second, De Brigard contends that the function of memory is not to provide

reliable access to past events but rather to provide raw material enabling simulation of counterfactual alternatives to past events. The simulation theory, in contrast, insofar as it is concerned with function, does not assign a privileged status to simulation of counterfactual episodes; again, chapter 11 will argue that it is likely that episodic future thinking, rather than episodic counterfactual thinking, is primary.

6.9 Objections to the Simulation Theory

Viewing memory as a form of mental time travel may push us in the direction of a simulation theory of remembering, but such a theory faces a number of philosophical objections. This section deals, first, with a pair of objections based on the metaphysics and the phenomenology of mental time travel; similar objections will apply to most simulationist views, including those just described. It then responds to an objection specific to the particular simulation theory developed here.

6.9.1 The Metaphysics of Mental Time Travel

According to the simulation theory, the only difference between remembering the past and imagining the future is that, in the former process, the episodic construction system takes a past episode as its target, while, in the latter, it takes a future episode as its target. Against this sort of view, which posits a fundamental symmetry between remembering the past and imagining the future, Debus (2014) argues that, though they may share a common neurophysiological basis, we should acknowledge a difference in kind between remembering the past and imagining the future, since, when a subject remembers a past event, he is experientially aware of the event, while, when a subject imagines a future event, he is not (and indeed could not be) experientially aware of it. Experiential awareness can only be awareness of particular events, and, for straightforward reasons, we cannot be aware of particular events that have not yet occurred. A similar argument can be run in terms of factivity: remembering the past, we might argue, is factive, in the sense that it requires that the remembered event actually occurred, whereas imagining the future is not; hence remembering the past is an occurrence of a different kind than imagining the future. And Debus's argument is similarly vulnerable to the reasons given above for rejecting the view that factivity is a necessary condition on remembering. The view discussed there concerned the alleged difference in kind between remembering the past and imagining the past, whereas Debus's view concerns the alleged difference in kind between remembering the past and imagining the future, but both theories introduce a distinction between kinds of states or processes that does not correspond to a psychologically real difference.

6.9.2   The Phenomenology of Mental Time Travel

Turning from metaphysics to phenomenology, one might object that the simulation theory downplays the importance of the form of consciousness characteristic of remembering. The concern here is not with an apparent difference between remembering the past and imagining the future, but rather with an important *similarity* between the two processes, a similarity that is left out by the simulation theory. Mental time travel research emphasizes the characteristic phenomenology—autonoesis, or consciousness of the self in subjective time—involved in both remembering the past and imagining the future, and Klein, in particular, has recently gone so far as to argue that this phenomenology—explored in detail in subsequent chapters—is essential to episodic memory. The claim is that remembering entails "the *experience* of the past *as* past" (Klein 2015).

If this is right, a reference to subjective temporal orientation should be built into the theory of remembering. Klein himself, however, reviews clinical evidence that the phenomenology *characteristic* of mental time travel is not in fact *essential* to it. He treats the relevant cases, in which patients are able to entertain representations of episodes from their personal pasts but in which they lack any sense that the episodes belong to them as suggesting merely that the feeling of pastness is not intrinsic to retrieved content, but in fact they seem to suggest, more strongly, that episodic remembering can occur even absent the feeling of pastness. In this context, it may be important to distinguish between two sorts of clinical case. On the one hand, there are cases in which a patient suffering from retrograde amnesia is able to relearn episodes from his personal past without, when he retrieves representations of the episodes in question, feeling that they belong to his personal past (e.g., Levine et al. 1998; Markowitsch and Staniloiu 2013). On the other hand, there are cases in which a patient does not suffer from episodic amnesia, in the sense that he is able to retrieve detailed representations of episodes from his personal past (without having to relearn them), without, when he retrieves them, feeling that they belong to his personal past (e.g., Klein and Nichols 2012; Simeon and Abugel 2006). Cases of the former sort are most naturally described as cases in which the subject relies on semantic learning as a substitute for episodic memory. Cases of the latter sort, in contrast, are most naturally described as cases in which episodic remembering occurs without its characteristic phenomenology. Hence, while there is evidence that the temporal dimension of remembering belongs to the phenomenology of remembering rather than to its content, it seems to accord better with the available evidence not to treat the feeling of pastness as being, strictly speaking, essential to remembering. This does not, however, imply that phenomenology does not play a central role in remembering. As we will see, it arguably plays a crucial role in explaining the reliability of remembering and hence the evolution of memory itself.

6.9.3   Memory without Experience

In contrast to the causal theory, the simulation theory implies that one can remember without drawing on information originating in one's experience of the remembered episode. As noted above, if the personal past can include nonexperienced episodes, it also implies that one can in principle remember even where one did not actually experience the relevant episode to begin with. The former implication will be hard for many to swallow. The latter implication is considerably harder to swallow than the former.

The causal theory of constructive memory already implies that one can remember *more* of an episode than one actually experienced. Given that boundary extension, for example, is a routine occurrence in healthy subjects, we have no principled reason for denying this implication, counterintuitive though it may be. The simulation theory simply goes (much) further in the same direction, allowing that one can in principle remember an entire episode that one did not experience—as long as the relevant representation is of an event belonging to one's personal past, and as long as it is produced by a properly functioning episodic construction system, one counts as remembering. Consider the sort of procedure used by eyewitness memory researchers to implant false memories of whole episodes, such as being lost in a shopping mall as a young child (Loftus 1993). According to the simulation theory, what goes wrong in such cases is not that the subject fails to remember, but simply that he *mis*remembers, relying on information received from other agents or information generated by his own imagination to construct a representation of an episode that did not actually occur. Suppose, now, that a subject on whom the procedure is used actually was lost in a mall as a young child, too young to count as having experienced the episode, strictly speaking. The simulation theory implies that in such a case, the subject does not even misremember—he simply remembers the episode. That he did not actually experience it makes no difference.[12]

Such cases make sense only given that we adopt a narrow notion of experience and, if no sufficiently narrow notion is available, in practice they will not arise. Given that a sufficiently narrow notion is available, however, it remains highly counterintuitive to say that one might remember without having experienced the relevant episode. For the same reason, where the subject did experience the episode, it is highly counterintuitive to say that he might remember it despite his apparent memory not drawing on any information originating in the relevant experience. It is only slightly less counterintuitive to say that the subject is remembering where his apparent memory draws both on information originating in the relevant experience and on information originating elsewhere. The following chapter will argue, however, that while there may be good practical reasons for denying that remembering occurs in cases of the latter sort, these do not translate into good theoretical reasons, and the same thing goes for the other cases as well.

At the same time, it is important to observe that the simulation theory does *not* suggest that one can episodically remember events that do not belong to one's personal past. While semantic memory may also have a constructive character, the simulation theory, in virtue of its reference to the episodic construction system, views episodic construction as a distinct cognitive process. It is thus consistent with the fact that I can episodically remember my own voyage from France to Turkey, while I can only semantically remember *that* my great-grandfather traveled from the Ottoman Empire to the United States. Unlike traditional theories of memory, however, it does call attention to the fact that I can episodically *imagine* my great-grandfather's voyage and to the fact that this episodic imagining has a great deal in common with my episodically remembering my own voyage. On the simulation theory, episodic memory is a *kind* of episodic imagination—namely, episodic imagination directed at the personal past—and, as a kind of episodic imagination, it draws on the same suite of cognitive resources that are involved in other kinds of episodic imagination. It remains meaningful, however, to distinguish between episodic memory—simulation of episodes in one's own past—and other forms of episodic imagination.

6.10   Remembering as Imagining the Past

The search for an adequate theory of memory was initially motivated by the aim of identifying a criterion capable of distinguishing between memory and imagination. We are now in a position to see that this aim was misguided. Recall that there are two senses in which we might want to identify such a criterion: we might want to identify a metaphysical criterion, a marker of the objective difference between remembering and imagining, or we might want to identify a metacognitive criterion, a marker (or markers) that subjects actually employ in order to judge, with whatever degree of accuracy, when they themselves are remembering and when they are imagining. If the simulation theory is right, the search for a metaphysical criterion is futile. We tend to assume that it is one thing to genuinely remember the past and another to imagine it, but that turns out not to be the case. The fact that the search for a metaphysical criterion is misguided might seem to imply that the search for metacognitive criteria is likewise a mistake, but this will turn out not to be the case. Episodic memory is a kind of episodic imagination, but it is only one kind of episodic imagination. Hence, while it is a mistake to ask how subjects tell the difference between remembering the past and imagining the past, we can still ask how they tell the difference between remembering and other kinds of imagining. The latter question has received relatively little attention, but an appreciation of the tight connection between episodic memory and other forms of episodic simulation lends it new urgency.

As noted above, the simulation theory supports radical generationism, the view that remembering can produce epistemic justification by producing new content, even more decisively than does the causal theory of constructive memory. The latter theory, by permitting the addition of content during encoding, consolidation, and retrieval, allows the content produced by remembering to go beyond the content of the relevant original experience. The simulation theory, by breaking the requirement of a causal connection, allows the content produced by remembering to be entirely new. If the simulation process is reliable, radical generationism follows. The question, then, is whether the simulation process is reliable. It is natural enough to suppose that it is not. Bartlett, for example, appears to favor the unreliability of memory when he remarks that it is "hardly ever really exact, even in the most rudimentary cases of rote recapitulation, and it is not at all important that it should be so" (1932, 213). The point that memory need not be *exact* in order to be functional is plausible, but this does not imply that it need not be reasonably accurate on average. The following part of the book therefore turns to the mechanisms responsible for ensuring the reliability of simulational remembering.

III   Mental Time Travel as a Source of Knowledge

Given that remembering is a matter of imagining the past, opportunities for error would seem to be widespread. In light of this, what accounts for the reliability of memory? It is natural to worry that, due to its simulational character, memory is not in fact reliable. A background assumption in this part of the book is that, while it is not feasible to obtain a precise measure of the reliability of memory outside of specific laboratory contexts, memory is reliable overall in ecological settings. This assumption will be defended in part III, which argues that, if the episodic construction system were unreliable, it would not have been selected for, given the complexity of the system and the fitness penalties that would accrue to agents prone to frequently misremembering (or misimagining) events. Before turning to evolution, the task of the present part of the book is to develop an account of the mechanisms responsible for ensuring the reliability of simulational remembering.

The account has two components. The first concerns the reliability of the constructive processes involved in remembering. Due to the involvement of these processes, "retrieved" episodic representations do, in many cases, differ considerably from the agent's original experience of the relevant episodes. Such differences are, however, compatible with reliability. Consider again the example of boundary extension: if the way in which remembering supplements the agent's representation of the scene is accurate with respect to the scene itself, boundary extension need not reduce the reliability of remembering. Indeed, it may actually increase its power by providing the agent with more information about the layout of the scene than he would otherwise have. Chapter 7 defends the claim that construction is compatible with reliability by considering in detail the effects of one constructive process in particular—namely, the unconscious incorporation of testimonial information into memory. Ideally, of course, the effects of many such processes could be explored in similar detail, but it is plausible that the account given here generalizes. There are individual cases in which constructive processes result in inaccurate memories, and there may even be specific constructive processes which tend to reduce reliability. But given the overall reliability of memory, it is most plausible to view constructive processes as contributing to reliability. This goes even for cases in which remembering occurs without any reliance on information originating in experience: opportunities for error may be greater in such cases, but it is no more impossible to accurately imagine a past episode on the basis of information that happens to be nonexperiential than it is to accurately imagine a future episode on the basis of (necessarily) nonexperiential information.

The second component of the explanation concerns metamemory—our capacity for metacognitive monitoring and control of memory processes. If the argument of chapter 7 is right, the incorporation of nonexperiential information into retrieved representations need not threaten the reliability of remembering. But it would do so were it to occur in a completely haphazard way. Memory stores and retrieves not only representations originating in experience but also representations originating in a range of other sources: we remember what we have seen with our own eyes, but also what we have imagined, read about, heard described, and so on. While remembering may draw on these sources of information to produce an accurate representation of a past episode, they represent a potential threat to the reliability of memory, since, were the agent unable to distinguish, say, between information derived from experiencing the past and information derived from imagining the future, remembering would regularly produce representations bearing no correspondence to past episodes. Chapter 8 appeals to the source-monitoring framework, a widely used and well-confirmed account of one form of metamemory, to develop an explanation of our capacity to cope with this threat. Now, it is one thing to imagine an episode and another to remember imagining an episode, and while the source-monitoring framework may explain how agents manage to avoid confusion between remembering experienced episodes and remembering imagined episodes, it does not explain how they avoid confusion between remembering and imagining as such. In addition to remembering the past, we imagine the future, entertain alternative outcomes to past episodes, fantasize about possible scenarios, and so on. Consequently, we run the risk of falling into confusion among different forms of episodic imagination—for example, confusing remembering the past and imagining the future. Chapter 9 describes the challenge this poses to the reliability of memory and argues that agents solve it due to their capacity for process monitoring, a form of metacognition which bears certain similarities to, but which is importantly different from, source monitoring.

Together, the two components of the explanation suggest that, in many cases, constructive processes need not interfere with the reliability of memory; while they do introduce a degree of uncertainty into remembering, metamemory processes may effectively compensate for this uncertainty.

7 The Information Effect

Episodic memories are rarely based entirely on experiential information—that is, on information originating in the agent's experience of the relevant episode. In some cases, episodic memory may not draw on experiential information at all. In most cases, while episodic memory draws primarily on experiential information, it also incorporates information originating in a variety of other sources, including experience of other episodes, information stored in semantic memory, and information received through communication with other agents—what epistemologists refer to as testimony. Thus, even where the content of a given retrieved episodic representation consists primarily of experiential information, it may also include a significant amount of testimonial information. We have seen that this is compatible with the occurrence of genuine *remembering*, but is it compatible with the *reliability* of remembering?

As long as the effects of the incorporation of testimonial information are limited, whether because it occurs infrequently or because only a small quantity of information is incorporated, it is clearly compatible with the overall reliability of memory, even if it lowers the average accuracy of the representations produced by memory retrieval. What this chapter aims to show, more strongly, is that the incorporation of testimonial information is compatible with reliability even if its effects are much more extensive—indeed, that there is reason to think that it may *increase* the reliability of memory. For methodological reasons, psychological research in this area tends to focus primarily on the incorporation of inaccurate information. If the argument of this chapter is right, however, incorporated information tends to be accurate, boosting not only the reliability but also the power of memory. Beliefs resulting from the incorporation of accurate testimonial information may nevertheless appear, when they are true, to be only luckily true. If so, they are defective in an important sense. The chapter therefore also looks at whether such beliefs satisfy an anti-luck condition (Pritchard 2005), arguing that, once we are armed with an adequate conception of epistemic luck, together with an adequate appreciation of the adaptive character of memory, it becomes clear that beliefs resulting from the incorporation of accurate testimonial information are not, in general, luckily true.[1]

7.1   The Misinformation Effect: Harmful Incorporation

Testimony has been defined in broader and narrower terms (Gelfert 2014; Michaelian 2010). In the present context, the appropriate definition is an extremely broad one, according to which testimony is a matter of any serious communication by an agent, regardless of whether the communication involves an explicit assertion. We communicate not only by means of assertions but also but means of gestures, implications, presuppositions, and so on. Adopting a conception of testimony sufficiently broad to cover such forms of communication allows our discussion to make contact smoothly with relevant research on eyewitness memory, which is concerned with the effects not only, or even primarily, of information that is directly asserted, but also with those of information communicated by more indirect means.

However communication occurs, the incorporation of inaccurate testimonial information received after the agent's experience of an event into his representation of the event—what we can refer to for convenience as "harmful incorporation"—will result in the production of an inaccurate (or a less accurate) memory representation, and thus, if the relevant aspect of the retrieved representation is endorsed by the agent, in the formation of a false memory belief. This is the process responsible for the occurrence of the *misinformation effect*, as Loftus refers to "the impairment of memory for the past that arises after exposure to misleading information" (2005, 361). In a typical experiment on the misinformation effect, the agent first witnesses a complex event. Next, he is exposed to inaccurate information about some aspect of the event. Finally, he is asked to remember the event. The misinformation effect is said to occur when he reports having seen what the misinformation describes. For example, the agent might see a stop sign at the scene of an accident but later be asked a question which presupposes that the sign in question was a yield sign. When he later recalls the event, he might remember a yield sign at the scene and end up believing that there was a yield sign at the sign. As Loftus (1996; 2005) points out, while it is easier to modify peripheral details, as in this example, memories for entire events can be implanted under the right condition.

The source-monitoring framework provides one plausible account of the process responsible for harmful incorporation (Lindsay 1994).[2] On this account, traces originating both in experience of an event and in testimony about the event can coexist in the subject's memory. During retrieval, source-monitoring processes may classify the latter as originating in experience, resulting in the incorporation of testimonial information into the retrieved memory representation of the event and thus, if the representation is endorsed, into the corresponding belief. The source-monitoring framework will be discussed in detail in the following chapter, but it is important to note here that source monitoring is typically an unconscious process. Consequently, in most cases, the agent is entirely unaware that the retrieved representation includes testimonial information. The misinformation effect can also occur when the agent deliberately chooses to accept testimonial information, but such cases seem importantly different from the central cases, in which incorporation occurs without the agent's awareness (see the discussion of delayed formation of testimonial belief below), and we may set them aside here. By the same token, in the cases of interest, it is the accuracy of the retrieved memory itself, as opposed to merely the agent's verbal report of what he remembers, that is impaired (Loftus 2005; Zaragoza and Lane 1994).

Note that, in order for the incorporation of inaccurate information to result in an impairment of memory, the agent must originally have stored either an accurate representation of the relevant aspect of the event or no representation of that aspect of the event. If inaccurate testimonial information replaces inaccurate experiential information about the relevant aspect of the event, no impairment occurs—it makes no difference to the overall accuracy of memory.

7.2   Helpful Incorporation

The overall epistemic status of beliefs produced by harmful incorporation is clear: since they are false, they fail to meet the standards for knowledge, whatever standards we adopt. The more interesting question concerns beliefs due to what we can refer to as "helpful incorporation," where helpful incorporation occurs in the same way as harmful incorporation, except that accurate rather than inaccurate information is incorporated. Cases of helpful incorporation need be no more complicated or artificial than cases of harmful incorporation, a point reinforced by work in the social contagion paradigm (Meade and Roediger 2002; Roediger et al. 2001) finding that, when subjects remember together, they acquire both accurate and inaccurate information from each other (Rajaram 2011). For example, an agent might see a complex event but misperceive or fail to perceive some aspect of it. Later, he might be exposed to accurate information about that aspect of the event. If this post-event information is incorporated into his memory representation of the event and, ultimately, endorsed, the resulting belief will be true. For example, the agent might misperceive a stop sign at the scene of an accident as a yield sign. If he is later asked a question with the presupposition that the sign in question was a stop sign, he might end up remembering the event as involving a stop sign and thus believing that it involved a stop sign.

7.2.1 The Contamination View

At first glance, the effects of helpful incorporation would appear to be beneficial. Just as harmful incorporation can result in an impairment to memory only given that the agent stored either an accurate representation of the relevant aspect of the event or no representation of that aspect of the event, helpful incorporation can result in an improvement to memory only given that the agent stores an inaccurate representation of the event or no representation of that aspect of the event. In cases where accurate testimonial information replaces inaccurate or missing experiential information, the agent may form a true belief where otherwise he would not. But do such beliefs meet reasonable standards for knowledge? Intuitively, the question must be answered in the negative. The natural view on the epistemic status of beliefs resulting from incorporation of testimonial information is what we might refer to as the "contamination view": the incorporation, without the agent's awareness, of testimonial information into a retrieved memory representation prevents the resulting belief from qualifying as knowledge. As stated, the contamination view covers both harmful incorporation and helpful incorporation. With respect to harmful incorporation, the view is right but uninteresting: beliefs resulting from harmful incorporation fail to qualify as knowledge simply because they are false. It is less obvious whether the contamination view is right with respect to helpful incorporation, but *something* does seem to go wrong, epistemically speaking, in cases of helpful incorporation.

7.2.2 Interactions between Testimony and Memory

It is important to avoid confusing beliefs resulting from incorporation with testimonial beliefs formed in a delayed manner, for the difference between the two cases means that one obvious reaction to the contamination view is misguided. While it is fairly uncontroversial that agents can acquire knowledge by accepting testimonial information, there is a debate between reductionists and anti-reductionists over whether agents enjoy a default entitlement to accept such information (Michaelian 2008). If we conflate beliefs resulting from incorporation with testimonial beliefs, it might appear that a standard anti-reductionist position in the epistemology of testimony implies that, in virtue of this default entitlement, incorporation is straightforwardly compatible with knowledge.

Consider, for example, Burge's "acceptance principle," according to which a "person is entitled to accept as true something presented as true and that is intelligible to him, unless there are stronger reasons not to do so" (1993, 467). Advocates of such anti-reductionist principles might be tempted to argue against the contamination view as follows. Since the agent has a default entitlement to accept testimonial information, nothing need go wrong, epistemically speaking, when he accepts such information without being aware that he is doing so—he is simply exercising his entitlement. Thus, as long as the information at issue is accurate, incorporation can, contra the contamination view, give rise to knowledge.

This line of reasoning is flawed. Above, cases in which the agent deliberately chooses to accept remembered testimonial information rather than remembered experiential information—which might occur, for example, because no experiential information is accessible or because the agent takes himself to have reason to trust accessible testimonial information over accessible experiential information—were distinguished from the cases of interest here, in which incorporation happens without the agent's awareness. Indeed, cases of the former sort appear not to be cases of memory belief at all but rather cases in which memory plays the role of an intermediary

in the delayed formation of a testimonial belief. In a case of incorporation without awareness, a testifier S tells the agent that P; the content later
retrieved from memory is $[P]$; the agent accepts the retrieved content, forming a memory belief that P. Contrast a case in which the subject consciously
chooses to accept remembered testimonial information: a testifier S tells
the agent that P; the content later retrieved from memory is $[S$ said that
$P]$; the agent accepts the retrieved content, forming a memory belief that
S said that P; the agent then accepts the content of S's testimony, forming
a testimonial belief that P. While, from an experimental point of view, it
will sometimes be difficult to distinguish between cases of these two types,
delayed formation of testimonial belief is nonetheless psychologically distinct from incorporation of testimonial information into memory without
awareness.

The psychological difference grounds an epistemic difference. Burge
remarks that "the justification of the Acceptance Principle says that
one is entitled to accept intelligible contents 'presented as true.' We must
perceive a speech act as involving a presentation-as-true in order to be
justified under the principle" (1993, 481). Under the acceptance principle, in order to be entitled to accept testimony, the agent must accept it
because it is presented as true (though Burge makes clear that this need
not involve consciously judging that it is being presented as true). This
condition may be satisfied in ordinary cases of formation of testimonial
belief, and it may be satisfied in cases of delayed formation of testimonial
belief, but it is not satisfied in cases of incorporation: in such cases, the
agent does not accept the testimonial content *because* it is presented as
true by the speaker—when he accepts the content, no trace of the presentation-as-true by the speaker is accessed, and indeed, in many cases,
no trace of the presentation by the speaker will remain in memory at all.
Nor can we argue that the endorsement of testimonial information in an
incorporation case is epistemically legitimate because the acceptance principle applies directly to contents delivered by the agent's own memory.
The idea here would be that an agent has a default entitlement to accept
something that is presented to him as true, regardless of whether the
source is internal or external. The problem is that contents retrieved from
memory are not presented as true—as we will see in chapter 8, retrieval
always involves a *decision* about the probable accuracy of the retrieved
representation.

7.3   Explaining the Appeal of the Contamination View

7.3.1   Incorporation and Reliability

Setting anti-reductionism aside, what accounts for the intuitive plausibility of the contamination view? One possibility is the thought that beliefs resulting from incorporation are bound to be *unjustified*. The contamination view, however, is compatible with the claim that beliefs resulting from incorporation are justified. Nor is it plausible to attempt to account for the intuition that something goes wrong, epistemically speaking, in cases of incorporation by claiming that the resulting beliefs are unjustified.

Whatever conception of justification one adopts, one might suspect that, in cases of belief resulting from incorporation, the agent typically has defeaters for the belief. Suppose that S remembers a stop sign at the scene of an accident and therefore forms the belief that there was a stop sign at the scene. Suppose that his memory of a stop sign at the scene resulted from incorporation. It might seem that there is a true proposition such that, if S were to believe it, his justification for believing that there was a stop sign at the scene would be defeated, namely, that his memory of a stop sign at the scene resulted from incorporation. If the argument below is right, however, this proposition does not in fact defeat S's justification, for there is nothing wrong, epistemically speaking, with forming a belief by endorsing a representation resulting from incorporation. Moreover, if the specific proposition that a memory results from incorporation were able to defeat the justification for a belief resulting from incorporation, so, presumably, would be the more general proposition that the memory results from a constructive process, and we should not take the latter proposition to defeat justification if we want to allow that there are any justified memory beliefs at all—memory is always constructive, regardless of whether it relies on testimonial information.

Of course, given the metaepistemological framework adopted in chapter 3, our concern here is not with a generic notion of justification but specifically with reliability, and one might suspect that the process responsible for producing memory beliefs incorporating testimonial information is unreliable, which would account for the intuition that even memory beliefs based on accurate testimonial information are epistemically defective. But this suspicion depends on the assumption that the process responsible for producing beliefs incorporating testimonial information can be distinguished from the process responsible for producing "ordinary" memory beliefs, and this assumption is untenable. Since incorporation is a routine part of the reconstructive retrieval process, we should classify the belief-producing process at work in cases of incorporation as being the same as that at work in cases of "ordinary" memory belief—incorporation should be viewed an optional step in the process responsible for the production of episodic memory beliefs. We have good reason to think that this process achieves an acceptable level of reliability. The challenge is to explain how it achieves this level.[3]

7.3.2 Incorporation and Truth

An alternative explanation of the intuitive plausibility of the contamination view is provided by the thought that beliefs resulting from incorporation must be *false*. But the contamination view is compatible with the accuracy of the episodic representations produced by helpful incorporation, and hence with the truth of the beliefs resulting from endorsing incorporated information—the claim is not that such beliefs must be false. Nor is it plausible to attempt to account for the intuition that something goes wrong in cases of helpful incorporation by claiming that beliefs resulting from incorporation must be false.

Certain views of episodic memory content do appear to imply that, when helpful incorporation occurs, it will normally result in a false belief. But there is independent reason to reject these views, and, even should one of them turn out to be right, the epistemological puzzle posed by helpful incorporation will reappear in a different form. As noted in chapter 3, reflexive views characterize the content of an episodic memory, and hence of an episodic memory belief, as referring to the agent's experience of an episode rather than directly to the episode itself. Fernández (2006), for example, defends a view according to which the content of a memory an agent S would express by saying that he remembers that P is an ordered pair <having had a veridical perception that P, S>; that is, something of the form [I saw that P]. Given the reflexive view, incorporation of accurate testimonial information will normally result in a false belief. Suppose, for example, that an agent either fails to perceive the stop sign at the scene of an accident or misperceives it as a yield sign. Suppose that he later incorporates the information that there was a stop sign at the scene and ends up forming the corresponding belief. If the reflexive view is right, his belief will have the content [I saw a stop sign at the scene], which is, of course, false.[4]

While reflexive views of episodic memory content have been popular, there is good reason to reject them. Subsequent chapters will make a case for viewing the self-referential character of episodic memory as being grounded in the form of consciousness involved in remembering, as opposed to the contents produced by memory retrieval. Moreover, when the perspectival character of episodic memories is taken into account, the reflexive view quickly leads to absurdities. As noted above, the perspective from which an agent remembers a scene is not always the perspective from which he originally experienced it. Consider the difference between field memories and observer memories (Nigro and Neisser 1983). In a field memory, the agent remembers the scene from (more or less) the point of view from which he experienced it. In an observer memory, he remembers the scene from the point of view of an external observer, seeing himself in the scene. While reflexive views are natural given that we have only field memories in mind, they are implausible with respect to observer memories—obviously, we do not want the content of an observer memory belief to come out being, for example, [I saw myself standing near a stop sign].

It may be possible to formulate a reflexive view capable of accommodating observer memories. But even should some reflexive view turn out to be right, this would simply introduce an additional complication into the argument. If episodic memory beliefs always have the form of [I saw a stop sign at the scene], so that beliefs resulting from incorporation are normally false, this does not mean that the embedded content [there was a stop sign at the scene] need be false. In cases of helpful incorporation, the embedded content will be true, and we can intelligibly ask about the epistemic status of this component of the belief. Committed proponents of the reflexive view may therefore take the argument of the following sections to apply to this component of the content.

7.3.3 Incorporation and the Anti-Luck Condition

Setting aside justification and truth, the intuitive appeal of the contamination view seems best accounted for by the thought that beliefs resulting from incorporation, if they are true, must be only *luckily* so, and to that extent epistemically defective. In a case of helpful incorporation, the relevant testimonial information happens to be accurate, but the agent does not incorporate it because he knows (or believes) that it is accurate—he cannot know this, since the incorporation occurs automatically, without his awareness. Due to this lack of awareness, if he were to have received inaccurate information rather than accurate information, he would likely have incorporated that information instead. It thus seems to be due to luck that he ends up forming a true belief.[5]

Indeed, beliefs resulting from helpful incorporation appear to be Gettiered. On Zagzebski's (1994) analysis, Gettier cases result when good epistemic luck cancels out bad epistemic luck. Consider Russell's (1948) example of the stopped clock. The subject looks at a clock. He knows that the clock is normally reliable and has no reason to doubt its accuracy on this particular occasion. The clock says that it is 9:00. He accepts this information and so comes to believe that it is 9:00. Everything is in order, epistemically speaking. Or nearly everything: the clock is in fact stopped, and it is not 9:00. Due to bad epistemic luck, the agent has formed a false belief. Now modify the case so that the agent just happens to look at the clock at 9:00. In the modified case, good epistemic luck counteracts bad epistemic luck, and he forms a true belief. But because the belief is true only due to luck, it does not qualify as knowledge.

Cases of helpful incorporation appear to have a similar structure. The subject retrieves a representation from episodic memory. He knows that his memory is normally reliable and has no reason to doubt its accuracy on this particular occasion. According to the retrieved memory, there was a stop sign at the scene of an accident that he witnessed. He accepts this information and so comes to believe that there was a stop sign at the scene. Everything is in order, or nearly everything: in fact, the component of the retrieved representation indicating that there was a stop sign at the scene results from harmful incorporation, and there was no stop sign at the scene. Due to bad epistemic luck, the agent has formed a false belief. Now modify the case so that there was a stop sign at the scene—that is, so that the incorporated information is accurate. In the modified case, good epistemic luck counteracts bad epistemic luck, and he forms a true belief. But because the belief is true only due to luck, it does not qualify as knowledge. Or so it would seem.

7.4 Skeptical Implications of the Contamination View

Despite its intuitive plausibility, the contamination view has a highly implausible skeptical consequence: it implies that we have far less episodic memory knowledge than we ordinarily take ourselves to have—that our episodic memory beliefs are epistemically defective in many cases where we would normally consider them to be in good standing. The contamination view does not imply the skeptical conclusion on its own, but rather in conjunction with two highly general empirical observations. What is at issue here is thus an empirically grounded form of skepticism about memory knowledge.

The first observation is simply that reconstruction in episodic memory is extremely pervasive: retrieval from episodic memory does not merely occasionally involve reconstruction; retrieval *always* involves reconstruction and thus routinely draws on information from sources other than experience. Previous chapters reviewed some of the evidence for this claim, but an additional example may help to make the point vivid. As noted above, an agent can remember a scene from either a field or observer perspective. It is tempting to think of field memories as privileged, even to think of field memories alone as being genuine memories, for, in an obvious way, observer memories fail to be true to the agent's original experience. Since observer memories depict the agent herself, they are clear reconstructions, departing significantly from the agent's original experience. It is natural to view field memories, on the other hand, as being more or less well-preserved copies of the agent's original experience. But this temptation is to be resisted, for, while there may indeed be a greater divergence between the original experience and the retrieved memory in the case of observer memories, this does not mean that field memories are any less the products of reconstruction. That field memories are, like observer memories, products of reconstruction is demonstrated by the ability of agents to switch between field and observer perspectives within a single episode of remembering (Rice 2010; Rice and Rubin 2009). As Sutton remarks, this ability "suggests that the difference in perspective is one of form rather than content, and that the same underlying ... representations can animate occurrent memories involving either perspective" (2010, 33). Stored information, in other words, does not determine perspective. The perspective of a retrieved memory is the product of a reconstructive process: just as, in the case of an observer memory, the episodic construction system makes its best guess as to what the scene must have looked like from the relevant observer perspective, in the case of a field memory, the system makes its best guess as to what the scene must have looked like from the agent's field perspective. Even memories which appear merely to preserve the original experience are themselves reconstructed.

The second observation is more mundane: each of us constantly receives testimony from others about an extremely wide range of topics, including events that we ourselves have experienced, and this testimony is often accurate. This point is familiar both from the literature on the epistemology of testimony and from the literature on human deception and deception detection (DePaulo et al. 1996; Michaelian 2012; Vrij 2008). Levine and colleagues, for example, provide evidence for a "principle of veracity" (Bok 2011)—what we might think of as an "honesty bias"—according to which honest communication is the default, with deceptive communication requiring special justification and hence occurring relatively infrequently (Levine et al. 2010; Serota et al. 2010).[6]

The pervasiveness of reconstruction in memory, together with the extent of our dependence on testimony, suggests that incorporation cannot be rare and that the representations produced by retrieval will often incorporate testimonial information. Thus, if the contamination view is right, in many perfectly ordinary cases of remembering, cases in which we would ordinarily take ourselves to have knowledge, we in fact lack knowledge. Assuming, in particular, that received testimony is fairly often accurate, in many ordinary cases of episodic remembering, we lack knowledge due to helpful incorporation. While this implication does not threaten all episodic memory knowledge, it does reduce the extent of episodic memory knowledge dramatically. Obviously, if our episodic memory beliefs turn out, due to harmful incorporation, to be false more often than we ordinarily take them to be, we will have no choice but to accept a reduction in the extent of our knowledge. The interesting question concerns helpful incorporation—here, there is room to maneuver, since the relevant beliefs are true.

7.5   Initial Attempts to Avoid Skepticism

One way of avoiding the skeptical conclusion is to adopt an unorthodox view on the compatibility of knowledge and epistemic luck. Hetherington (1999), for example, argues that, strictly speaking, some degree of epistemic luck is inevitable in belief formation, in which case we should grant that knowledge is compatible with epistemic luck. Making this move would allow a defender of the contamination view to avoid the skeptical conclusion: he could maintain that, while beliefs resulting from helpful incorporation are defective to the extent that they are luckily true, such beliefs are, since they are reliably produced, nevertheless knowledgeable.

If we accept the standard view of epistemology as being in the business of developing a unified theory of knowledge, this strategy is unattractive. While Hetherington's view on the compatibility of knowledge and epistemic luck is coherent, it represents a radical departure from the consensus among epistemologists. The strategy should thus appeal only to those already convinced by Hetherington's argument. The strategy is equally unattractive given the pluralistic metaepistemology adopted here. The fact that beliefs resulting from helpful incorporation have one epistemically valuable property—namely, reliability—does not lessen the importance of their apparent failure to have another epistemically valuable property, non-luckiness. Of course, we might, following Hetherington's lead, attempt to minimize the importance of epistemic luck, but non-luckiness is clearly a property that we want our beliefs to have, so this can only go so far.

An initially more promising strategy is to resist the move from the two empirical observations given above to the conclusion that helpful incorporation, viewed as the automatic inclusion of testimonial information in retrieved episodic memory representations, occurs frequently. The idea is that, though the availability of accurate testimonial information to the reconstructive retrieval process does mean that something like helpful incorporation will occur on a regular basis, it does not mean that incorporation is not under the agent's control: while agents are normally not *aware* that they are incorporating testimonial information, incorporation is nevertheless in an important sense under their *control*, for agents are implicitly sensitive to the honesty and competence of testifiers and therefore to the accuracy of received testimonial information. Assuming that control is sufficient to rule out luck, this strategy—which is suggested, for example, by Fricker's local reductionist position in the epistemology of testimony, according to which agents are entitled to accept testimonial information because they are sensitive to signs of dishonesty and incompetence (Fricker 1994, 2006)—would provide a way of avoiding the skeptical conclusion.

As we will see, it is a mistake to equate control with the absence of luck. But even if we set this point aside, the strategy turns out to be empirically untenable, for agents in fact have little sensitivity to the honesty and dishonesty of testifiers. As the work of Park and Levine and their colleagues, among others, shows, it can appear that we are sensitive to honesty in particular, since there is a high probability that, given that an item of testimony is honest, the recipient will judge that it is honest (Levine et al. 2006, 1999; Park and Levine 2001). But this is simply an effect of the "truth bias" of recipients: we tend to judge that honest testimony is honest because we tend to judge that any given item of testimony is honest, regardless of its actual honesty (Michaelian 2010, 2013).[7]

7.6   Incorporation and Epistemic Luck

While the contamination view thus seems to make the skeptical conclusion inevitable, there turns out to be independent reason to reject the view. In order to see this, we need to look more carefully at the notion of epistemic luck.

7.6.1   The Modal Conception of Epistemic Luck

The motivation for the contamination view given above relied implicitly on an understanding of luck in terms of control. As Pritchard (2005) points out, this is a natural conception of luck (defended, e.g., by Statman 1991). In the epistemic case, viewing luck in terms of control would amount to something like the following: good (bad) epistemic luck occurs when an agent forms a true (false) belief, the truth value of the belief being beyond the agent's control. The idea, roughly, is that good epistemic luck occurs when the agent does not see to it that he forms a true belief. While this control conception of luck is natural, it is, as Pritchard argues, inadequate. Many events that are beyond an agent's control—for example, the rising of the sun (Latus 2000)—clearly are not due to luck. More importantly, as the implausibility of doxastic voluntarism indicates, belief formation, in particular, is typically not (and possibly is never) under the agent's control, so that a control conception of *epistemic* luck, in particular, is especially misguided, as it would imply that virtually all true beliefs, and certainly all basic perceptual beliefs, are lucky. Since we want a unified conception of luck (so that if the control conception is inadequate with respect to perceptual beliefs, it is simply inadequate), this is not necessary for the present argument, but note that an analogous point can be made with respect to memory beliefs: formation of many memory beliefs (though perhaps not those that result from a conscious decision by an agent to endorse the content of a retrieved memory representation) is beyond the agent's control, for much the same reason as formation of basic perceptual beliefs is beyond the agent's control—he finds himself seeming to remember that P, and this is already enough to produce a belief that P, just as seeming to see that P is sufficient to produce a belief that P.

In place of the control conception, Pritchard proposes a modal conception of luck, according to which, if an outcome is lucky, then, first, it is an outcome which occurs in the actual world but which does not occur in most nearby possible worlds and, second, it is significant to the agent concerned. Presumably, the truth of an agent's memory beliefs is virtually always significant to him, so we may set the second of these conditions aside. Luck thus boils down to an event's occurring in the actual world but not in most nearby possible worlds. Given this generic modal conception, there are a number of varieties of specifically *epistemic* luck, many of them benign (e.g., serendipitous discovery). The malignant, knowledge-blocking variety with which we are concerned here is *veritic* epistemic luck, the sort of luck at work when "it is a matter of luck that the agent's belief is true" (Pritchard 2005, 146). On the modal conception, if a belief is luckily true, the agent forms it in the actual world but instead forms a false belief in most nearby possible worlds.[8]

An important virtue of the modal conception is that it explains the intuitive plausibility of the control conception. Though control is not necessary for non-luckiness, it tends to be sufficient for non-luckiness (Pritchard 2005). This association between absence of control and luck explains why it is natural to assume that beliefs resulting from helpful incorporation are luckily true (and hence epistemically defective). In cases of helpful incorporation, the agent does not see to it that he forms a true belief, since the truth of the belief depends on the accuracy of the testimonial information that he unknowingly incorporates; that is, the truth of the belief is beyond his control. Given the close association between absence of control and luck, this makes it natural to assume that his belief is veritically lucky. The association also helps us to understand how the intuition that helpful incorporation involves epistemic luck could be mistaken: because control, though sufficient for the absence of luck, is not necessary for it, the truth of the agent's belief might not be due to luck despite his lack of control over it. If a belief resulting from helpful incorporation is not luckily true, the explanation for the absence of luck, since the agent lacks control, should be sought not in the agent himself but rather in his environment or in the way in which he interacts with his environment.

Given the modal conception of epistemic luck, a given belief resulting from helpful incorporation will be luckily true only if the agent does not also form a true belief in most relevant nearby possible worlds. We can assume that the relevant nearby possible worlds are those in which the agent receives and incorporates testimony. Obviously, we should not assume that only worlds in which the agent receives *accurate* testimony are relevant. Thus whether the agent forms a true belief in most nearby worlds depends on whether he receives accurate testimony in most of those worlds. This point is crucial: given the modal conception, it is possible that, despite the agent's lack of control over the formation of a true belief in incorporation cases, beliefs resulting from helpful incorporation are not luckily true; if it is not a matter of luck that the agent receives true testimony (i.e., if he receives true testimony in most nearby worlds), then the beliefs in question will not be luckily true. The suggestion developed below is that, once we focus on the nature of the interaction between agents and their environments, including the other agents who provide them with testimony, it becomes clear that it is, in most cases, not in fact a matter of luck that the agent receives true testimony.

7.6.2   The Honesty Bias

The suggestion is grounded in two general methodological assumptions. First, we should adopt an adaptive perspective on cognition in general and on memory in particular (Anderson 1990), including the reconstructive character of retrieval (Schacter 2012, 2013): complex cognitive capacities such as memory can be assumed to be adaptations. Second, we should assume that, in general, true belief is adaptive and false belief is maladaptive (McKay and Dennett 2009): while there are exceptions, and while adaptivity does not require perfect accuracy, cognitive capacities are typically adaptive in virtue of their tendency to produce accurate representations.[9]

We are sometimes inclined to see memory as being extremely prone to failures of various kinds, as a flawed system in need of constant surveillance and correction. On the adaptive approach, however, memory, like other cognitive systems, should be seen as a system evolved to serve the needs of the organism of which it is a component. Given this approach, when we encounter a feature of memory that initially appears to be a defect, we should, rather than immediately concluding that it is in fact a defect, first look to see whether it functions adaptively. In particular, given that true belief is in general adaptive, when we encounter a feature of memory that initially appears to be a defect, we should first look to see whether it serves the production of true beliefs by the system. As the argument of part II emphasized, though the constructive character of remembering can give rise to distortion under certain circumstances, construction is compatible with the accuracy of memory. Though this point is simple and should not be controversial, it is often overlooked (Ost and Costall 2002), and it is, perhaps, a failure fully to acknowledge the point that has led researchers to focus on the misinformation effect without considering the possibility that it is a byproduct of the overall adaptive functioning of memory.

Evidence in support of this possibility comes from research on human deception and deception detection. As noted above, this research suggests that we are truth-biased—that is, that we tend to evaluate testimony as being honest, regardless of its actual honesty. The truth bias was anticipated by Reid, in a passage that has often been cited in recent work on the epistemology of testimony:

> The wise and beneficent Author of nature, who intended that we should be social creatures, and that we should receive the greatest and most important part of our knowledge by the information of others, hath, for these purposes implanted in our natures two principles that tally with each other … [We have] a propensity to speak the truth, and to use the signs of language, so as to convey our real sentiments. … [We have] a disposition to confide in the veracity of others, and to believe what they tell us. (Reid 1764, 428–430)

Reid's claim is that the truth bias does not operate in isolation: we also have an honesty bias, a tendency to give mostly honest testimony. Just as work on deception detection has confirmed Reid's suggestion that we are biased in favor of accepting testimony, work on deception in everyday life is beginning to confirm his suggestion that we do not lie easily (DePaulo et al. 1996; Levine et al. 2010; Michaelian 2010, 2012). Recent brain imaging work, for example, suggests that "truth constitutes the default response of the brain, and … lying involves intentional suppression of the predominant truth response" (Verschuere et al. 2011).[10]

Given the existence of the honesty bias, the tendency of reconstructive retrieval to automatically incorporate testimonial information straightforwardly emerges as adaptive. While the honesty bias will obviously sometimes be overridden by other factors, most of the testimony received by an agent will be accurate. And if most of the testimony received by an agent is accurate, then the incorporation of testimonial information into episodic memory representations need not diminish the reliability of memory. This assumes that agents are largely competent about the topics about which they testify, or at least that we have some capacity to filter our incompetent testimony (since honest but incompetent testimony will normally be inaccurate). There is room to contest this assumption, but there is reason for optimism here. There is evidence that we have a degree of sensitivity to testifiers' competence (Mascaro and Sperber 2009) and that we tend to allow testimony to influence memory when we believe that the relevant testifiers are likely to be more accurate than we are (Gabbert et al. 2007).

Given the existence of the honesty bias, moreover, it likewise becomes apparent that beliefs resulting from helpful incorporation are typically not lucky, despite the relevant agents' lack of control. Give that a testifier is honesty-biased on a particular occasion, he will also testify honestly in most nearby possible worlds on that occasion. In other words, it is not a matter of luck that he testifies honestly. Thus it will usually be the case that, when an agent forms a true belief due to the incorporation of accurate testimonial information, he also forms a true belief in most nearby possible worlds. In short, it is not a matter of luck that his belief is true, despite his lack of control over the truth value of his belief. As Reid foresaw, the agent's tendency to incorporate testimonial information "tallies with" an environment populated by honesty-biased testifiers, eliminating the role of luck in most cases.

Consider again the example of the stopped clock. Given the modal conception of epistemic luck, the agent's belief that it is 9:00 is luckily true because, in many nearby possible worlds, the agent forms a false belief instead. If the clock stops at a slightly different time, or if the agent looks at it at a slightly different time, he ends up with a false belief. Typical cases of helpful incorporation are not like this. Assuming the operation of the honesty bias, the testifier tries to tell the truth and usually succeeds. It is not a matter of luck that he tells the truth, so it is not a matter of luck that the agent forms a true belief. Typical cases of helpful incorporation are, instead, like cases in which an agent forms a true belief by relying on a properly functioning clock. Just as it is not normally a matter of luck that the agent relies on a properly functioning clock when forming a belief about the time, it is not normally a matter of luck that the agent's memory incorporates testimonial information when forming a belief about a witnessed event. And just as it is not a matter of luck that a properly functioning clock tells the right time, it is not a matter of luck that an honesty-biased testifier provides accurate testimony.

7.7   The Information Effect

Table 7.1
Impact of the positive and negative information effects on the reliability and power of memory

	Accurate information stored	Inaccurate information stored	No information stored
Accurate information incorporated	no effect	positive effect + power + reliability	positive effect + power + reliability
Inaccurate information incorporated	negative effect —reliability —power	no effect	negative effect —reliability

If beliefs resulting from helpful incorporation are not usually epistemically lucky, the source of the appeal of the contamination view is undermined. The view should thus be rejected. By the same token, the focus in eyewitness memory research on the misinformation effect begins to look misplaced. The misinformation effect will occur relatively rarely in natural settings. Indeed, the incorporation of testimonial information will typically improve memory for the past, rather than impairing it.

This suggests that the misinformation effect is best viewed as a special case of a broader *information effect*. A negative information effect—that is, the misinformation effect—occurs when the incorporation of inaccurate testimonial information results in the production of a false memory belief that the agent otherwise would not have had, because he otherwise would have formed either a true belief or no belief at all. If inaccurate testimony is incorporated but the agent would have formed a false belief anyway, no effect (in terms of overall accuracy) occurs. A positive information effect can be said to occur when the incorporation of accurate testimonial information results in the production of true memory belief that the agent otherwise would not have had, because he would otherwise have formed either a false belief or no belief. If accurate testimonial information is incorporated but the agent would have formed a true belief anyway, no effect occurs. Whether the information effect is epistemically beneficial on the whole depends on the relative frequency with which the positive and negative effects occur. As table 7.1 illustrates, if the negative effect usually occurs, then incorporation diminishes the reliability, or both the reliability and the power, of memory. (Power refers to the ratio of true beliefs to total beliefs, plus cases in which the system fails to produce a belief.) If, on the other hand, the positive information effect usually occurs, as is suggested by the argument of this chapter, then incorporation improves both the reliability and the power of memory.

Do other constructive processes have a similarly beneficial epistemic impact? In some cases, constructive processes may decrease the reliability of memory. In imagination inflation, for example, repeatedly imagining an episode increases the likelihood of falsely taking the episode to have occurred (Garry et al. 1996). Thus the constructive character of remembering introduces a role for monitoring in memory. This role is investigated in detail in the following two chapters. In many cases, however, constructive processes are consistent with and may even promote the reliability and power of memory. Consider false recognition. In the DRM paradigm, subjects remember nonpresented lure words closely related to presented lists of words (Gallo 2010). While false recognition would seem straightforwardly to decrease the accuracy of memory, it may actually increase its power, giving rise to memory for "information concerning the meaning or critical feature of an experience" (Schacter 2013, 57). Similarly, while the argument of this chapter has focused on reconstructive retrieval, which allows the misinformation effect to occur, constructive encoding appears to give rise to an analogous problem, as it allows a reversed misinformation effect to occur (Holliday and Hayes 2002; Lindsay and Johnson 1989). While the misinformation effect occurs when post-event information is incorporated into memory, the reversed misinformation effect occurs when *pre*-event information is incorporated. The argument of this chapter has concerned only the standard misinformation effect, but it should be possible to extend it to cover the reversed misinformation effect as well.

7.8   Avoiding Skepticism

Appealing in part to the limitations of eyewitness memory, Shanton (2011) has defended a view which appears to be opposed to that defended here, arguing that episodic memory beliefs fail to meet otherwise reasonable standards for knowledge. Her focus is on the standards contained in Sosa's virtue epistemology (Sosa 2007), according to which a belief is knowledgeable if it is the product of an exercise of an epistemic competence, where competence is a matter of both reliability and "security"; the security condition is satisfied on a given occasion if no false beliefs are produced in nearby possible worlds on that occasion. Shanton argues that, typically, neither the reliability condition nor the security condition is satisfied by episodic memory beliefs—memory belief formation is an unreliable process, *and* many memory beliefs are insecure. Rather than concluding that we have no episodic memory knowledge, she recommends rejecting the reliability and security conditions. This is one way of avoiding skepticism about memory knowledge, though it comes at a high price. Fortunately, if the argument of this chapter is right, the situation is not quite as dire as she takes it to be.

Rather than the security condition, this chapter has focused on the anti-luck condition. It may be the case that episodic memory beliefs fail, with some frequency, to meet the security condition. But, whereas security means no false belief in a nearby possible world, absence of luck means no false beliefs in very many nearby possible worlds, a significantly less demanding standard. If memory beliefs fail to satisfy the security condition, the condition must indeed be abandoned, on penalty of skepticism. But even if Shanton's argument—which appeals to the mere possibility of memory errors—shows that beliefs resulting from helpful incorporation fail to satisfy the security condition, it does not show that they fail to satisfy the anti-luck condition. If the argument of this chapter is right, they do not. Replacing the security condition with the anti-luck condition thus may allow us to avoid lowering our standards to an unacceptable level.

When it comes to reliability, Shanton provides little reason for thinking the condition is not met. Essentially, she points out that, due to its constructive character, episodic memory is fallible in some surprising ways and then asks us whether it strikes us as reliable. Our tendency, of course, is to answer this question in the negative, but that tendency is largely a product of our reaction to the divergence between the reality of simulational memory and our folk-psychological "filing cabinet" picture of memory, to use Shanton's term. The argument depends on the sort of prejudice described above, according to which construction can only be a source of inaccuracy. Pointing out that, due to its constructive character, episodic retrieval sometimes produces inaccurate beliefs simply does not establish that episodic retrieval is an unreliable process, any more than, say, giving examples of visual illusions establishes that vision is an unreliable process. An imperfectly reliable process can be reliable overall.

Of course, this does not amount to a demonstration of the overall reliability of memory. That no noncircular demonstration of memory's reliability can be given is a familiar point, made recently by Alston (1986) and earlier by Reid, who remarked that "every kind of reasoning for the veracity of our faculties, amounts to no more than taking their own testimony for their veracity," a point that applies as much to memory as it does to other core cognitive systems (1785, 593). In practice, we have no alternative but to take the reliability of memory for granted (Hamilton 2003).

This familiar point should not be thought to undermine the project of this book. Reid's point concerns our justification for our reliance on memory: there can be no noncircular demonstration of the reliability of memory, hence no justification for our reliance on memory. That we cannot provide such a justification does not, however, mean that we can say nothing at all about the reliability of memory. If the argument of this chapter (and the following two) is right, we have an explanation of the compatibility of constructive processes with the reliability of episodic memory. If the argument of part IV is right, we have general theoretical reasons to take episodic memory to be reliable. Thus, while no demonstration can be given, the view that episodic memory is reliable is the safer bet, suggesting that avoiding skepticism does not require giving up the reliability condition.

8 Metamemory and the Source Problem

8.1 The Source Problem

The previous chapter argued that the incorporation of nonexperiential information into retrieved representations is compatible with (and may even promote) the reliability of memory. But the argument pertains specifically to testimonial information, and there is no guarantee that it generalizes to information from other sources. Indeed, in some cases it clearly does not. Again, consider imagination inflation, which occurs when the subject mistakes an episode that he merely imagined for one that actually occurred. If we are to explain how agents succeed in avoiding imagination inflation and similar traps, we must consider how they solve the "source problem," the problem of determining whether remembered information originates in a reliable source.

This chapter argues that a capacity for metacognition—the monitoring and control of mental processes[1]—plays a crucial role in enabling agents to solve the source problem. The argument makes two general claims. First, though metacognition is not always necessary for ensuring reliable belief formation—if the source problem for a given source is sufficiently mild, the agent can "solve" it trivially—a capacity for metacognition can enable the agent to form beliefs with a high level of reliability where this would otherwise be impossible. Second, reliability is not the only epistemically valuable property of beliefs: power and speed, among other properties, matter as well (Goldman 1992), and metacognition can likewise play an important role in enabling agents to attain high levels of power and speed in belief formation. After making a case for these general claims, the chapter argues that the form of metacognition known as source monitoring (Johnson,

Hashtroudi, and Lindsay 1993; Mitchell and Johnson 2009) explains our ability to solve the source problem for episodic memory, in particular.[2]

8.2   Metacognitive Belief-Producing Systems

8.2.1   Two-Level Systems

Reliabilists have not always kept the internal structure of belief-producing processes clearly in view, failing to consider the separate contributions of the various stages of processing performed by a system to the reliability of the overall process by which it produces beliefs. For many purposes, it may be appropriate to view belief-producing processes at this level of abstraction, but the focus on overall processes has the unfortunate consequence of obscuring the fact that it is often useful, when we are after more than a shallow explanation of how a belief-producing process achieves a given level of reliability, to conceive of many processes as having a two-level structure, in which a first process produces information "intended" to serve as the content of a belief (in the sense that, in the absence of intervention, the agent will tend to end up endorsing the information), while a second process "chooses" (in a nonhomuncular sense) between endorsing the produced information—in which case a belief having the information as its content is produced—and rejecting it, in which case no belief is formed. In a two-level system, the second process in effect functions as a filter on the first.

Refer to the component of a two-level system responsible for producing information as its "information producer," and to the component responsible for determining endorsement/rejection as its "endorsement mechanism." It is useful to conceive of the endorsement mechanism as implementing a policy (which need not be explicitly represented) consisting of a set of criteria against which produced information is evaluated, together with a rule determining whether a given item of information is to be evaluated as accurate given the extent to which it satisfies these criteria.[3] The reliability of belief production in a two-level system is determined by the interaction of its information producer and its endorsement mechanism. But while the reliability of the information producer (the ratio of accurate representations produced by it to total representations produced by it) affects the reliability of the system as a whole, the reliability of the endorsement mechanism (the ratio of cases in which it accurately evaluates a representation as accurate or inaccurate to total cases in which it evaluates a representation as accurate or inaccurate), strictly speaking, does not. Since the production of a representation by the information producer eventuates in the production of a belief by the system as a whole only given that the representation is evaluated as accurate by the endorsement mechanism, it is only the reliability of the endorsement mechanism's evaluation of representations as accurate (the ratio of cases in which it accurately evaluates a representation as accurate to total cases in which it evaluates a representation as accurate) that affects the reliability of the system as a whole. In other words, the reliability of the larger system is determined, first, by the frequency with which the information producer produces accurate representations and, second, by the frequency with which the endorsement mechanism accurately evaluates produced representations as accurate. In what follows, references to the reliability of an endorsement mechanism will therefore be to its reliability with respect to evaluations of information as accurate.

An endorsement mechanism need not produce explicit beliefs that a given representation is accurate or inaccurate. If it does, the overall process which produces the beliefs output by the system will be belief-dependent, taking both received information and beliefs about its accuracy as input (Goldman 2012). In such cases, the reliability of the overall process will depend in part on the frequency of true beliefs among beliefs about accuracy. If the second process does not produce such explicit beliefs, the overall process will be, strictly speaking, belief-independent. But even in such cases, the reliability of the overall process will depend on the frequency of correct *evaluations* of accuracy. Such a belief-independent process can therefore still be modeled as a belief-dependent process. Indeed, any two-level process can be modeled as a belief-dependent process in which a first process generates a belief, a second process produces a belief about the accuracy of the first belief, and, depending on the content of this second belief, the first belief is either ratified, so that the total process outputs a belief with the same content, or rejected, so that the overall process outputs no belief.

Though it can be useful, for heuristic purposes, to view two-level processes this way, care is required when doing so, for while it is natural to suppose that a belief-dependent process can be reliable only given that it takes only reliably produced beliefs as input, this is a mistake. As noted above, in the case of a two-level process, a belief is produced only when information is evaluated as accurate—it is not the reliability as such of the second process, but only its reliability with respect to evaluations of information as accurate that affects the reliability of the overall process. And, as will be made clear below, in the case of a two-level process, if the second process is sufficiently reliable with respect to accuracy, the overall process can turn out to be highly reliable even if the first process is highly unreliable.

8.2.2 Metacognition

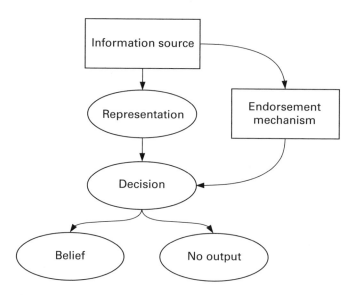

Figure 8.1
Structure of a metacognitive belief-producing system.

One way of ensuring a high level of reliability in a belief-producing system is to equip it with a highly reliable information producer—that is, to ensure that it produces a high base rate of accurate representations. In a system with a highly reliable information producer, an endorsement mechanism will be redundant.[4] If there are few inaccurate representations to filter out, then no additional activity is required to ensure reliable belief production, and the endorsement mechanism might as well employ a policy of automatic endorsement. But real agents do not in general have near-perfect information producers. Their information producers regularly produce inaccurate representations, and there is thus a potential role for an endorsement mechanism to play in ensuring reliable belief production.

One way for an endorsement mechanism to play this role is for it to employ metacognitive monitoring and control. In any metacognitive system, we can distinguish between an object-level and a meta-level, connected by relations of monitoring, in which information flows from the object-level to the meta-level, and control, in which information flows from the meta-level to the object-level, potentially changing the state of the latter. Nelson and Narens describe these relations by means of an analogy with using a telephone. Control can be compared to speaking:

> The basic notion underlying control—analogous to speaking into a telephone handset—is that the meta-level modifies the object-level. In particular, the information flowing from the meta-level to the object-level either changes the state of the object-level process or changes the object-level process itself. This produces some kind of action at the object-level, which could be (1) to initiate an action, (2) to continue an action ..., or (3) to terminate an action. (Nelson and Narens 1990, 127)

Since the source problem concerns the response of agents to already produced information, the discussion to follow will focus on control operations of the latter two types; that is, on the capacity of a metacognitive mechanism to either terminate an object-level process or allow it to run to conclusion, setting aside initiation of new processes.[5]

Monitoring, in turn, can be compared to listening:

> The basic notion underlying monitoring—analogous to listening to the telephone handset—is that the meta-level is informed by the object-level. This changes the state of the meta-level's model of the situation, including "no change in state." ... However, the opposite does not occur, i.e., the object-level has no model of the meta-level. (Nelson and Narens 1990, 127)

In addition to the source-monitoring processes described below, metacognitive monitoring includes processes producing ease of learning judgments, judgments of learning, feelings of knowing, and retrospective confidence judgments, among other evaluative states (Arango-Muñoz and Michaelian 2014; Dunlosky and Metcalfe 2008).

In general, metacognition may draw on either type 1 (heuristic, unconscious, fast) processing or on type 2 (reflective, conscious, slow) processing; that is, control operations can be based on either automatic or systematic monitoring.[6] Metacognitive systems incapable of systematic processing are possible, but the systems on which the discussion will focus here and in the following chapter are capable of both types of processing. Even in these systems, (cheaper) type 1 processing executed by the relevant system itself occurs by default. But (more costly) type 2 processing executed at the level of the agent can also occur under certain circumstances: the agent can deliberately initiate systematic processing, or systematic processing might be triggered by the system itself under certain conditions.

A two-level system need not be a metacognitive system. Though any endorsement mechanism by definition controls an object-level information-producing process, its control need not be based on monitoring the process. Endorsement and rejection might be determined in some other way—for example, on the basis of information about environmental conditions. But if endorsement and rejection are determined on the basis of monitoring, the components make up a metacognitive system in which they stand to each other in the relationship described by Nelson and Narens: the information producer produces representations, while the endorsement mechanism, on the basis of its monitoring of the information producer, either intervenes to prevent a produced representation from being accepted, preventing the formation of a belief, or permits it to be accepted, allowing the formation of a belief. Figure 8.1 depicts the basic structure of a metacognitive belief-producing system.

8.3   Reliability in Metacognitive Systems

Though a number of other forms of metacognitive monitoring and control have been studied (e.g., metaperception; see Loussouarn, Gabriel, and Proust 2011), metamemory remains the paradigmatic example of metacognition. From an epistemological point of view, this suggests looking to communication research for a means of clarifying the role of metacognition, for memory and communication are in certain respects analogous. Though the analogy has definite limits, it is sometimes useful to think of retrieved memories as being like testimony received from one's past self. This, in turn, suggests that it might be useful to think of inaccurate memories as being like dishonest testimony. And research on dishonest communication—specifically, research on human deception detection— indeed turns out to provide a model: Park and Levine's probability model of deception detection accuracy (Levine et al. 2006; Park and Levine 2001), which can be generalized to provide an account of the reliability of two-level belief-producing systems, including metacognitive belief-producing systems.

Deception detection research is concerned in part with *deception detection accuracy*, the ratio of true judgments by a subject that a speaker is honest or dishonest to total judgments that a speaker is honest or dishonest. Where *H* stands for "the hearer judges that the speaker is honest" and *T* stands for "the speaker is in fact honest," a hearer's deception detection accuracy is determined by simply summing $P(H \& T)$ and $P(\sim H \& \sim T)$, which, in turn, can be calculated as follows.

$$P(H \& T) = P(H|T) \times P(T) \tag{8.1}$$

$$P(\sim H \& \sim T) = P(\sim H|\sim T) \times (1 - P(T)) \tag{8.2}$$

This is the core of the Park-Levine model. The epistemology of testimony requires us to extend the model slightly. Since it is concerned primarily with the reliability of forming beliefs by accepting received testimony, and since we can assume that a testimonial belief is formed only when the hearer judges the speaker to be honest (Fricker 1995; Michaelian 2010), the epistemology of testimony is concerned with what we can refer to as *honesty detection accuracy*, or the ratio of true judgments that a speaker is honest to total judgments that a speaker is honest:

$$P(H \& T) / (P(H \& T) + P(H \& \sim T)). \tag{8.3}$$

In order to calculate honesty detection accuracy, we need $P(H \& \sim T)$, which can be calculated as follows.

$$P(H \& \sim T) = P(H|\sim T) \times (1 - P(T))$$

$$= (1 - P(\sim H|\sim T)) \times (1 - P(T)) \tag{8.4}$$

The virtue of this model is that it makes clear that honesty detection accuracy varies as a function of *both* the base rate of honesty—that is, $P(T)$—*and* the hearer's sensitivity to honesty and dishonesty—that is, the conditional probability of judging that a speaker is honest, given that he is honest, or $P(H|T)$, and the conditional probability of judging that a speaker is dishonest, given that he is dishonest, or $P(\sim H|\sim T)$.

Now, factors other than honesty (including competence) determine the accuracy of a speaker's testimony. But if we abstract away from these factors, the ratio given in eq. (8.3) refers simply to the reliability of the process used to form testimonial beliefs. And since any two-level process shares the same basic structure (production of a representation, followed by endorsement/rejection of the representation according to whether it is evaluated as accurate/inaccurate), the same ratio can be used to describe the effects of an endorsement mechanism on the reliability of belief production in the system of which it is a component. In other words, if H stands for "the endorsement mechanism evaluates the produced information as accurate" and T stands for "the produced information is in fact accurate," then, assuming that the endorsement mechanism endorses only those representations it evaluates as accurate, eq. (8.3) refers to the reliability of the two-level belief-producing system. Note that this model does not assume that the endorsement mechanism actually produces explicit evaluations of the accuracy of representations, but only that we can describe its behavior as if it does. In the context of deception detection, $P(T)$ refers to the base rate of honesty, while $P(H|T)$ and $P(\sim H|\sim T)$ reflect agents' deception detection abilities: the greater the prevalence of honesty, the higher $P(T)$, and the greater agents' sensitivity to honesty and dishonesty, the higher $P(H|T)$ and $P(\sim H|\sim T)$, respectively. Analogously, in the case of a two-level belief-producing system, $P(T)$ is determined by the workings of the system's information producer, while $P(H|T)$ and $P(\sim H|\sim T)$ are determined by the workings of its endorsement mechanism: the more reliable the information producer, the higher $P(T)$, and the more sensitive the endorsement mechanism to accuracy and inaccuracy, the higher $P(H|T)$ and $P(\sim H|\sim T)$.

It is easy to verify that, given a perfect information producer, there is no role for an endorsement mechanism to play, just as there is no need to monitor for deception when dealing with perfectly honest testifiers: if $P(T) = 1$, then overall reliability = 1, no matter how sensitive or insensitive the endorsement mechanism might be. At $P(T) = 1$, in other words, all endorsement policies are equivalent to a policy of automatic endorsement. As $P(T)$ decreases, the endorsement mechanism has the potential to play an increasingly important role in ensuring an acceptable level of overall reliability. In order for it to play such a role, however, it must be sensitive to both accuracy and inaccuracy. Consider the cases illustrated in figure 8.2. The 0.75/.35 curve shows the effects of a hypothetical endorsement mechanism employing a policy such that $P(H|T)$ and $P(\sim H|\sim T)$ are 0.75 and 0.35, respectively. Such a policy is truth-biased in a manner analogous to that in which hearers are truth-biased when evaluating testimony (the numbers are the estimates given in Levine et al. 1999). As a result, the overall reliability of the system is nearly equivalent to that of a system employing a policy

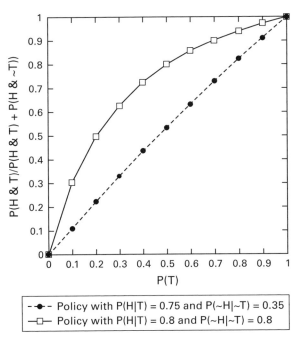

Figure 8.2
Effects of different hypothetical endorsement mechanisms on the reliability of belief-producing systems.

of automatic endorsement—it essentially mirrors the base rate of accurate information. In other words, the endorsement mechanism is almost completely ineffective. The 0.8/.8 curve, on the other hand, shows the effects of a hypoethical endorsement mechanism employing a policy such that $P(H|T)$ and $P(\sim H|\sim T)$ are both 0.8. Such a mechanism, while far from perfectly sensitive to accuracy and inaccuracy, can have a dramatic effect on the overall reliability of the system, improving reliability at any base rate of accurate representations and even compensating for an absolutely unreliable information producer. For example, such a system would produce true beliefs more than 70% of the time despite relying on an information producer that is right only 40% of the time.

How might such an effective endorsement mechanism be designed? In principle, sensitivity sufficient to enable a significant improvement in reliability could be achieved even by a nonmetacognitive endorsement mechanism—that is, a mechanism without access to information about the operation of the information producer. But in practice, it is unclear how such a system might work, as it would in effect have to predict the occasions on which the endorsement mechanism will deliver an inaccurate representation in advance. In a metacognitive system, in contrast, information about the operation of the information producer is transmitted to the endorsement mechanism, where it can serve as the basis for endorsement decisions sensitive to accuracy and inaccuracy. The information producer need not perform operations designed to transmit the necessary information. Instead, the features of its operation which indicate the accuracy of the representations that it produces may be by-products of its normal operation, features which can be interpreted by an external mechanism as indicating the accuracy of the representations it produces. For example, the fluency with which some information is retrieved is treated as an indicator of its accuracy (Reber and Unkelbach 2010), but information is not retrieved fluently by the system *in order to* indicate accuracy. If the mechanism employs an appropriate endorsement policy—for example, treating fluency as an indicator of accuracy in cases where it genuinely indicates accuracy—it can intervene at the object-level to prevent belief formation when the information producer delivers an inaccurate representation and can refrain from intervening, thus permitting belief formation, when the information producer delivers an accurate representation.

Of course, the effect that metacognitive monitoring and control actually have on reliability in a given case—including memory—is an empirical question. The point, for now, is simply to clarify the role that metacognition can in principle play in ensuring reliable belief formation in agents dependent on imperfect information producers.

8.4   Power and Speed in Metacognitive Systems

The pluralistic framework developed in chapter 3 stresses that reliability is only one epistemically valuable property of cognitive systems. As Goldman (1992) has argued, power and speed are also important, though these properties are perhaps less central to our epistemic evaluations.

Reliability is a matter of avoiding false beliefs, and thus the reliability of a system is compatible with its not producing very many beliefs. But there is a clear sense in which a system which is reliable but forms very few beliefs may be epistemically deficient. In other words, we care not only about the reliability of belief-producing systems, about whether they tend to produce *mostly* true beliefs, but also about their power, about whether they tend to produce *many* true beliefs. Whereas reliability is defined as the ratio of cases in which the system produces true beliefs to total cases in which it produces beliefs (whether true or false), power is defined as the ratio of cases in which the system produces true beliefs to total cases in which it produces beliefs (whether true or false) *plus* cases in which it fails to produce a belief.[7]

Even a system that is both highly reliable and highly powerful might be deficient if it is unacceptably slow—given a choice between two equally reliable and powerful systems, one of which produces beliefs more quickly than the other, we will obviously prefer the faster system. There is thus a role for speed in epistemic evaluations as well. Though speed tends to contribute to power, since processes in a faster system will more seldom need to be interrupted to divert resources to other tasks, there are often trade-offs between power and reliability, since additional power can often be secured at the expense of forming additional false beliefs, thereby decreasing reliability. The balance of reliability, power, and speed that is appropriate at a given time is plausibly determined by the agent's current context, which affects the agent's cognitive and practical goals, the consequences of forming false beliefs (or failing to form true beliefs) on certain topics, and so on. For example, a high level of reliability might be imperative in a context in which it is crucial to avoid forming false beliefs, but, when the consequences of forming false beliefs are less severe, it might be appropriate to settle for a lower level of reliability if doing so increases the power of the system. An epistemically satisfactory cognitive system, in short, will be capable of flexibly adjusting its levels of reliability, power, and speed in line with the demands of the agent's current context.

Setting speed aside for the moment, it is easy to see that, in a system with a perfect information producer, there is no role for an endorsement mechanism to play in achieving an acceptable balance between reliability and power. In such a system, there is no need to negotiate trade-offs between reliability and power, as simply automatically accepting all representations delivered by the information producer ensures both a 1:1 ratio of true beliefs to total beliefs (maximizing reliability) and a 1:1 ratio of true beliefs to total outcomes (maximizing power). In a system with an imperfect information producer, in contrast, reliability and power can come apart. One way for a system to achieve high reliability despite depending

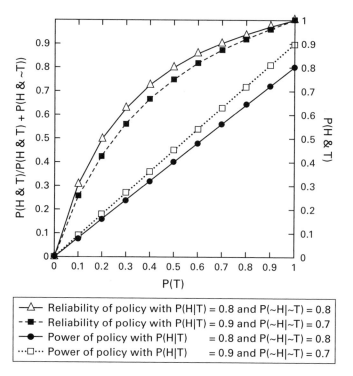

Figure 8.3
Effects of different hypothetical endorsement policies on power and reliability.

on an imperfect information producer is for its endorsement mechanism to employ a highly conservative or risk-averse policy, rejecting any representation which has even a slight chance of being inaccurate. A system employing such a policy will typically be less powerful than an otherwise similar system employing a more liberal or risk-tolerant policy. By the same token, increasing power tends to decrease reliability, for the cost of accepting additional accurate representations is normally also accepting additional inaccurate representations. The effects of the hypothetical endorsement policies depicted in figure 8.3 illustrate this trade-off. Since the power of a process is defined as the ratio of cases in which it produces a true belief to cases in which it produces a (true or false) belief plus cases in which it produces no belief, and since in a two-level system a belief is produced only if its endorsement mechanism evaluates a produced representation as accurate, the power of a two-level system is equivalent to

$P(H \& T)$. In general, by increasing the endorsement mechanism's truth bias, it is possible to secure additional power at the expense of decreasing reliability—adopting a more liberal policy increases $P(H|T)$ but tends to decrease $P(\sim H|\sim T)$. By the same token, by decreasing the truth bias of the mechanism, it is possible to secure additional reliability at the expense of decreasing power.

In principle, $P(H|T)$ and $P(\sim H|\sim T)$ might vary independently, in which case there need be no trade-off between reliability and power, allowing both to be maximized simultaneously. But it is unlikely that any feasible endorsement mechanism would allow the conditional probabilities to vary independently in this way, at least in any cognitive system with an information producer that provides only imperfect indications of the accuracy of the representations that it produces. Given that it is not possible to improve reliability without decreasing power, and vice versa, and given that in different contexts the agent might prioritize either, how might a system negotiate the necessary trade-off? It is useful to consider speed at this point. Like the optimal levels of reliability and power, the optimal level of speed is contextually variable. Though a high level of speed is in general desirable for memory retrieval, in particular, a lower level will sometimes be acceptable if the particular item that the agent is attempting to retrieve is sufficiently important. In metacognitive systems, recall, endorsement can be determined by either automatic or systematic monitoring. Typically, the policy employed in automatic monitoring will be fixed and relatively simple, ensuring that it is computationally inexpensive and therefore fast. Given these advantages, we can assume that metacognitive systems employ automatic monitoring by default, shifting to systematic monitoring only sparingly. The fixed character of the automatic policy, however, means that it will be largely insensitive to changes in the agent's context. While the automatic policy might assure an appropriate balance of reliability and power in most contexts, it cannot adjust that balance in order to ensure a balance appropriate for atypical contexts. Systematic monitoring (executed at the level of the agent), on the other hand, can allow the temporary adoption of a policy better suited to an atypical context: by altering the criteria for endorsement or the thresholds that need to be crossed on certain criteria, the agent can adopt a more or less risk-averse policy according to the requirements of his current context.[8] For example, the agent might temporarily adopt extremely strict source-monitoring criteria if he has special reason to think that his memory might be deceiving him.

The switch to systematic monitoring might be triggered either by the endorsement mechanism itself or by the agent, perhaps in response to discrepancies between expectations for the operation of the information producer and its observed operation or in response to changes in interest or environmental cues. Consequently, the ability of metacognitive monitoring to contribute to epistemically adequate belief production depends in part on features of the agent beyond the relevant system. The agent himself must have enough understanding of his current context and enough metacognitive knowledge (knowledge of the workings of his own information sources) to enable him temporarily to adopt endorsement policies that ensure appropriate levels of reliability and power in atypical contexts.

8.5   The Source-Monitoring Framework

The foregoing argument is meant to show that, if endorsement of the representations delivered by the information producer is based on metacognitive monitoring, if monitoring is sufficiently sensitive to (in)accuracy, and if the system appropriately employs both automatic and systematic monitoring, metacognition can enable a two-level system to attain an appropriate balance of reliability, power, and speed. How does this apply to episodic memory?

We know that memory stores information originating in a variety of sources, in addition to perceptual experience. While some of these sources (such as testimony, if the argument of the preceding chapter is right) may be reliable, others are not. In particular, memory stores information originating in a variety of forms of episodic imagination—we remember not only episodes experienced in the past but also imagined counterfactual episodes, imagined future episodes, and so on. Representations originating in any of these sources may be retrieved in response to a given cue. Thus episodic memory, considered in isolation, is an imperfect information producer. Remembering agents therefore face a version of the source problem, the problem of determining whether remembered information originates in a reliable source, and there is a potential role for metacognition to play in ensuring the reliability of remembering.

The remainder of this chapter reviews work on the form of metacognition known as source monitoring, arguing that Johnson and collaborators' source-monitoring framework provides a plausible explanation of how agents solve the source problem. Due to uncertainty about both the base rates of representations originating in different sources and the precise degree of sensitivity of source monitoring to the origins of remembered information, this explanation cannot be established with certainty. Nevertheless, the explanation receives support from its place in an empirically well-supported framework.[9]

8.5.1 Effects on Reliability

As emphasized in previous chapters, while it is natural for epistemologists to view remembering as a simple belief-preserving process, a process which, when all goes well, takes a belief as input, stores it, and later delivers the same belief as output, this view oversimplifies by ignoring both the constructive, simulational character of remembering and the role of metamemory in producing memory beliefs. In virtue of the involvement of metamemory, in particular, remembering, rather than being a simple belief-preserving process, has the two-level structure described above: information is first produced, and a memory belief is formed only when it is endorsed—in many cases, retrieved information is rejected, resulting in the formation of no belief. The source-monitoring framework focuses on the decision process that intervenes between the retrieval of a representation and the formation of the corresponding memory belief. The constructive character of memory raises the question of how the memory system can "remain functional and not deteriorate into a pathological quagmire of real and imagined experiences or recombinations of features of real experience" (Mitchell and Johnson 2000, 180). According to the source-monitoring framework, subjects are able to discriminate the origins of remembered information by means of attributional judgment processes, monitoring processes that take us from properties of a retrieved representation to a judgment that it originates in a given source and is thus likely (or unlikely) to be veridical.

The severity of the source problem for episodic memory depends on both the reliability of the various sources of information stored in memory and on the frequency with which reconstructive retrieval draws on information originating in any given source. If the system stores and draws on a high proportion of records originating in unreliable sources, then the base rate of accurate representations produced by retrieval will be relatively low. Given that the system stores records originating in a range of external and internal sources, and given that reconstructive retrieval tends to draw on all relevant information in response to a given cue, the base rate is likely relatively low.

How do agents solve the source problem? One natural suggestion—embodied, for example, in the reflexive view of memory content discussed in chapters 3 and 7—is that retrieved representations themselves point to their origins. As we have seen, this sort of view is problematic. According to the source-monitoring framework, in contrast, though memory does not normally store explicit source information, memories typically *do* bear implicit marks of the sources in which they originate:

> Different types of acquisition processes (e.g., reading, thinking, inferring) and different types of events (e.g., movie, newspaper, dream) tend to produce memorial representations that are characteristically different from each other. For example, memories of imagined events typically have less vivid perceptual, temporal, and spatial information than perceived events and often include information about intentional cognitive operations (e.g., active generation and manipulation of visual images during problem solving). Memories of dreams are often perceptually vivid, typically do not include information about the cognitive operations that created them, and are often inconsistent with knowledge or other memories. (Mitchell and Johnson 2000, 180)

The presence of these marks means that though information about the source of information is not typically stored along with the information itself, it is nevertheless often possible to determine the source of a record:

> We infer source. We use heuristic source monitoring processes to attribute a source to information based on an evaluation of various features of the information. If activated information from the memory being evaluated has qualities that we expect memories from a certain source to have, we attribute the information to that source. (Johnson and Raye 2000, 39)

The source-monitoring framework, in short, suggests that agents solve the source problem for episodic memory by endorsing retrieved representations only when they are evaluated as having originated in experience.

Experience itself is presumably a reliable source of information, but, unfortunately, we cannot be very precise about the reliability of classifications of information as having originated in experience. The source-monitoring framework suggests that our evaluations are fairly reliable; if this is right, then source monitoring likely enables an adequate overall level of reliability in remembering. But it is important to note that evaluations based on the characteristics of retrieved information are bound to be less than perfectly reliable (Robin 2010). As Mitchell and Johnson (2000) note, "because of variability within ... source types, the distributions of features of memories from different processes and events overlap."

Given the occurrence of memory errors, however, what we need is precisely a framework that explains not only why source judgments are usually accurate, but also why they are sometimes inaccurate. So, for example, we are more likely to misclassify repeatedly imagined episodes as having been experienced, and the source-monitoring framework predicts this tendency, since repeated imagination will tend to result in stored representations having high levels of perceptual, temporal, and spatial information, characteristic marks of representations originating in experience. But note that imagination is not necessarily a source of inaccurate information. In particular, attempts to simulate episodes from the personal past may result in largely accurate representations, even when they themselves are not based on experiential information. Subsequent attempts to remember an episode may thus draw on content generated during previous attempts without any necessary loss of accuracy.

8.5.2 Effects on Power and Speed

To ensure sufficient speed—and hence power—a metacognitive belief-producing system should employ type 1 monitoring by default, since type 1 monitoring is in general faster than type 2 monitoring. As Johnson and Raye point out, source monitoring does indeed employ type 1 processing by default: "We are not always conscious of these processes. Heuristic source attributions take place constantly without notice, and are relatively automatic or effortless" (2000, 39). The source-monitoring framework is not always clear about whether heuristic monitoring is executed by the memory system itself, or, instead, at the level of the agent. Given the automaticity of the processing in question, which is normally triggered without intervention by the agent and typically concludes without the agent becoming aware that it has occurred, however, it is more plausible to view it as occurring at the level of the system.

Type 2 source monitoring, occurring at the level of the agent, is also engaged under certain circumstances: the source-monitoring framework "posits that source monitoring sometimes also entails more systematic processes that are typically slower and more deliberate, involving, for example, retrieving additional information, discovering and noting relations, extended reasoning, and so on" (Mitchell and Johnson 2000, 180–81). Given that agents sometimes engage in type 2 source monitoring, when do they do so? In particular, do they tend to engage in systematic monitoring when the current context calls for a non-default balance of reliability and power? The framework suggests that the need for a higher-than-usual level of reliability is normally responsible for the initiation of systematic monitoring. Discussions of cases in which reliability is sacrificed for additional power are less frequent, but the framework clearly allows for this—there is nothing that prevents agents from temporarily adopting more relaxed source-monitoring criteria. But it is important to note that our capacity to initiate type 2 source monitoring when it is called for, and to adjust our policy so as to achieve appropriate levels of reliability and power, depends both on our appreciation of our own current context and on our metacognitive knowledge of the workings of our own memory systems (Johnson 1997; Johnson and Raye 2000). Given that type 2 monitoring is sensitive to the requirements of the agent's current context, and assuming that type 1 monitoring achieves appropriate default levels of reliability and power, then, it is plausible that source monitoring enables agents to attain an appropriate balance of reliability, power, and speed in memory belief formation, though this ultimately depends on the details of the manner in which the endorsement policy is adjusted in systematic monitoring.

While this review obviously does not conclusively establish that source monitoring enables agents to solve the source problem, it seems clear that some form of metacognitive monitoring must be invoked here. Even given that the source-monitoring framework provides a sufficient explanation of how agents solve the source problem, however, it is not the whole story about the role of metacognitive monitoring in grounding the reliability of remembering; the following chapter will show that a distinct form of metamemory must also be invoked.

8.6   Metacognition in Internalism and Externalism

The approach to the source problem developed in this chapter is couched entirely in terms of externalist epistemic norms—reliability, power, and speed—but the idea that metacognitive monitoring plays an important role in enabling epistemically adequate memory belief formation may seem to be particularly congenial to internalism. While internalists may ultimately be able to adopt something like the account of the role of metamemory developed here, it is nonetheless worthwhile to caution against one particularly appealing but misguided internalist reinterpretation of the argument of this chapter.

It might be tempting for internalists to argue that the role of metamemory in solving the source problem shows that agents are able to form justified memory beliefs not (or not only) because the process at work when they do so is reliable but (also) because it provides them with internally accessible justifiers for their memory beliefs—namely, source judgments. This reinterpretation of the argument would require that even type 1 metacognitive monitoring produce explicit evaluations—representations to which the agent at least in principle has access—but, while it is often convenient to think of monitoring as producing such evaluations, nothing in the argument of this chapter requires that it actually do so. The argument requires only that metacognitive control be sensitive to the relevant features of produced representations, and this sort of sensitivity need not be mediated by representations. Indeed, the meta-level need not contain a representation of the object-level at all—all that is required is that there be an appropriate mapping between object-level events and meta-level responses (Lepock 2007). In other words, meta*cognition* need not involve meta*representation* (Arango-Muñoz 2011; Proust 2007).

Whether or not type 1 source monitoring ultimately ends up being appropriately classified as metarepresentational will depend in part on the general conditions that a system needs to satisfy in order to count as representational. The question of what it takes for a system to count as representational is well beyond the scope of this book, but even if type 1 source monitoring turns out to involve metarepresentation, the representations in question appear to be encapsulated and hence unavailable at the level of the agent. Thus, even if we assume that type 1 source monitoring involves explicit, representational evaluations of retrieved information, the internalist reinterpretation of the argument is unworkable. Standard versions of internalism require that the justifiers for a belief be accessible to the agent himself, but the evaluations produced by type 1 source monitoring are not thus available. (One is not aware of having classified information as originating, say, in experience, unless one has consciously attempted to do so.) Indeed, while the question we started with was how agents "solve" the source problem, this is merely a sort of shorthand. In general, agents need not *do* anything in order to solve the source problem. The explanation of how agents form memory beliefs in an epistemically adequate manner despite storing information originating in both reliable and unreliable sources is given primarily in terms of the design of cognitive systems that operate below the level of the agent.

Nevertheless, subsequent chapters will argue that source monitoring and process monitoring interact to produce a feeling of remembering which, in turn, drives the agent's decision to accept or reject an apparent memory. The feeling of remembering, like other metacognitive feelings, has what Koriat (2000) refers to as a "crossover" mode of operation in that, while it is produced by unconscious processing, it is available to consciousness. If internalists are willing to allow such metacognitive feelings to play the role of justifiers, they may be able to adopt the overall account of the role of metamemory defended here.

9 Metamemory and the Process Problem

Chapters 7 and 8 examined mechanisms contributing to the reliability of episodic memory considered in isolation from other episodic constructive processes. As we saw in part II, however, episodic memory ultimately should not be considered in isolation: agents capable of constructive episodic memory are likewise capable of a range of forms of episodic imagination, and a full explanation of the reliability of remembering must take this broader episodic constructive capacity into account. This chapter therefore turns to the question of how one knows whether one is remembering, rather than imagining—or rather, if the simulation theory is right, how one knows whether one is remembering, rather than engaging in some other form of episodic imagination. Typically, one does not take oneself to be remembering when one is in fact imagining, or vice versa; that is, we reliably distinguish between remembering and imagining. Given that remembering and imagining are tightly interlinked, however, it is far from obvious *how* we reliably distinguish between them. The chapter develops a process-monitoring framework, modeled on but distinct from the source-monitoring framework, designed to answer this question. The notion of process monitoring, in turn, will play a central role in the approach to the evolution of memory developed in part IV.

9.1 The Process Problem

How does one know whether one is remembering or imagining? The question is doubly ambiguous. To illustrate, Hume argued that memory is distinguished from imagination by its greater vivacity. As noted above, Hume's criterion can be taken either as an account of the objective difference between memory and imagination, or as an account of the subjective difference on which agents rely to discriminate between remembering and imagining. Even if we take it in the latter sense, resolving the first ambiguity, there is a second ambiguity: the vivacity criterion, like any other criterion for distinguishing between memory and imagination, might be invoked to answer either of two questions. First, given that a subject is remembering, how does he determine whether the *content* of a given representation originates in experience or, instead, in imagination? Second, how, in the first place, does the subject determine whether the *process* that generates a given representation is an instance of remembering or, instead, an instance of imagining? Before remembered information is endorsed, the agent must determine whether it originates in a reliable source; this is the source problem discussed in the previous chapter. Before the source of remembered information can be meaningfully determined, however, the agent must determine whether he is remembering at all; this is what we can refer to as the process problem. An agent capable of both remembering and imagining must reliably solve both problems in order to be in a position to have reliable access to his personal past. As we saw in the previous chapter, the source-monitoring framework provides a plausible explanation of how agents solve the source problem. As we will see in what follows, the source-monitoring framework cannot simply be extended to explain how agents solve the process problem. Nevertheless, it does provide a useful model for approaching process monitoring.

Before the explosion of research on memory distortions in recent decades, the existence of source error and the need for an explanation of how it is normally avoided was recognized by philosophers such as James Mill, who remarked, "It is said that there are men, who, by often telling a mendacious story as true, come at last to believe it to be true. When this happens, the fact is, that a case of the memory of *ideas*, comes to be mistaken for a case of the memory of *sensations*" (1869, 333). Mill goes on to sketch an explanation of how source errors are avoided that appeals to the fact that memories of sensations tend to be accompanied by information about related objects of sensation, while memories of ideas tend to be accompanied by information about related ideas.

The suggestion that memories of ideas can be distinguished from memories of sensations by features of their content, while simple, prefigures the explanation given by the source-monitoring framework. To review, the core claims of the framework are the following:

- Information about the source of a record is typically not stored along with the record itself, so that it can be read off during retrieval. In particular, representations originating in imagination are normally not tagged as having originated in imagination, and representations originating in experience are normally not tagged as having originated in experience.

- Source is, rather, inferred using heuristics relying on average differences among records originating in different sources.

- As in Mill's suggestion, these differences are mostly content-based. In particular, representations originating in imagination often contain records of cognitive operations, which is normally not the case for representations originating in experience, while representations originating in experience will normally include more sensory, contextual, semantic, and affective details.

- Source monitoring can involve either type 1 or type 2 processing, but is usually accomplished by type 1 processing.

The source-monitoring framework provides an elegant explanation both of how agents distinguish between representations originating in experience and representations originating in other sources, including imagination, and of why they sometimes fail to do so. It does not, however, explain how agents solve the process problem—nor is it designed to do so, despite occasional ambiguity on this point in the literature. This ambiguity may be due simply to the conceptual awkwardness of distinguishing the process problem from the source problem: whether a subject commits a source error in which he confuses a memory based on imagination with a memory based on experience, or a process error in which he confuses the process of imagining with the process of remembering, we tend to say simply that he mistakes imagining for remembering, making it tempting to lump the process problem in with the source problem.

To illustrate the temptation, consider imagination inflation (Garry et al. 1996), in which imagining an event leads to falsely remembering that it took place. A standard explanation of imagination inflation has it occurring due to source-monitoring failure: roughly, source-monitoring processes fail to determine that a retrieved representation originates in imagination rather than experience because, after repeated imaginings, the representation takes on characteristics normally associated with representations originating in experience (e.g., Goff and Roediger 1998). Schacter argues that, though the phenomenon of imagination inflation shows that imagination can be a threat to the reliability of memory, in general the ability to imagine events that have not occurred is adaptive (an idea discussed further in part IV). He then points to recent research on mental time travel, which has identified similarity at the cognitive and neural levels between remembering the past and imagining the future, arguing that "these similarities can help to explain why memory and imagination are easily confused: they share common neural and cognitive underpinnings" (2012, 605). But this runs together two distinct types of error that a subject might make. The cognitive- and neural-level similarities between remembering and imagining that have been uncovered by research on mental time travel concern the ongoing processes of remembering and imagining: remembering the past and imagining the future involve, at the time at which they occur, similar cognitive processes and draw on similar brain regions. Confusion between remembering and imagining due to such similarities will amount to process error. This does not explain imagination inflation, which reflects the subject's judgment about whether a given memory representation corresponds to his past experience. The confusion between memory and imagination here is of a different sort: the subject is not mistaken about whether he is now remembering or imagining (he knows he is remembering *something*), he is confused about where the remembered content comes from—that is, he commits a source error.

Another illustration is provided by McDonough and Gallo's discussion of the role of reality monitoring (a special case of source monitoring; see Johnson and Raye 1981) in distinguishing between memory for experienced past events and memory for imagined future events. They point out that, due to source-monitoring error, subjects can mistake memories of imagined future events for memories of experienced past events. Referring to the recent literature on mental time travel, they ask: because past memories and future imaginations "share so many cognitive and neural processes, how are we able to effectively discriminate between the two in our daily lives? How do we avoid constantly confusing the past and the future?" (McDonough and Gallo 2010, 3). While their own experiments clearly focus on the processes involved in distinguishing between memories originating in experience and memories originating in imagination (i.e., on the source problem), McDonough and Gallo's formulation of the question is ambiguous between the source problem and the process problem. The cognitive- and neural-level similarity between remembering past events and imagining future events is directly relevant only to process judgments, not source judgments.

The relation between source monitoring and process monitoring will be discussed in more detail in chapter 11. For the moment, the point is that, despite the temptation to lump process error in with source error, the two types of error should be distinguished. Process error might provide a distinct explanation for a range of memory errors and distortions, both errors due to mistaking imagining for remembering and errors due to mistaking remembering for imagining. False recovered memories (Lindsay and Read 2005) provide one potential example of process error due to mistaking imagining for remembering. One standard explanation of false recovered memories is that they arise in part due to source-monitoring errors. The subject vividly imagines a scene, perhaps in therapy. This creates a stored representation satisfying source-monitoring criteria for memories originating in experience. When the subject later retrieves the representation, he therefore takes it to originate in experience. Use of relatively lax criteria in type 2 source monitoring may also play a role. But in some cases, false recovered memories may instead arise due to process-monitoring error. The details of the explanation will depend on the details of the process-monitoring framework, but a subject might imagine something especially vividly or effortlessly, as opposed to retrieving a representation generated by imagination at an earlier time and now stored in memory. If the process satisfies process-monitoring criteria for remembering, the subject might therefore take himself to be remembering. The error is not about *where* the content of the representation originally comes from—it might come primarily from experience—but about *how* the representation is being generated.[1]

On the other hand, cryptomnesia, a form of unconscious plagiarism (Brown and Murphy 1989; Marsh, Landau, and Hicks 1997), might provide an example of error due to mistaking remembering for imagining. Cryptomnesia can be explained in terms of source-monitoring error: the subject retrieves a stored representation but, perhaps because it lacks the level of detail characteristic of representations originating in experience, takes it to have originated in imagination. Process monitoring error provides an alternative explanation (again, the details will depend on how the framework is developed): the subject might, for example, remember something only with difficulty and therefore take himself to be imagining—that is, generating a new representation—rather than retrieving a previously generated representation.

Whether false recovered memories, cryptomnesia, or other memory distortions are indeed caused by process error is an open question. These examples are intended merely to illustrate the point that, because process error is distinct from source error, it can in principle provide an alternative explanation of memory distortions. Determining in which cases process error provides a better explanation of memory distortions than source error and exploring those distortions that do arise due to process error are tasks for experimental research. The goal here is the preliminary one of describing the nature of process monitoring in general terms.

9.2   Do Agents Face the Process Problem?

Before turning to potential process-monitoring criteria, several worries about the necessity of a process-monitoring framework should be addressed.

To begin with, while it is natural to view remembering and imagining as distinct cognitive processes—including where imagination produces a representation of an episode from the personal past—the simulation theory implies that remembering is just a special case of imagining, and one might worry that, if remembering is just a special case of imagining, the process problem disappears. On the commonsense conception of memory, if we set aside cases of malfunctioning memory systems, remembering can go wrong in either of two ways: on the one hand, the process of remembering might end up producing an inaccurate representation; on the other hand, the process of remembering might be replaced with a process of imagining that, in the case at hand, is indistinguishable from remembering, perhaps even producing an accurate representation. On the simulation view, in contrast, the only meaningful distinction to be made between remembering the past and imagining it is between memory/imagination of the past that produces an accurate representation and memory/imagination of the past that produces an inaccurate representation. Since the process problem is about determining the nature of the process, as opposed to the accuracy of the representation it produces, it might appear that, given the simulation theory, agents simply do not face the problem.

But this is a mistake. If remembering the past is not distinct from imagining the past, we need not account for how subjects distinguish between remembering the past and imagining the past. But we still need to explain how subjects distinguish between the form of imagination dedicated to reconstructing past episodes—that is, remembering—and other forms of episodic imagination. These include both forms of non-past-directed imagination (e.g., episodic future thought) and forms of past-directed imagination other than remembering (e.g., episodic counterfactual thought).

9.3   How Hard Is the Process Problem?

A distinct worry is that, while we might need to posit a capacity to distinguish between remembering and other forms of imagining, such a capacity is trivial and requires no deep explanation. Recent work on the extensive overlap at the phenomenal, cognitive, and neural levels between memory and other forms of episodic imagination, however, makes clear that the capacity to reliably distinguish between remembering and imagining represents a nontrivial cognitive ability.

As we saw in chapter 6, remembering the past and imagining the future appear to be functions of a single episodic construction system, responsible for multiple forms of episodic imagination, in which the hippocampus plays a central role. For example, damage to the hippocampus impairs mental time travel into both past and future, while damage to other regions, at least partially sparing the hippocampus, results in confabulation about both the personal past and the personal future (Dalla Barba and La Corte 2013). There are, to be sure, differences in the extent to which different brain regions are involved in different forms of episodic imagination. For example, regions associated with prospective memory are more heavily involved in future-oriented than in past-oriented mental time travel. But these appear to be differences of degree, with imagining the future requiring greater activation than remembering the past, perhaps reflecting the greater constructive demands of the former task (Schacter and Addis 2007b). Of course, the same neural mechanism may implement multiple different functions (Anderson 2010), but activation of highly similar regions during remembering and during other episodic constructive processes supports the view that all episodic constructive processes are implemented by a single system. Indeed, given an approach grouping remembering the past together with imagining the future, along with mindreading, planning, imagining fictional scenes, mindwandering, and other forms of episodic imagination, it is plausible that, rather than related but distinct forms of episodic construction, what is at issue, strictly speaking, is a single, general simulational process capable of taking multiple types of episode as its target. But even if, more conservatively, we assume that we can meaningfully distinguish among different episodic constructive processes, these forms of episodic construction overlap along various dimensions, not only at the neural level but also in terms of their cognitive demands and their phenomenal features. Given this overlap, the agent cannot trivially "see" the type of the constructive process, and it is unclear how agents, usually effortlessly, manage to avoid confusing remembering the past with other forms of imagination.

There is no generally agreed-upon list of episodic constructive processes. Table 9.1, by allowing both the identity of the relevant agent and the location of the target episode in subjective time to vary, and by taking into account whether the constructive process attempts to produce a representation corresponding to reality or instead to produce a representation of a merely possible event, provides a framework for exploring episodic constructive processes in a relatively systematic way. These processes are discussed in the remainder of this section.

9.3.1   Mental Time Travel

In imagining his own past, an agent may, in addition to attempting to match an actual past episode—that is, to remember—imagine counterfactual scenarios (De Brigard et al. 2013; Van Hoeck et al. 2013). For example, one might imagine how things would have gone had one made a different decision in a given situation. Future-oriented mental time travel may likewise take on a variety of forms. In some cases, it may amount to an attempt to predict the future—to single the agent's actual personal future out from among the various possible futures that remain accessible to him. More commonly, it is a matter of imagining personal futures that are currently accessible but which may or may not be realized, depending on whether certain conditions are met. We most often imagine more probable futures, but in other cases we may imagine highly unlikely futures. The agent may also imagine "counterfactual futures"—futures that in some sense belong to him but that are inaccessible (perhaps futures that were accessible to him at a previous point in time but are no longer so). For example, Szpunar (2010) restricts mental time travel to plausible personal futures but groups

Table 9.1
Remembering and other episodic constructive processes

| | | | Time | Impure ———————————→ Pure | | |
			Present	Past	Future	Unspecified
Agent Impure ———→ Pure	**Self**	Actual	(grayed out)	MTT— actual past	MTT— possible futures	
		Counterfactual		counterfactual pasts	inaccessible futures	
	Specific other	Actual	mindreading			
		Counterfactual				
	Unspecified other					

Note: Cells are left blank where there is no obvious name for the relevant process. The grayed-out cell indicates that episodic construction is not responsible for the corresponding form of knowledge (knowledge of one's own current mental states).

mental time travel, so defined, with imagining possible but irrelevant future events.

9.3.2   Mindreading and Related Processes

As Perrin (2011), Shanton and Goldman (2010), and Buckner and Carroll (2007) have noted, mental time travel seems to draw on many of the same capacities as mindreading. Mindreading typically amounts to an attempt to imagine the experience of a specific agent, but one might also attempt to imagine an experience without attributing it to a definite agent. For reasons given in section 9.10 below, it is unlikely that reading one's own mind—that is, representing one's own current experience—should be included here as a constructive process, though nothing in the following argument depends on this. In contrast, imagining alternatives to one's own current experience (Eacott and Easton 2012) can be grouped here, along with imagining counterfactual past and future experiences. These capacities—imagining alternatives to one's current experience and imagining counterfactual past and future experiences—are clearly related, though they appear to be distinct.[2] Consider Hoerl's example of a diner arriving at a restaurant and seeing someone at another table who is already eating his dessert. He might imagine already (now) being at the dessert stage of the meal—that is, an alternative to his current experience, or he might imagine the anticipated future experience of being at the dessert stage of the meal—that is, a possible future experience (Hoerl 2008). Hoerl suggests that one might engage in the former sort of construction, but not the latter, without having a grasp of tense; a similar point might be made in terms of the sense of subjective time described below. Finally, just as an agent can imagine alternatives to his own past, present, or future, he can imagine the experiences of another individual, not in an attempt to represent their actual experiences, but rather in order to imagine counterfactual alternatives to those experiences, though we may use this capacity relatively rarely.

9.3.3   Pure Forms of Imagination

Finally, an agent might simply imagine an episode occurring at an unspecified time (De Vito, Gamboz, and Brandimonte 2012) or involving an unspecified agent (Hassabis et al. 2007a; Romero and Moscovitch 2012). The distinction between counterfactual and factual construction is blurred in the case of imagining episodes at an unspecified time, and it breaks down entirely in the case of imagining the experiences of an unspecified agent. These cases represent especially "pure" or unconstrained forms of episodic imagination and may be important in some forms of mindwandering, including some fantasizing, daydreaming, and so on (Regis 2013).

9.4   Do Agents Need to Solve the Process Problem?

The overlap among the various forms of episodic imagination of which we are capable suggests that distinguishing among them is likely to be error prone to some extent. A distinct worry is that, while agents might indeed be prone to confusions among episodic constructive processes, the reliability of remembering can nevertheless be explained without invoking process monitoring as a distinct form of metacognition. In particular, if the base rate of remembering relative to episodic imagination in general (i.e., remembering plus other episodic constructive processes) is sufficiently high, there will be no need to posit a capacity to reliably distinguish between remembering and imagining in order to explain the reliability of remembering. Given a sufficiently high base rate of remembering, memory belief formation would be (imperfectly) reliable even if the agent regularly mistook representations produced by other episodic constructive processes for memory representations.

Even if the base rate of remembering is high, this worry turns out to be unfounded. In order for an agent to solve the process problem, it is not sufficient for him to be able to distinguish remembering from other forms of episodic imagination: he must be able to distinguish *each* form of imagination from the others. An agent unable to distinguish between, say, representations of counterfactual alternatives to past episodes and representations of actual past episodes would be prone to unreliable episodic counterfactual thinking, even if not unreliable remembering. An agent unable to distinguish between representations of accessible personal futures and representations of purely hypothetical future scenarios would be prone to unreliable future-oriented mental time travel. And so on. Thus, even if the base rate of remembering, in particular, is high, agents still face the process problem.

Moreover, it is implausible that the base rate of remembering is so high that we need not posit a capacity to reliably distinguish between remembering and other episodic constructive processes in order to account for the reliability of remembering. Everyday life includes a great deal of time spent imagining alternatives to past events, planning future events, considering possible events located at no particular point in time, and so on. Research on mindwandering (Baird, Smallwood, and Schooler 2011; Finnbogadóttir and Berntsen 2013; Mason et al. 2007; Smallwood and Schooler 2006) confirms this intuitive picture, showing that subjects spend a large fraction of their time engaged in stimulus-independent thought. While some of this mindwandering amounts to remembering, a great deal of it involves future-oriented mental time travel and other forms of imagination (Berntsen and Jacobsen 2008; D'Argembeau, Renaud, and Van der Linden 2011; Smallwood, Nind, and O'Connor 2009; Smallwood and Schooler 2015).

9.5   Do Agents Solve the Process Problem?

Hence it appears that, in order to explain the reliability of memory, we need to assume that agents reliably solve the process problem. A final worry is that we do not know whether memory is in fact reliable, in which case it remains to be shown that we need to posit a capacity for process monitoring. As noted above, the question of the overall reliability of episodic memory is too general to be straightforwardly empirically tractable. But there are evolutionary reasons to expect our cognitive processes to be globally reliable, and we can observe that a creature capable of both remembering and imagining but not of distinguishing between them would lose the advantages associated with each capacity. As McDonough and Gallo put it, the "ability to play out alternative scenarios would be in vain if we then thought that we had already completed each action (i.e., confused future imagination with past occurrences)" (2010, 10). The point was anticipated by Holland:

Had [the difference between memory and imagination] existed clandestinely … then although memory and imagination would have been different, we should never have learned to distinguish them: the difference between them would have been useless, would have meant nothing to us. … There must be some mark or sign whereby a remembering state of mind can be distinguished from an imagining state of mind. (1954, 65)

Indeed, the constructive capacity underlying remembering and imagining would likely *decrease* fitness, absent an ability to reliably distinguish between them. Part IV of the book will develop this argument in more detail.

9.6   Formal Process-Monitoring Criteria

If the argument so far is on track, an agent capable of constructive episodic memory and hence of other forms of episodic imagination faces a form of mental uncertainty in addition to that compensated for by source monitoring, namely, uncertainty about what kind of episode he is simulating at a given point in time. Given that we are capable of simulating not only our past but also our future experiences, how, as McDonough and Gallo ask, "do we avoid constantly confusing the past and the future?" (2010, 3). Given that the episodic construction system underwriting episodic memory also gives rise not only to imagining the future but to episodic imagination in general, how, more generally, do we know whether we are remembering or engaged in some other kind of imagining?

The philosophical literature on memory and imagination contains a number of suggestions that can be interpreted[3] as proposals regarding the mechanisms that enable agents to solve the process problem. These can be grouped into formal, content-based, and phenomenal solutions. Though none of these proposals is adequate on its own, collectively they identify a set of plausible process-monitoring criteria. Let us begin by looking at several formal criteria: flexibility, intention, and spontaneity.[4]

9.6.1   Flexibility
In addition to vivacity, Hume proposed flexibility as a criterion for distinguishing between memory and imagination. The idea is that they are distinguished by the latter's flexibility: whereas memory is constrained to preserve the subject's original experience, imagination is free "to transpose and change its ideas" (Hume 1739, 25), recombining information originally derived from experience.

In its simplest form, the flexibility criterion would seem to depend on a view of memory as essentially preservative, a view which, as we have seen, is inadequate, since remembering, like other kinds of imagining, involves the flexible recombination of stored information. The mere fact of flexibility, then, cannot be used as a criterion for distinguishing between remembering and imagining. This problem can be avoided if the criterion is modified to refer to the greater level of flexibility involved in other forms of imagining relative to remembering; that is, to refer to a quantitative rather than a qualitative difference. Even granted that imagination is more flexible than remembering, however, the criterion appears to face a second problem, noted by Hume himself, at least when viewed as a process-monitoring criterion: the criterion is unusable, for it is impossible "to recall the past impressions, in order to compare them with our present ideas, and see whether their arrangement be exactly similar" (Hume 1739, 152–153).

Now, while the agent obviously cannot compare a current representation to a previous experience in order to determine whether it closely resembles the experience, if he has access to information about the level of flexibility of the process responsible for producing his current representation, such information might play a role in allowing him to determine whether he is remembering or imagining. Given that the inferences involved in remembering are relatively constrained, carrying out less extensive transformations of stored content, flexibility may play a role in process monitoring. It will, however, have limited validity as a process-monitoring criterion, for, while remembering is certainly less flexible than relatively pure forms of imagination, it may not be much more flexible than other relatively impure forms, which likewise are highly constrained by available information. Moreover, flexibility does not distinguish among relatively pure forms of imagination.[5]

9.6.2 Intention

Proposing a different formal criterion, Urmson argues that memory and imagination are distinguished by the agent's intentions. Indeed, he argues, intention allows the agent to determine whether he is remembering or imagining not only reliably but *infallibly*, for "all we have to do is to know what criteria of success are applicable, and this is a question which depends upon our own intentions. We are recollecting not if we did [have a certain experience] but if it matters whether we did. We are imagining if some such criteria of success as general verisimilitude, or interestingness are the relevant ones" (1967, 87–88; cf. Earle 1956). Restated in our current vocabulary, the idea is that a given constructive process is a process of remembering if the agent intends that it produce an accurate representation of a past experience. Otherwise, it is some other form of episodic construction. Since the agent, presumably, knows his own intentions, this grounds reliable process judgments. Munsat (1967) defends a similar view, as does Pears, who argues that the subject need not rely on criteria at all to determine whether he is remembering or imagining: "You just *mean* your mental image in one way rather than the other" (1990, 42).

While this proposal is elegantly simple, intention, like flexibility, turns out, on closer examination, to have only limited validity as a process-monitoring criterion. First, it ignores involuntary remembering, remembering not initiated or accompanied by an intention to remember. Remembering is not always, or even usually, voluntary (Berntsen 2009). If Urmson's proposal were the whole story, an agent could not know, in cases of involuntary remembering, whether he is remembering or imagining, simply because there is no intention to remember (or intention to imagine) for him to consult in such cases. But presumably we are able to determine whether we are remembering or imagining even in such cases. An analogous point holds for other forms of imagination; much mindwandering, for example, is initiated automatically. Thus, in an important class of cases, the intention criterion cannot account for formation of process judgments.

Second, where the criterion does apply, in cases of voluntary remembering, Urmson's proposal makes process error all but impossible, as he himself emphasizes. The agent simply consults his own intention and decides on that basis whether he is remembering or imagining. Since all that matters, on this view, is the intention to remember or imagine, process error will only be possible in cases where the agent misclassifies his own intentions. This sort of error may be possible (Bernecker 2008), but it is surely extremely rare at best. This is not a virtue of the proposal, since errors are indeed possible in process monitoring, as they are in any form of metacognitive monitoring.

If we allow that the agent's intentions do not suffice to determine whether he is remembering or instead engaged in another form of episodic construction, however, intention may play a role without making process error all but impossible. And the view that the only difference between remembering and imagining lies in the corresponding intention is indeed implausible, as long as we are interested in psychologically real processes, as opposed to a sort of first-person authority over whether one is remembering or imagining. Thus, allowing intention to correspond imperfectly to process type, intention may play an important but limited role in process monitoring: in cases of involuntary remembering/imagining, intention makes no contribution, but, in cases of voluntary remembering/imagining, intention might be weighted heavily in the formation of process judgments (while still being defeasible), with most process errors occurring in cases of involuntary remembering.

9.6.3 Spontaneity

Furlong provides us with a final formal criterion: "What happens in both [semantic memory and episodic memory] is that what I recall presents itself to my mind, independently of sensation or inference, with a certain spontaneity or involuntariness; and it is this chiefly which exacts my belief. When a belief arises in this way, then I am said to remember. *Per contra*, if this involuntary quality were to disappear, we would approach the region of imagination, of supposition and make-belief" (1948, 26). The proposal is essentially that the agent can distinguish between remembering and imagining because the latter process is launched by him voluntarily, while the former is involuntary. As noted above, remembering is indeed often involuntary. However, this does not enable the subject to distinguish between remembering and imagining, for the straightforward reason that remembering is also often voluntary. Moreover, imagination is also often involuntary, triggered automatically by environmental cues; involuntary mental time travel into the future (Berntsen and Jacobsen 2008), in particular, may be as frequent as involuntary remembering. Thus it appears that the fact that a process is voluntary or involuntary cannot be used by the agent to determine its type.

Furlong is, of course, aware that remembering is often voluntary and argues that, in cases where the agent deliberately tries to remember an event, he succeeds "only in so far as the act of imaging occurs with some degree of spontaneity": "this spontaneity is indeed one factor influencing the strength of our belief that the remembered event did occur; when this factor shrinks to zero, we have reached the border-line between memory and imagination" (Furlong 1951, 82). This suggests an alternative version of the proposal: remembering and imagining are distinguished not because the former is launched automatically rather than deliberately but instead because, while both processes may be launched deliberately, the *course* taken by the former, but not the latter, is characterized by a sort of spontaneity (Szpunar and McDermott 2008). There is support for the view that imagining the future is more spontaneous, in this sense, than is remembering the past (Van Boven et al. 2008). But while remembering is plausibly more spontaneous than relatively pure or unconstrained forms of imagination, other

relatively impure, constrained forms of imagination are likewise characterized by a high degree of spontaneity. Thus spontaneity, like flexibility, may
play a limited role in distinguishing between more and less pure forms of
episodic construction. In fact, it is not clear whether these should be treated
as two separate criteria: access to information about the level of flexibility
involved in a given episodic constructive process might manifest itself precisely in a sense that the process unfolds more or less spontaneously.

9.7   Content-Based Process-Monitoring Criteria

Moving beyond formal criteria, a number of criteria pertaining to the
content of the representations produced by remembering and imagining,
including their level of detail, their internal and external coherence, and
their emotional content, may play a role in process monitoring.

9.7.1   Vivacity

Bernecker refers to Hume's vivacity criterion as a phenomenal criterion, but
the label is potentially misleading, as we saw in chapter 4, since at least on
one reading, vivacity refers to features of the content of remembered and
imagined episodes (Bernecker 2008): "The ideas of memory are much more
lively and strong than those of the imagination, [and] the former faculty
paints its objects in more distinct colours, than any which are employ'd
by the latter. When we remember any past event, the idea of it flows in
upon the mind in a forcible manner; whereas in the imagination the perception is faint and languid, and cannot without difficulty be preserv'd by
the mind steddy and uniform for any considerable time" (Hume 1739, 24).
The reference to the "forceful manner" characteristic of remembering and
the difficulty of preserving a stable representation characteristic of imagining suggests a formal criterion similar to flexibility or spontaneity. Other
passages suggest that Hume may have viewed vivacity as being a *feeling*,
rather than a matter of more detailed content, which would indeed make
it a phenomenal criterion. This possibility is discussed below. But the main
thrust seems to be that remembering is distinguished from imagining by
the greater level of detail contained in representations produced by the
former process. Russell (1921) defends a similar view, arguing that memory
and imagination are distinguished by the amount of "contextual detail"
they respectively involve.

Bernecker notes several potential problems for the vivacity criterion. First, he argues that vivacity is a matter of degree, and therefore provides no clear cut-off point between remembering and imagining. Were this a genuine problem, it would disqualify not only vivacity but most other potential process-monitoring criteria, but the fact that vivacity (or any other criterion) is not binary need not prevent it from playing a role in process monitoring. Just as source-monitoring criteria can be flexibly adjusted, it is plausible that process-monitoring criteria can be flexibly adjusted, raising or lowering the standards that need to be met before a given episodic constructive process is judged to be an instance of remembering. One way of ensuring flexibility is by allowing process-monitoring heuristics to require more or fewer criteria to be satisfied before a given process is classified as an instance of remembering. Another way is by allowing the heuristics to vary the *extent* to which the relevant criteria need to be satisfied. On a conservative setting, they may require a very high level of detail before the process is classified as an instance of remembering; on a more liberal setting, a lower level of detail may be sufficient. The fact that vivacity is a matter of degree, therefore, does not disqualify it from playing a role in process monitoring.

Second, Bernecker argues that vivacity cannot accommodate cases of what we might refer to as "embedded construction"—remembering remembering, imagining remembering, remembering imagining, and so on. The thought here is that, because a memory representation of imagining an episode will not in general be more vivid than the original imagined representation of the episode, the vivacity criterion tends to break down in cases of embedded construction. But vivacity may nevertheless play a role in nonembedded cases, which presumably account for the overwhelming majority of cases of episodic construction. Moreover, accurate process discriminations would in fact seem to be more difficult to make in embedded cases, and the fact that vivacity breaks down here may help to explain certain process-monitoring errors.

Third, there is a problem originally noted by Hume himself (see also Holland 1954): ideas of memory are not always more vivid than ideas of the imagination, which sometimes leads to confusion. The first point to note here is that Hume is right, both about the existence of imagination representations that are more detailed than memory representations, and about the possibility of process-monitoring errors in such cases. The second point to note is that these observations do not suggest that vivacity does not play an important role in process monitoring. Assuming that process judgments are reliable but only imperfectly so, we want a theoretical framework that can explain both why process judgments are accurate as often as they are *and* why they are sometimes inaccurate. Thus what matters here is whether remembered episodes are *on average* more detailed than imagined episodes.

Finally, while it is intuitively plausible that remembered episodes are on average more detailed than imagined episodes, a problem first noted by Reid shows that the role played by vivacity in process monitoring must nevertheless be limited. Reid remarks that he "would gladly know … how one degree of vivacity fixes the existence of the object to the present moment; another carries it back to time past; a third, taking a contrary direction, carries it into futurity; and a fourth carries it out of existence altogether" (1764). The crucial point here is that vivacity must contribute not only to the agent's ability to distinguish between memory and relatively pure forms of imagination, but also to his ability to distinguish among remembering the past, imagining the future, and other relatively impure episodic constructive processes. While there will be exceptions to the rule—for example, as Vandekerckhove and Panksepp (2009) emphasize, while episodic memory is characterized by contextual detail and sensory detail of a sort that is absent from semantic memory (Berntsen and Bohn 2010; D'Argembeau and Van der Linden 2004; Gamboz, Brandimonte, and De Vito 2010), episodic memories are gradually semanticized with repeated retrieval (Piolino et al. 2006), decreasing in level of detail—it is plausible that memory on average produces more detailed episodic representations than do purer forms of imagination, and this is sufficient to allow a high level of detail to provide some evidence that the agent is remembering rather than imagining. But it is less clear that level of detail can play a role in allowing the agent to discriminate between remembering the past and imagining the future or other relatively constrained forms of episodic imagination. It does appear that representations of past and future episodes tend to be more detailed than representations of counterfactual events (De Brigard and Giovanello 2012)—though there will be exceptions to this rule as well—with events closer to the present time being more detailed (D'Argembeau and Van der Linden 2004, 2006; Trope and Liberman 2003), perhaps because temporally close events tend to occur in more familiar settings (Arnold, McDermott, and Szpunar 2011; D'Argembeau and Van der Linden 2012). But, while the mental time travel literature does suggest that a representation of an episode at a certain temporal distance from the present will, on average, be more detailed when the event lies in the past rather than the future (D'Argembeau and Van der Linden 2004; Szpunar 2010), this is not enough to enable level of detail to distinguish between mental time travel into the past and mental time travel into the future, since we remember/ imagine events at various distances from the present (with events closer to the present being more frequent; Spreng and Levine 2006), which means that there will be many cases in which a representation produced by mental time travel into the future is more detailed than a representation produced by mental time travel into the past, simply because the past event is further away in time than the future event. Moreover, in cases where the imagined future event corresponds closely to an experienced past event (a possibility emphasized by Gamboz et al. 2010), there may be few content-based differences of any sort between remembering the past and imagining the future.

Reid's point thus reinforces the view that vivacity by itself cannot ground reliable process-monitoring judgments. Nevertheless, given that representations produced by relatively pure forms of imagination (at the extreme: imagining the experience of an unspecified agent at an unspecified time) tend to be less detailed than representations produced by relatively impure forms of imagination (at the extreme: remembering recent, well-encoded events from one's own past), information about level of detail may play a role as one member of a larger set of criteria contributing to reliable process monitoring. For example, level of detail may contribute to the ability to distinguish between imagining more and less likely personal futures, as future events occurring in more detailed settings give rise to a stronger feeling of pre-experiencing (Szpunar and McDermott 2008).

9.7.2 Coherence

While there are many similarities between the contents produced by future- and past-oriented mental time travel—for example, both past and future representations tend to cluster around periods of self-development (Rathbone, Conway, and Moulin 2011)—content-based features other than level of detail may play a role in process monitoring. In certain cases, imagined episodes can trivially be identified as such by bringing them into contact with the agent's other knowledge. For example, imagining sometimes produces episodes inconsistent either with the agent's semantic knowledge in general or with his semantic autobiographical knowledge in particular. In addition to this sort of external incoherence, representations produced by imagination may be somewhat more likely to be internally incoherent than representations produced by memory. Thus a form of coherence checking may play a role in process monitoring, just as it plays an evaluative role in other areas, including communication (Sperber et al. 2010).

For several reasons, however, it is likely that coherence, like the other criteria examined so far, plays only a limited role. First, though both internal and external incoherence may be more likely in imagination than in memory, memory, too, is often incoherent (in part due to its constructive character). Second, process evaluations typically occur rapidly and automatically; given that coherence checking is a cognitively costly procedure (the costs increasing rapidly as the size of the body of knowledge against which the given representation is assessed for coherence increases), it is likely that produced representations are not systematically checked for external coherence—at least, not against very much of the agent's remaining knowledge. Finally, in many cases, even if coherence is assessed, it need not unambiguously decide between memory and imagination. An imagined episode may be perfectly coherent, both internally and with respect to the agent's remaining knowledge. With respect to external coherence, in particular, in many cases there will be little in the agent's knowledge that might allow him to determine whether he is remembering or imagining. Consider, for example, the task of distinguishing between the processes producing two representations of highly similar episodes, one occurring in the past and one occurring in the future, as in the case of oft-repeated actions. In such cases, the contents of the representations may be nearly identical. (I remember coming into the office yesterday; I imagine coming into the office tomorrow. How do I tell the difference?) The importance of this point is reinforced by the finding that mental time travel into the future tends to focus on near-future events occurring in familiar settings (D'Argembeau et al. 2011; D'Argembeau and Van der Linden 2004; Spreng and Levine 2006).

9.7.3 Affective Valence and Intensity

Affective valence and intensity may provide additional process-monitoring criteria. As Boyer (2008) has pointed out, affect is central to episodic memory. Positive or negative emotional tenor does not suffice to distinguish remembering from other forms of construction, as episodic memories may be either positive or negative in tenor, but emotional tenor may play a role in process monitoring if, as a number of studies have found, imagined future episodes tend to be rated as more positive (D'Argembeau et al. 2011; D'Argembeau and Van der Linden 2006; Finnbogadóttir and Berntsen 2013).

In addition to their positive or negative valence, the intensity of the accompanying emotions may also play a role. Sharot and her collaborators have shown that emotion plays a role in generating remember/know judgments (Phelps and Sharot 2008; Sharot, Delgado, and Phelps 2004; Sharot, Verfaellie, and Yonelinas 2007), and it may likewise play a role in generating process judgments, helping to distinguish past from future episodes. Somewhat counterintuitively, it appears that emotions are more intense in future-oriented mental time travel than in past-oriented mental time travel (Caruso 2010; Caruso, Gilbert, and Wilson 2008; Van Boven and Ashworth 2007). Affective intensity may also contribute to distinguishing between mental time travel and other forms of episodic construction. De Brigard and Giovanello (2012) found that constructed counterfactual events are less emotionally intense than constructed past or future events, in line with Boyer's suggestion that "emotion is crucial to the intuition that an event represented actually occurred" (2008, 219).

9.8   Phenomenal Process-Monitoring Criteria

As noted above, Hume can be interpreted as suggesting that memory and imagination are distinguished by how they respectively feel. For example, he argues that "since [memory and imagination] are only distinguish'd by the different *feeling* of the ideas they present, it may be proper to consider what is the nature of that feeling. And here I believe that every one will readily agree with me, that the ideas of the memory are more *strong* and *lively* than those of the fancy" (1739, 133). The nature of the relevant feelings of "strength" and "liveliness"—Hume also refers to the supposed superior "*force*, or *vivacity*, or *solidity*, or *firmness*, or *steadiness*" of memory (1739, 146)—is not especially clear, but it may be that this amounts to an attempt to describe an overall *feeling of remembering*. The idea of an overall feeling of remembering will be discussed in section 9.9; the remainder of this section considers the potential role of other feelings in process monitoring.

9.8.1 The Feeling of Prior Belief

James suggested that "the object of memory is only an object imagined in the past ... to which the emotion of belief adheres" (1890, 652). Similarly, Audi has defended a view of the justification of memory beliefs which assumes that remembering is accompanied by a feeling of having previously believed the relevant proposition: "As I consider the proposition, I have a sense not only of believing it but also of *having believed* it" (1995, 35). Taken as a process-monitoring criterion, the feeling of prior belief is a non-starter, simply because remembering does not in general produce previously accepted representations. Much of the information stored in episodic memory is stored not because it was accepted by the agent but because it was of interest for some other reason. And given that remembering is a matter of constructing a new representation of an episode rather than simply retrieving a stored representation, the agent may have never previously entertained the relevant representation, even when it is based primarily on previously accepted information. Moreover, memories may persist even when the agent explicitly rejects them (Mazzoni, Scoboria, and Harvey 2010; Otgaar, Scoboria, and Mazzoni 2014)—memories need not be believed, much less have been previously believed. Thus it is unlikely that a feeling of prior belief serves as a process-monitoring criterion. To the extent that the contrary suggestion seems plausible, this is likely due to the fact that, after a representation has been identified as a memory of an episode from the personal past, we tend to form the corresponding belief.

9.8.2 The Feeling of Familiarity

In addition to the feeling of prior belief, Audi (1995) invokes a feeling of familiarity, echoing a phenomenal approach suggested by a number of other theorists. James, for example, argued that memory is characterized both by "warmth and intimacy" and a "general feeling of the past direction of time" (1890, 650). Similarly, Russell referred to "the feeling of *familiarity*" and argued that "there may be a specific feeling which could be called the feeling of 'pastness,' especially where immediate memory is concerned" (1921, 161–162).[6] Writing around the same time as Russell, Broad likewise refers to the feeling of familiarity, arguing that pastness is inferred from familiarity (1925, 266–267). Since repeatedly contemplating, for example, a future episode does not normally incline us to experience it as past, and since an unfamiliar episode may be experienced as past, Broad's suggestion that pastness is inferred from familiarity seems unworkable, and it is preferable to treat the feelings of familiarity and pastness as independent.

Pastness is discussed below. Though familiarity is neither necessary nor sufficient for pastness, a feeling of familiarity might nevertheless serve as a process-monitoring criterion if we assume that the fact that a constructed episode seems familiar is treated as a cue that it has been encountered before, providing some evidence that it was previously experienced—and so that it is a product of remembering, rather than another form of episodic imagination. Such a feeling of familiarity (which must be distinguished from the feeling of familiarity involved in déjà vu experiences; Brewer 1996; Hamlyn 1970) might in principle be determined by the fluency of construction. Remembering should, on average, be easier—that is, less cognitively effortful—than other forms of imagination, given that in general the representations produced by remembering are closer to the available stored information, requiring less recombination and transformation than representations produced by other forms of construction (Schacter and Addis 2007a). The greater fluency of remembering might give rise to a feeling of familiarity and hence an inclination to trust the produced representation, just as, in the perceptual domain, more fluent processing of stimuli tends to give rise to judgments of familiarity and an inclination to accept the stimuli (Unkelbach 2007). Reber and Unkelbach (2010) argue that, in the perceptual domain, this occurs because fluency is experienced as pleasurable (Reber, Schwarz, and Winkielman 2004), or perhaps because fluency increases relevance (Sperber and Wilson 1995); similar mechanisms might be at work in the fluency of construction.[7]

9.8.3   The Feeling of Pastness and the Feeling of Futurity

While the idea of a feeling of familiarity is somewhat speculative, the suggestion that remembering involves a feeling of pastness is well supported by work on the role of the sense of subjective time in episodic memory. Consciousness of subjective time, or chronesthesia (Tulving 2002), and the related notion of consciousness of the self, or autonoetic consciousness (Wheeler, Stuss, and Tulving 1997), are a major focus of recent episodic memory research. Chronesthesia and autonoetic consciousness are developing concepts, and the terms are not always used in consistent ways. On one view, they refer to the same capacity but emphasize different aspects of that capacity, autonoesis putting the accent on the subject who mentally travels in time, while chronesthesia puts the accent on the subjective time in which the subject travels (Szpunar 2011). On an alternative view, it may ultimately be more useful to define autonoetic consciousness purely in terms of awareness of one's self, whether or not in subjective time, and to define chronesthesia purely in terms of awareness of episodes in subjective time, whether including one's self or not.

Chapter 11 will argue for the latter view. But whether it ultimately turns out that we are dealing with two forms of awareness here or only one, what is crucial at this stage of the argument is that there appears to be not only a sense of subjective *past* time, corresponding to the hypothesized feeling of pastness, but also a sense of subjective *future* time (Dalla Barba 2001; Szpunar and Tulving 2011)—a feeling of *futurity*. The feelings of pastness and futurity are tightly interlinked. For example, amnesic patients are typically unable not only to remember the personal past but also to imagine the personal future (Dalla Barba et al. 1997); Dalla Barba and Boissé (2009), for example, argue that this reflects a general deficit in time consciousness. While we now have a reasonably good understanding of the brain regions necessary for chronesthesia and autonoesis (Nyberg et al. 2010), we have a limited understanding of how these forms of consciousness are actually generated. As Klein (2015) and Dalla Barba (2001; following Merleau-Ponty 1945) have argued, pastness is not contained in or directly determined by retrieved information. Regardless of how the feelings of pastness and futurity are determined, the fact that they normally accompany past- and future-oriented mental time travel is enough for present purposes, as it enables them to play a role as additional process-monitoring criteria. In particular, the agent may rely on them to discriminate between mental time travel into the past and mental time travel into the future, thus explaining how we avoid "constantly confusing the past and the future" (McDonough and Gallo 2010).

Like the other criteria discussed so far, however, they have only limited validity. While the involvement of the sense of subjective time in episodic constructive processes other than mental time travel into the actual past and the predicted future has so far been little studied, it is plausible that the sense of subjective time is involved in many forms of episodic construction. For example, when one imagines a counterfactual alternative to a given past experience, one may have the sense that it belongs to the *past*, though it does not belong to one's *actual* past. Likewise, when one imagines an episode belonging to an inaccessible (or no-longer-accessible) personal future, one may have the sense that the episode in question belongs to the future. And when one imagines an episode involving another agent, one may likewise have the sense that it belongs to the past or the future, though it does not belong to one's own personal past or future. Thus, while chronesthesia may be able to locate episodes in subjective time, this only goes so far: it does not tell the agent whether he is imagining an actual or a counterfactual episode, and it does not tell him whether he is imagining his own experience or the experience of another subject.

Since autonoetic consciousness—viewed as a form of *self*-awareness—need not be involved in some of these forms of episodic construction, it might narrow things down further, but even autonoetic consciousness and chronesthesia, viewed as independent forms of awareness, do not uniquely single out forms of episodic construction. For example, remembering the past (imagining the actual personal past) and episodic hypothetical think-ing (imagining counterfactual personal pasts) would appear to be indis-tinguishable on the basis of autonoetic consciousness and chronesthesia alone. Moreover, these forms of subjective awareness may sometimes be weak or absent, further limiting their validity as process-monitoring cri-teria; for example, the feeling of pastness varies in intensity, and may be weaker for memories of more temporally distant events (Crawley and Eacott 2006; Eacott and Easton 2012), even when these have not been fully semanticized.

9.9   Toward a Process-Monitoring Framework

Which of the formal, content-based, and phenomenal criteria reviewed above are actually employed in process monitoring, how they are weighted, and how they interact are matters that can only be settled by experimental research, but given what we know about other forms of metacognition, we are in a position to predict some general features of process monitoring.

Subjectively, one normally "just knows" whether one is remembering or imagining. This characteristic of process judgments suggests that, rather than being based on type 2 monitoring of episodic constructive processes, they are typically based on type 1 monitoring. Koriat (2000) has argued for a distinction between a conscious, information-based form of metacogni-tion and an unconscious, experienced-based form, the former involving conscious inference and the latter depending on subjective feelings, the central example here being the feeling of knowing. Such subjective meta-cognitive, epistemic, or noetic feelings are based on the unconscious appli-cation of heuristics (Arango-Muñoz 2014). In line with this view, process monitoring may be seen as a matter of the unconscious application of heu-ristics, likely drawing on at least some of the process-monitoring criteria described above, and resulting in certain metacognitive feelings.

The metacognitive feelings resulting from process monitoring are dis-tinct from autonoesis and chronesthesia, as the latter are among the cues on which the heuristic monitoring responsible for the production of the relevant metacognitive feelings draws. As Koriat points out, though meta-cognitive feelings are based on unconscious monitoring, they are them-selves conscious and can thus serve as a basis for controlled action by the agent. In the context of process monitoring, the relevant feelings may serve as the basis for epistemic control decisions, shaping the agent's decision to adopt a certain attitude toward a given simulated episode. In practical terms, they may tell him whether he should assume that he previously experienced the episode, anticipate experiencing it in the future, or adopt some other attitude toward it. A large number of different metacognitive feelings have been hypothesized (Arango-Muñoz and Michaelian 2014; de Sousa 2008; Dokic 2012)—feelings of knowing, of certainty, of familiarity, and so on—but the process-monitoring framework requires extending the list considerably. The proposal is that a distinct feeling tends to be gen-erated for each distinct kind of episodic imagination; so there will be a *feeling of remembering*, as well as a range of *feelings of imagining*. These feel-ings are distinct from the feelings serving as process-monitoring criteria. For example, the feeling of remembering resulting from monitoring the process of remembering is distinct from the feeling of pastness involved in that process: the latter feeling accompanies not only remembering but also other forms of past-directed episodic construction, and serves as one criterion monitored by the metacognitive process that generates the feeling of remembering.

In parallel with the source-monitoring framework, the process-monitor-ing framework can be summed up as follows:

•   An episodic constructive process of a given type is not "tagged" with information specifying its type—the target of the process (i.e., the kind of episode that it aims at simulating) is not given directly to the agent.

An episodic constructive process constituting remembering does not directly announce to the agent that it aims at reconstructing a past experience; a process constituting episodic hypothetical thinking does not announce that it aims at determining how an event would have unfolded, had certain counterfactual conditions been met; and so on.

- Instead, process type is inferred using heuristics relying on average differences among constructive processes of different types.

- In contrast to the differences among records originating in different sources on which source monitoring draws, which are primarily content-based, these differences concern a range of formal, content-based, and phenomenal features of episodic constructive processes.

- Process monitoring may occasionally be a type 2 process (as when the agent consciously attempts to determine whether he is imagining instead of remembering a scene), but it is usually accomplished by type 1 processing, resulting in metacognitive feelings of remembering and imagining that can then ground process judgments.

Process monitoring can be viewed as being prior to source monitoring, in the sense that source judgments are only relevant given that process monitoring evaluates a given process as one of remembering.

Fleshing out the process-monitoring framework would require experimental work to determine which potential criteria are used, their respective default weights, and how they interact, as well as to determine which conditions trigger a shift from type 1 to type 2 monitoring. There are likely to be significant challenges involved in such research. Ideally, we would be able to manipulate various formal, content-based, and phenomenal features of episodic constructive processes in order to achieve dissociations between process types and process judgments, so that, for example, a subject who is remembering the past might judge that he is in fact imagining the future, or vice versa. But it may be difficult to achieve such dissociations, and it may be equally difficult to determine that they have been achieved. First, while content-based features can be manipulated relatively easily (e.g., level of detail can be manipulated by requiring subjects to imagine novel events unfolding in familiar or unfamiliar locations), formal and phenomenal features would be more difficult to manipulate. Formal features, in particular, pose a problem. In order to achieve a dissociation here, it would be necessary, for example, to lead the subject to form the intention to imagine (and hence to judge, on the basis of his access to his intention, that he is imagining) when in fact the process is one of remembering. It is unclear how this might be done. It should be possible to manipulate phenomenal features, such as the feeling of pastness and the feeling of futurity, in such a way that they mislead subjects about process type, but it may be difficult to do this until more is known about how the relevant feelings are generated. Second, even where a dissociation occurs—and the framework predicts that dissociations should occur occasionally even in ecological settings—how is the experimenter to verify that it has occurred? Suppose, for example, that the subject is led to imagine a future episode but misclassifies himself as remembering an episode from the past. How is the experimenter to verify that the process judgment is inaccurate?

For both of these reasons, testing the process-monitoring framework is more difficult than testing the source-monitoring framework. In the case of source monitoring, only content-based features are at issue, and these can be manipulated by exposing the subject to information, asking him to repeatedly imagine an episode, and so on. And since source monitoring produces judgments about the source of remembered information, the experimenter can in many cases verify the accuracy of source judgments—source, unlike process type, is (at least sometimes) publicly accessible. Nevertheless, a start might be made by manipulating those features that can be manipulated and observing the effects on process judgments. Based on the discussion so far, we can make the following tentative suggestions about formal features:

- Level of flexibility may contribute to distinguishing between more and less pure forms of construction.
- Spontaneity, if construed as spontaneity in the course of the process (as opposed to spontaneity in the launching of the process), may play a similar role, though, so construed, it is not clear that it is a distinct criterion.
- Intention applies only in cases of voluntary construction; where it applies, however, it seems likely to be weighted heavily.

We can make the following suggestions about content-based features:

- The role played by affective content is unclear, but it may play a limited role.
- Coherence, both internal and external, may likewise play a limited role.

- The most heavily weighted content-based criterion is likely to be level of detail, serving primarily to distinguish between more and less pure forms of construction.

Finally, we can make the following suggestions about phenomenal features:

- The feeling of familiarity may have limited validity in distinguishing remembering from other forms of construction.
- The main role is likely played by the feelings of pastness and futurity, perhaps in combination with a distinct form of autonoetic consciousness.

Adopting an evolutionary perspective on episodic memory will shed additional light on the way in which process-monitoring criteria—and source and process monitoring themselves—interact. Part IV of the book is devoted to developing such a perspective.

9.10   Process Monitoring and Mindreading

To know whether one is remembering or imagining is to know something about one's own mental states. Our discussion of process monitoring thus intersects with philosophical discussions of self-knowledge, and, before turning to the evolution of episodic memory, a brief digression on the relationship between process monitoring and self-knowledge is in order.

Philosophers have traditionally endorsed a doctrine of privileged access, according to which there is an asymmetry between one's knowledge of one's own mental states and one's knowledge of the mental states of others. While articulating the precise sense in which self-knowledge differs from other-knowledge is a challenging task (Alston 1971), it is generally assumed that knowledge of the mental states of others is inferential and hence fallible in a way that knowledge of one's own mental states is not. Setting aside Wittgensteinian approaches, which make privileged access into an artifact of the rules of our language (which permit each of us to "make up" his own mind), the idea is that one has an especially reliable form of direct, introspective access to one's own mental states (Goldman 2006). Discussions of privileged access typically focus on belief and other propositional attitudes, but the doctrine can easily be extended to apply to episodic thought in addition to propositional thought. Applied to episodic thought, it says that, just as one is able to tell, with an especially high degree of reliability, whether one believes (or disbelieves, or merely entertains) a given proposition, one is able to tell, with an especially high degree of reliability, whether one is remembering (or anticipating, or merely imagining) a given episode.

The doctrine of privileged access is in tension with certain contemporary accounts of "mindreading" or "theory of mind," as the process by which one comes to know mental states is variously called. In particular, theory theorists (e.g., Gopnik 1997) argue that knowledge of the mental states of others is inferential in a strong sense: the mindreader applies a largely tacit psychological theory to the observed behavior of his target, and on that basis infers that the target must have certain mental states. Many theory theorists offer a unified account of self-knowledge and other-knowledge: applying the same theory to one's own observed behavior, one infers, on that basis, that one must have certain mental states. If such a view were right, privileged access would be effectively undermined—self-knowledge might be marginally more reliable than other-knowledge, but there would be no qualitative difference between the two.

In contrast to theory theorists, simulation theorists argue that knowledge of the mental states of others is inferential in a weaker sense: rather than applying a folk psychological theory, the mindreader puts himself in his target's shoes, employing his own cognitive faculties in an offline mode to predict the target's mental states. Unlike theory theorists, simulation theorists tend to offer an account of self-knowledge that is distinct from their account of other-knowledge—a "dual-method" account of mindreading (Goldman 2006). Though, as we have seen, one might in principle simulate one's own past mental states, it is implausible to maintain that one comes to know one's own current mental states by simulating them. Instead, one presumably employs some more direct form of introspective access. The simulation theory thus allows us to hold on to the doctrine of privileged access.

The framework developed here aligns naturally with the simulation theory. But when situating it with respect to the simulation theory, it is important to distinguish between knowledge of the mental states of others and knowledge of one's own mental states. Concerning other-knowledge, it may be possible to combine a standard simulationist account of mindreading with the account, sketched above, of mindreading as a form of episodic imagination or simulation. Since standard simulation theorists view mindreading as a matter of the offline employment of cognitive faculties, whereas the present account of mindreading as a form of episodic imagination treats it as an active, constructive process, however, this combination may ultimately prove unworkable.

We can be more confident about the compatibility of the two approaches when it comes to self-knowledge, as the process-monitoring framework can be seen as one way of filling out the dual-method account with respect to knowledge of one's own mental states. Nichols and Stich (2003) provide one influential version of the account, arguing that we can explain privileged access as the result of the operation of a simple monitoring mechanism. On their view, each of us is endowed with a monitoring mechanism capable of taking a copy of a belief that P from his "belief box," appending the comment that the proposition in question is believed, and depositing the result—"I believe that P"—back in the belief box. This view provides an attractively simple method of accounting for privileged access, but ultimately it is too simple. As Goldman points out, it provides no explanation of how the subject is able to distinguish among attitude types, in addition to attitude contents. How does one know whether one believes that P or disbelieves that P? We might in principle multiply monitoring mechanisms (positing one mechanism for belief, one for disbelief, one for suspension of judgement, and so on), but this would result in an extremely unparsimonious theory. Widening the scope of privileged access to include episodic thought, in addition to propositional thought, worsens the problem dramatically.

Goldman himself favors an alternative version of the dual-method account, on which introspection is sufficiently sensitive to a variety of properties of attitudes to enable it to reliably classify propositional thoughts. Focusing on episodic rather than propositional thought, the process-monitoring framework can be seen as a suggestion in the same general spirit: process monitoring is a form of introspection which, on the basis of sensitivity to a variety of properties of episodic processes, is able to reliably classify episodic thoughts. A key difference between the two accounts is that, whereas Goldman views classification as based on neural properties, the process-monitoring framework views it as based on formal, content-based, and phenomenal properties. Additional work would thus be required to determine whether the two approaches can be combined. Nevertheless, since both accounts acknowledge a difference in method between self-knowledge and other-knowledge, while acknowledging that self-knowledge is imperfectly reliable, together they may provide a coherent account of the asymmetry between self-knowledge and other-knowledge.

IV The Evolution of Mental Time Travel

If the argument of part III is on track, we have the ingredients necessary for an explanation of how episodic memory might achieve an acceptable level of reliability despite the fact that its simulational character provides ample opportunity for the formation of false beliefs. Though remembering regularly draws on nonexperiential information, this need not adversely affect its reliability if the nonexperiential information in question tends to be accurate. Source monitoring tends to filter out inaccurate nonexperiential information. And process monitoring reduces the risk of confusing remembering with other kinds of episodic imagination.

Process monitoring appears to depend on autonoesis and chronesthesia. These forms of consciousness appear to be uniquely human; that is, they distinguish human episodic memory from the forms of episodic-like memory that have been demonstrated in a number of nonhuman species. The final part of the book turns the spotlight directly on this subjective, conscious dimension of human episodic memory. Until recently, the evolution of episodic memory was not a major research focus, but, due in part to growing interest in episodic-like memory in animals, the literature now contains a significant number of proposed explanations of the evolution of episodic memory and mental time travel more generally. Part IV reviews these explanations and argues that they either do not address or fail to fully account for the subjective dimension of human episodic memory. It defends an alternative explanation of the emergence of the subjective dimension in terms of its metacognitive function.

10 The Puzzle of Conscious Episodic Memory

In Lewis Carroll's *Through the Looking Glass*, the White Queen declares to Alice that one great advantage of living backward is that "one's memory works both ways," to which Alice naturally replies that she "can't remember things before they happen." The White Queen retorts, "It's a poor sort of memory that only works backward."

Mother Nature, it appears, does not entirely agree with the White Queen: evolution, as far as we know, has been content to produce memories that work in one direction only—backward—in all species other than man. And yet there is an element of truth in the White Queen's remark, for the development of the one form of memory that "works both ways"—episodic memory—apparently conferred significant adaptive advantages, perhaps even being a key precondition for the very emergence of human culture and civilization (Tulving 2005).

Obviously, Alice was, strictly speaking, right: it is impossible to remember things before they happen. Equally obviously, it *is* possible to *imagine* things before they happen. What the research reviewed above shows is that both capacities—remembering the past and imagining the future—are functions of a single episodic construction system, or at least of heavily overlapping systems. This much is now firmly established, even if many computational, algorithmic, and implementational-level details of the system remain to be explored. What is not at all well established is *why* evolution produced this system in humans, given that nonepisodic forms of memory—semantic memory, as well as more basic forms such as perceptual memory, priming, procedural memory, and primitive forms such as habituation and sensitization (Markowitsch and Staniloiu 2011)—and simpler forms of episodic-like memory seem to be sufficient for most purposes.[1] This chapter looks at the ongoing debate over the evolution of episodic memory, showing that the conscious character of human episodic memory poses an especially difficult puzzle. The following chapter will argue that solving this puzzle requires taking the metacognitive role played by consciousness in episodic memory into account.

10.1 When Did Episodic Memory Evolve?

We can ask two basic questions about the evolution of episodic memory:

- The "when question": When in evolutionary history did episodic memory emerge? Is the capacity for episodic memory uniquely human, or is it shared by other species?
- The "why" question: Why did episodic memory emerge? Assuming that episodic memory is adaptive, what makes it adaptive?

Though the focus here is ultimately on the why question, it will be helpful to begin with the when question, as a review of the debate over where episodic memory first emerges in evolution will serve to clarify the nature of the capacity the adaptivity of which needs to be explained.

The when question is somewhat more amenable than the why question to direct empirical investigation, though, as the now extensive literature on mental time travel in animals demonstrates, there is ample room for debate here as well (Cheke and Clayton 2010; Feeney and Roberts 2012; Templer and Hampton 2013). All parties agree that episodic memory depends on and is evolutionarily more recent than semantic memory—presumably, episodic memory evolved out of semantic memory (Tulving 1983, 1984)—but this is more or less where agreement ends. On the one hand, Tulving has consistently and influentially argued that episodic memory is evolutionarily recent—in fact, uniquely human (Tulving 2002b, 2005; Tulving and Markowitsch 1998). This is in line with the Bischof-Köhler hypothesis (Suddendorf and Corballis 1997), according to which nonhuman animals are essentially "stuck in time" (Hoerl 2008). On the other hand, while Tulving's view has been influential, the Bischof-Köhler hypothesis has been challenged (e.g., Naqshbandi and Roberts 2006; Paxton and Hampton 2009), and there is considerable evidence in favor of the opposed position.

Allen and Fortin (2013), for example, have made a thorough case for the view that episodic memory has a long evolutionary history.[2] They review behavioral evidence that "strongly suggests" (2013, 2) that core properties of episodic memory are present in mammals (e.g., rats; Babb and Crystal 2006; and nonhuman primates; Hoffman et al. 2009; Martin-Ordas et al. 2010), as well as in some bird species (e.g., scrub jays; Clayton and Dickinson 1998; Griffiths, Dickinson, and Clayton 1999; and chickadees; Feeney, Roberts, and Sherry 2009). For example, Clayton and Dickinson's well-known study demonstrated that scrub jays remember not only *what* food items—either worms or peanuts—they have stored and *where* they have stored them, but also *when* they stored them, searching for perishable worms when permitted to do so shortly after caching but longer-lasting peanuts after enough time has elapsed to allow the worms to decay (Clayton and Dickinson 1998). As impressive as this research is, the possibility remains, as Suddendorf and Corballis (2007) underline, that scrub jays have a specialized capacity related to food-caching, rather than a more general capacity analogous to human episodic memory (Redshaw 2014). Nevertheless, several lines of converging evidence suggest that some nonhuman species may be capable of genuine memory for past episodes. Allen and Fortin review anatomical and functional evidence suggesting that the basic brain structures involved in episodic memory in humans exist across mammals (Manns and Eichenbaum 2006) and that analogous structures exist in birds (Rattenborg and Martinez-Gonzalez 2011). Additionally, they argue that the neural circuit responsible for episodic memory is present across mammals and that birds have a similar circuit (though they grant that less is known about the neural mechanisms of episodic memory in birds).

What are we to make of the persistence of these opposed views? To some extent, the disagreement over the existence of episodic memory in animals may be merely verbal. While Allen and Fortin, like other partisans of animal episodic memory, rely on a minimal definition of episodic memory as simply memory for the *what, when,* and *where* of events—memory for events in context, or what other researchers have referred to as episodic-like memory (Clayton and Dickinson 1998)—Tulving and those who follow him employ a richer definition of episodic memory, on which it is characterized not only by the *kind* of information that it makes available to the subject, namely information about specific experienced past events, but also by the *way* in which it makes that information available, that is, by its subjective, conscious, or phenomenological dimension. Evidence of the sort reviewed by Allen and Fortin does not speak to the involvement in animal episodic-like memory of a subjective dimension analogous to that characteristic of human episodic memory. Hence, if we build the subjective dimension emphasized by Tulving into the definition of episodic memory, this sort of evidence will be insufficient to determine when episodic memory emerged. The way we answer the when question thus depends in part on how we *define* episodic memory.

10.2 From Episodic-like Memory to Conscious Mental Time Travel

10.2.1 Contextual versus Phenomenological Definitions

The what-when-where (www) definition of episodic memory is in the spirit of Tulving's own original "contextual" definition of episodic memory, according to which

episodic memory is an information processing system that a) receives and stores information about temporally dated episodes or events, and about temporal-spatial relations among these events, b) retains various aspects of this information, and c) upon instructions transmits specific retained information to other systems, including those responsible for translating it into behavior and conscious awareness. (Tulving 1972, 385)

As knowledge of episodic memory has accumulated over time, Tulving's definition has shifted, and he no longer characterizes episodic memory in strictly information-processing or functional terms:

Episodic memory is a recently evolved, late developing and early deteriorating, past-oriented memory system, and probably unique to humans. It makes possible mental "time travel" through subjective time, from the present to the past and to the future, and it allows re-experiencing, through autonoetic awareness, experiences as such. Its operations depend on semantic memory, and it is subserved by multiple brain regions including medial temporal lobes and prefrontal cortex. (Tulving 2001, 20)

This newer definition bundles a number of ideas together. The claims about the relation of episodic to semantic memory and the brain regions responsible for episodic memory are relatively uncontroversial, so we can set these aside. In the current context, it would be question-begging to build human uniqueness into a definition of episodic memory, so we can set this aspect of the definition aside as well. The claim that episodic memory is late developing not only in phylogenetic but also in ontogenetic terms—children develop the ability to remember specific events located in time between three and five years of age—is important, in part because it helps to account for childhood amnesia, but will not play a role in what follows.

Thus the key aspect of the definition, for present purposes, is its reference to the forms of consciousness characteristic of episodic memory. On this "phenomenological" definition (McCormack 2001), what ultimately makes the difference between full-blown human episodic memory and the episodic-like www memory the existence of which has been demonstrated in a range of other species is its subjective dimension, its mode of presentation of past episodes (Rowlands 2009): human episodic memory involves a specific form or forms of consciousness, and there is no evidence that broadly analogous forms of remembering in other species involve similar forms of consciousness. It is in view of the centrality of the subjective dimension to episodic remembering that Tulving maintains that only human beings possess the capacity for genuine episodic memory.

10.2.2   The Phenomenology of Episodic Memory

Which of these two definitions should we adopt? Some researchers have argued against adopting the phenomenological definition on the ground that it is impossible for us to get even indirect access to the phenomenology of episodic remembering in nonhuman animals (Eacott and Easton 2012). Due to this impossibility, the phenomenological definition implies that the hypothesis that episodic memory is uniquely human cannot be decisively confirmed or disconfirmed. Since the phenomenological definition clearly captures something important about human episodic remembering, however, the fact that it has implications that cannot be subjected to a straightforward empirical test seems insufficient as a reason to reject it.

One might attempt to provide further motivation for rejecting the phenomenological view by claiming that human episodic memory and animal episodic-like memory are functionally equivalent, regardless of any phenomenological differences between them, in the sense that the relevant nonhuman species, as well as humans, satisfy purely behavioral criteria for episodic memory (Crystal 2010; Eichenbaum et al. 2005; Sellers II and Schwartz 2013). But while the view that human episodic and animal episodic-like memory are functionally equivalent has appeal as a way of making the question of animal episodic memory experimentally tractable, bracketing the subjective dimension of episodic memory overexaggerates the functional similarity of episodic and episodic-like memory. The www criterion, in fact, is neither necessary nor sufficient for human episodic memory. On the one hand, as emphasized above, humans are capable not only of remembering the actual past but also of a much broader range of forms of mental time travel, while there is no evidence that animals have a comparably broad capacity for episodic imagination. In other words, the www criterion is not sufficient. On the other hand, as Suddendorf and Corballis (2007) point out, the criterion is not even necessary for episodic memory, as one can episodically remember a given event while being unable to retrieve information about what happened, when it happened, or where it happened.

In short, concerns about experimental tractability notwithstanding, a phenomenological definition is preferable to a contextual www definition—the subjective dimension of remembering should be included as a central feature of human episodic memory. Whether it is, strictly speaking, necessary is another question. While there is a case to be made for its necessity (Gennaro 1992), it may be possible, for reasons given in chapter 6, to remember without undergoing the standard phenomenology. The present point is not that the subjective dimension is, strictly speaking, necessary, but simply that it is a prominent feature of human memory, such that creatures incapable of experiencing it should not be viewed as sharing the capacity for human-like episodic memory, and such that an account of the evolution of episodic memory must account for its occurrence.

Might it turn out, despite the lack of direct evidence, that some non-human species are capable of a form of memory with phenomenological features analogous to those characteristic of human episodic memory? Some species may be capable of precursors to conscious mental time travel (Corballis 2013; Newen and Bartels 2007), but in light of the cognitive sophistication presupposed by the phenomenology of mental time travel, which involves both a sense of self and a sense of subjective time, it seems unlikely that nonhuman species are capable of undergoing the relevant phenomenology.

As Markowitsch and Staniloiu (2011) argue, episodic memory is tightly bound up with the creation of a robust sense of self (cf. Droege 2013). A robust sense of self appears to be evolutionarily recent (Boyer 2008; Cosentino 2011), and the sort of cognitive (Howe and Courage 1993) or autobiographical selves (Gallagher 2000) that are a prerequisite for episodic memory (Markowitsch and Staniloiu 2011) are late-developing in humans. While nonhuman animals may possess more basic forms of self, including a primitive proto-self (Panksepp 1998) and in some cases an affective core self (Northoff and Panksepp 2008), they presumably do not have these relatively sophisticated self-concepts, making it plausible that human-like mental time travel is unavailable to nonhuman species.

It is similarly unlikely that nonhuman species have a sense of subjective time sufficiently sophisticated to enable mental time travel. As Stocker (2012) suggests, our ability to engage in mental time travel appears to depend on our possession of a spatialized representation of time. At the empirical level, there is evidence that the direction of perceived self-motion—forward or backward—influences our propensity to think future- or past-oriented thoughts (Miles et al. 2010). At the theoretical level, "once time is conceptualized as a spatial path, then time can be traveled forward or backward—at least in our imaginations" (Merritt, Casasanto, and Brannon 2010, 200), and it is unclear how this might occur without a spatialized conception of time. While the claim is difficult to test directly, it is unlikely that nonhuman species have such a spatialized conception of time. From a developmental perspective, for example, McCormack and Hoerl (1999) argue that the grasp of subjective time involved in episodic memory presupposes the ability to temporally decenter oneself; that is, to consider alternative temporal perspectives and to understand their relationship to one's current temporal perspective. The cognitive sophistication that this ability presupposes is likely to rule out nonhuman species.

Thus, while the remainder of the argument does not strictly presuppose this, there is a convincing case to be made for Tulving's claim that conscious episodic memory is uniquely human. Given the implausibility of attributing the forms of consciousness characteristic of episodic memory to nonhuman species, if these forms of consciousness are crucial not only to remembering past episodes but also to imagining future episodes, it seems clear that animals equally lack the capacity for future-oriented forms of episodic imagination. Admittedly, there is evidence that certain nonhuman species do have a capacity for future-oriented mental time travel (Roberts 2007; Zentall 2006), but the evidence at present is too weak to establish this conclusion with any confidence (Roberts and Feeney 2009; Suddendorf and Corballis 2007). More importantly, even if it were sufficient, the evidence in question, which is analogous to the evidence for www memory, would speak only to the existence of a form of www future-oriented episodic thought, as opposed to conscious future-oriented mental time travel.

10.3   Subjective Time

The argument so far has made do with a very rough description of the subjective dimension of episodic memory. Given the centrality of the subjective dimension to what follows, it is necessary at this point to be more precise about the nature of the relevant forms of consciousness. As we saw above, early attempts to characterize the subjective dimension of episodic memory referred to feelings of "warmth and intimacy," "familiarity," and "the past direction of time" (Broad 1925; James 1890; Russell 1921). But it is Tulving's treatment of the forms of consciousness related to subjective time that serves as the starting point for contemporary discussions.

Subjective time, for Tulving, refers to "the thought-about time in which one's personal experiences take place" (2002a, 313). Beyond general formulations along these lines, there is a certain level of vagueness in the way the concept of subjective time is employed in the mental time travel literature. For example, Tulving links our sense of the ongoing flow of the time in which we live, "an ever-present awareness of one's being existing in a subjective sea of time, always in transition from what is now becoming the past to what was once the future" (2005, 29), to mental time travel. That form of subjective time, however, appears to be more closely related to what Husserl (1990) described as internal time consciousness than to the form of subjective time involved in mental time travel. The structure of this form of subjective time corresponds roughly to McTaggart's A-series, in which events are defined as past or future in relation to the present moment, the present being held fixed while events approach from the future and recede into the past (McTaggart 1908). Though a number of formulations in the literature (e.g., Klein 2013a; Klein et al. 2002) suggest that it is this form of subjective time that is involved in mental time travel, this seems to be a mistake: the sense of subjective time in question provides the temporal structure of our unfolding experience, rather than our mental travels into past and future.

In addition to Husserlian time consciousness, we also have a sense of a second form of subjective time, a sense of the time in which we move when we mentally travel back to past events or forward to possible future events. The notion of subjective time at issue here corresponds more closely to McTaggart's B-series, in which events are ordered by an objective earlier than/later than relation (as opposed to moving closer to the present, coinciding with it momentarily, and then receding ever further into the past). The relevant form of subjective time does, however, have features of the A-series, in that events continue to be viewed as future or past with respect to the present, as opposed to being ordered simply by an earlier than/later than relation, as in the B-series. In this form of subjective time, it is not events that move (from future to past) in relation to the observing self, but rather the self that moves (forward or backward) in relation to a fixed temporal structure to "re-experience" or "pre-experience" events. It is this form of subjective time consciousness which is central to episodic remembering—when I mentally travel in time, I do not have a sense of events moving toward the present or receding into the past, but rather a sense that I myself am (imaginatively) moving toward an earlier or a later event.[3]

While they provide a useful heuristic, the A- and B-series are too simple to capture the structure of the form of subjective time involved in mental time travel, since subjects do not simply mentally travel into the actual past and the "actual" future. Thus, though it is often invoked in the literature, the idea that mental time travel involves "re-experiencing" and "pre-experiencing" events is misleading. Obviously, subjects do not literally pre-experience events. Even if the future is not metaphysically open, it is epistemically open, in the sense that we can have no contact with (and hence no experience of) events before they occur (Ismael 2011). In other words, even if some form of determinism is true, the future remains undetermined as far as our knowledge of it is concerned.

But there is no real danger of being misled here. The problematic aspect of the notion of pre-experiencing is rather that it suggests that subjects mentally travel into a unique, determinate personal future, whereas future-oriented mental time travel in fact consists of the mental exploration of a range of possible futures. These range from Dalla Barba's "probable possible" (futures that are open and likely to occur) to what we might refer to as the improbable possible (futures that are open but unlikely to occur) and even the impossible (futures that are no longer open, having been closed off by some present or past event).

The past, unlike the future, is fixed. But subjects likewise do not mentally travel only into the actual past. As we saw above, past-oriented mental time travel also involves mentally traveling into counterfactual pasts. As in future-oriented mental time travel, these alternatives may be closer to or more distant from the actual. In episodic counterfactual thought, the subject may revisit past experiences, altering them to imaginatively bring about a different outcome. Additionally, the subject may travel into counterfactual pasts that are more distant (in modal or probabilistic terms) from the actual past, including pasts that in some sense belong to him but that may never have been accessible to him. As figure 10.1 makes clear, the branching structure of subjective time means that the notions of re-experiencing and pre-experiencing are inapplicable here.[4]

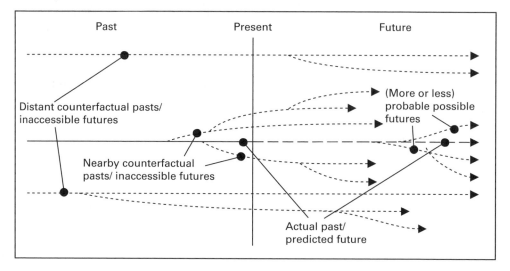

Figure 10.1
The structure of the form of subjective time involved in mental time travel. The subject, situated in the present, mentally travels into pasts and futures more or less distant from the actual past and the predicted future. The subject can mentally travel into both the personal past/personal future (i.e., his own past/future), and what we can refer to as the impersonal past/impersonal future (i.e., pasts/futures belonging to other subjects), where the subjects in question may be more or less indeterminate.

More generally, though subjective time is often treated as if it were equivalent to *personal* subjective time, subjective time is in fact a feature not only of mental travel into the personal past or personal future (i.e., the mentally traveling subject's own past or future), but also of mental travel into the pasts and futures of other subjects. The other subjects might be definite others, for example, friends or acquaintances (Grysman et al. 2013). But we can also mentally simulate the experience of more or less indeterminate subjects (subjects having certain features but lacking definite identities). Finally, though we arguably cannot simulate an episode without adopting *some* point of view on it, we can simulate an episode without *attributing* the point of view from which it is simulated; that is, we can mentally travel into the past or future of a completely indeterminate subject. Thus the structure depicted in figure 10.1 applies not only to personal subjective time but also to a more general, impersonal form of subjective time.

10.4 Consciousness of Subjective Time

The mentally time traveling subject's grasp of the subjective time in which he moves depends in part on his capacity for autonoesis. While the concept of autonoetic consciousness is widely used, it lacks a precise definition. Nevertheless, there is a rough consensus on the core features that distinguish it from noetic and anoetic consciousness.

10.4.1 Anoetic Consciousness

Anoetic consciousness can be viewed as a pure capacity to experience. Vandekerckhove (2009) characterizes it as a form of "procedural, sensory, and primary affective level consciousness," an unreflective consciousness of the ongoing flow of external events and internal bodily and mental activity. Indeed, in contrast to "knowing"—that is, noetic and autonoetic—forms of consciousness, this form of consciousness, possessed even by newborn infants, does not require a self-aware, reflective subject capable of distinguishing itself from the world; it is, rather, a matter of direct response to the world. Vandekerchove and Panksepp view the content of this form of consciousness as primarily affective, determined by primitive emotional and survival values but connected to sensory-perceptual experience (Panksepp 1998; Vandekerckhove and Panksepp 2009, 2011). Anoetic consciousness is ever-present but may barely translate into outright awareness even in subjects who are capable of higher forms of consciousness (Vandekerckhove 2009). It may thus include aspects of what James referred to as the "fringe of consciousness" (James 1890; Mangan 2001). In the domain of memory, anoetic consciousness is associated with procedural memory, which enables the organism to respond directly to its environment without any need for mediation by internal representations.

10.4.2 Noetic Consciousness

Whereas anoetic consciousness refers to a pure capacity to experience, noetic consciousness involves a richer phenomenology. At its core, noetic consciousness refers to a relatively sophisticated consciousness of one's own mental life. The noetically conscious subject not only represents the world but is aware of his representations (Tulving 2001). Noetic consciousness thus requires a grasp of the relationship between one's representation of the world and the world itself, and it is therefore a considerably more advanced capacity than anoetic consciousness. Unsurprisingly, it appears later both phylogenetically and ontogenetically. In the domain of memory, noetic consciousness is associated with semantic memory, referring to a specific subjective dimension of memory retrieval: when I retrieve a representation from semantic memory, I am or can become aware of the retrieved representation as a representation. Noetic consciousness can give rise to a feeling of knowing—but not yet remembering—as when I judge that a word was present on a list because it seems familiar, or when I say that Sofia is the capital of Bulgaria without retrieving information about any specific episode involving Sofia (Gardiner 2001).

10.4.3 Autonoetic Consciousness

Autonoetic consciousness, in turn, is associated uniquely with episodic memory. On Tulving's approach, what ultimately distinguishes human episodic memory from animal episodic-like memory is that the former but not the latter involves consciousness of the self in subjective time. When one episodically remembers, one is not only aware of one's representation as a representation, one is also (potentially) aware of it as a representation of a particular episode from one's personal past. That is, when I episodically remember an event, the constructed representation is presented to me both as representing an event that occurred at a particular time and as representing an experience of that event that belongs to me—I am aware of myself as the very subject who was involved in the event. It is in part due to this distinctive subjective dimension that it is not redundant to say that a subject *episodically remembers a given episode*: I can also semantically remember an episode, even an episode belonging to my personal past, but when I do so the retrieved representation typically lacks the feeling of warmth and intimacy which mark it as belonging to my personal past. For example, an amnesic patient may relearn information about his past, while still lacking a sense that the relevant experiences were his (Dalla Barba et al. 1997). The retrieved information may originate in an external source (e.g., someone may have told me about the episode) or it may originate in my experience of the episode, but if it is not imbued with warmth and intimacy by autonoesis, I will lack the sense that the memory belongs to me, that the represented experience was *my* experience.

While the concept of autonoesis was initially developed in connection with episodic memory, it is associated with mental time travel more generally, including future-oriented mental time travel. As Wheeler et al. emphasize, "autonoetic consciousness is not limited to the past; ... it encompasses the capacity to represent the self's experiences in the past, present, and future" (1997, 335). For example, the well-known patient KC, who seems to lack not only access to episodic information but also autonoetic consciousness, when asked what it was like for him to attempt to imagine his personal future, remarked (using a formulation that has since often been quoted) that he experienced "the same kind of blankness" that he experienced when he attempted to remember his personal past (Rosenbaum et al. 2005).

10.4.4   Chronesthesia

In addition to autonoesis, Tulving has argued that mental time travel involves chronesthesia, a form of consciousness of the subjective time in which mental time travel occurs. Originally, chronesthesia was explicitly defined in contrast to autonoesis, on the ground that "time can be dealt with, and usually is dealt with, independently of the self, and self can be dealt with independently of time" (Tulving 2002a, 315). While the distinction between autonoesis and chronesthesia is necessary, and for precisely the reason given by Tulving, it is often not respected in the literature. In particular, the distinction is often presented as a matter of degree or emphasis, rather than a qualitative distinction between two separable capacities. As Szpunar views the matter, for example, chronesthesia "emphasizes awareness of the subjective time in which one's self exists," whereas autonoesis "emphasizes awareness of one's self existing in subjective time" (2011, 410). Similarly, Vandekerckhove argues that "autonoetic consciousness departs from the self in subjective time, whereas in chronesthesia awareness of time itself comes to the fore" (2009).

Despite the tendency to blur the distinction between autonoesis and chronesthesia, we have good reason to treat them as separable (but interacting) capacities. As we saw in chapter 6, for example, Klein and Nichols (2012) have described a patient who appears to have a sense of events as occurring in subjective time but who does not experience those events as belonging to him. They treat the case as one in which the patient has normal episodic memories, except for the fact that his memories lack "a special kind of self-representation," but it is more parsimonious (while still being consistent with the patient's own reports) to treat him as having a deficit in autonoetic consciousness, while having intact chronesthesia, so that his episodic memories are accompanied only by the sort of noetic consciousness that accompanies semantic memory, along with a normal sense of subjective time. If so, the case suggests that autonoesis and chronesthesia can be dissociated.

Ideally, in order to establish a qualitative distinction between autonoesis and chronesthesia, we would also be able to identify cases in which the subject has a sense that imagined episodes do (or do not) belong to him but in which he is unable to place them in subjective time. If Dalla Barba and La Corte (2013) are right, some cases of confabulation may have this profile, but even if we cannot decisively identify such cases, it remains plausible that autonoesis and chronesthesia should be treated as distinct. It is one thing to know where in the structure of subjective time an imagined episode is located; it is another to know the subject to whom it belongs. Moreover, as argued above, one can simulate an episode without assigning it to a location in subjective time, just as one can simulate an episode without assigning it to the personal past or future of a definite subject; autonoesis, but not chronesthesia, would seem to be involved in simulation of the former sort, while chronesthesia, but not autonoesis, is involved in simulation of the latter sort.

10.5 Why Did Episodic Memory Evolve?

While autonoesis and chronesthesia are involved in forms of episodic imagination other than episodic memory, their roles in these processes have so far not been investigated in depth; this point is important as we move from the when question to the why question. Reserving "episodic memory" for full-blown episodic memory as found in humans and "episodic-like memory" for animal www memory, we can interpret the why question as referring to either form of memory:

- Why did episodic-like memory evolve?
- Why did episodic memory evolve?

While it is relatively easy to answer the "episodic-like" version of the why question, the answer to the "episodic" version of the question is far from evident. It is relatively easy to construct a convincing theoretical story about why a capacity to remember specific events from one's past should have been adaptive, but things are much less straightforward when it comes to explaining what might be gained by adding novel forms of consciousness to that capacity.

Tulving put the problem clearly early on: "If recovery of information about past events can occur independently of episodic memory and autonoetic consciousness, why should the episodic system and autonoetic consciousness have emerged at all in the course of evolution? Wherein lies their adaptive advantage?" (1985, 9). Relatively little progress has been made since Tulving wrote. Thus Klein recently posed essentially the same question: "If episodic recollection enables its possessor to re-live his or her past, what selective advantage does such ability confer? Why cannot the same or comparable benefits be obtained from semantic memory-based knowledge of time, place, and self, absent the additional experiential component of re-experiencing the events surrounding the acquisition of knowledge?" (2013b, 256). The challenge, in short, is to account for the evolutionary emergence of autonoesis and chronesthesia.

Tulving argues that the fact that nonhuman animals do not have the ability to mentally travel back in time suggests that the sense of subjective time is "an evolutionary frill" (2002b, 2). But the suggestion that the subjective dimension of mental time travel is an evolutionary frill (perhaps a spandrel; i.e., a mere adaptively neutral by-product, not itself selected for, of something that does qualify as an adaptation; Gould and Lewontin 1979) is implausible. Given the complexity of the episodic construction system, we can assume that mental time travel—including autonoesis and chronesthesia—is adaptive. It is possible in principle that the subjective dimension of episodic memory is epiphenomenal—that autonoesis and chronesthesia do not have an evolutionary function—but this is unlikely. First, given the complexity of the relevant forms of consciousness and the possibility of selective impairment, they seem unlikely to be mere by-products of other, functional capacities. Second, impairments to autonoesis and chronesthesia interfere with the normal functioning of memory. It is therefore reasonable to assume that the subjective dimension of episodic memory is not a mere spandrel.

The episodic version of the why question ultimately boils down to a question about survival-relevant problems encountered by remembering organisms: what problem or problems does conscious mental time travel solve that cannot be solved by episodic-like memory? The next chapter turns to this question.

11 Consciousness and Memory Knowledge

Existing explanations of the evolution of episodic memory can be grouped into past-oriented, future-oriented, and social categories. While the available explanations go some distance toward answering the episodic-like version of the why question, none provides a satisfactory answer to the episodic version of the question: why did *conscious* mental time travel evolve?

11.1 Past-Oriented Explanations

Bracketing the subjective dimension, it is plausible that episodic memory is adaptive simply because it enables organisms to recall information about specific past episodes, information which can then be of use in guiding future behavior. From this point of view, the specific episodic content provided by episodic memory can be seen as a useful supplement both to general patterns of behavior grounded in procedural memory and to the kind of general information stored in semantic memory. Both versions of this past-oriented strategy have been defended in the literature.[1]

11.1.1 Episodic versus Procedural Memory

Adopting a functional perspective, Sherry and Schacter argue that procedural memory (their "system I") and episodic memory ("system II") are functionally incompatible, in the sense that the problems that they respectively solve cannot be efficiently solved by a single memory system: whereas procedural memory, responsible for the formation of habits and skills, must be sensitive to features that are invariant across episodes, episodic memory functions "to preserve the contextual details that uniquely mark individual experiences—to preserve *variance* across episodes, rather

than invariance" (1987, 448). Memory for unique episodes would presumably confer adaptive advantages on organisms capable of it, so the explanation may be adequate with respect to episodic-like memory. But in light of
our current understanding of episodic memory as a phenomenologically
rich form of episodic imagination, the explanation is at best incomplete
with respect to episodic memory, strictly understood. First, it does not take
into account the fact that episodic memory appears as part of a larger pack-
age of constructive capacities, including future-oriented mental time travel.
Second, it does not take into account the subjective dimension of episodic
memory: supposing, as seems plausible, that certain adaptive advantages
are conferred by the capacity to recall specific episodes from one's past,
why can these advantages not be conferred (presumably more cheaply) by
mere episodic-like memory? As we will see, the latter limitation is shared by
most available explanations of the emergence of episodic memory, and the
former is shared by all but the future-oriented explanations.

11.1.2   Episodic versus Semantic Memory

An explanation in the same general spirit as Sherry and Schacter's appeals
to functional incompatibilities between episodic and semantic (rather
than procedural) memory. Anticipating the social explanations considered below, for example, Szpunar (2010; following Pillemer 2003) points
out that a memory of a past error in a given social interaction might
provide information sufficient to enable the agent to avoid committing
similar errors in future interactions. Another possibility is that deviations
from scripts representing the way familiar types of situation unfold may be
stored, along with the scripts themselves, in order to allow for more precise shaping of future behavior (Schank 1999). Along the same lines, Klein
et al. have argued that episodic memory may be useful primarily because
it delimits the scope of the generalizations stored by semantic memory:
"generalizations from semantic memory allow speedy decisions, but at the
cost of accuracy, whereas episodic memories provide accurate—that is, situ-
ationally specific—information, but at the cost of speed" (2002, 318). These
explanations share the limitations of Sherry and Schacter's explanation:
while the benefits of having access to information about specific past episodes may account for the adaptivity of episodic-like memory, they do not
explain the emergence of conscious, simulational mental time travel.

11.2   Social Explanations

There have been a number of attempts to provide specifically social accounts of the evolution of episodic memory—explanations according to which episodic memory is adaptive in virtue of its benefits for members of a highly social species. While most of these have a past-oriented character, in the sense that they attempt to explain the adaptivity of episodic memory entirely in terms of benefits accruing to the agent in virtue of being able to recall information about specific past events, some begin to take into account the fact that, in humans, the ability to remember the past is bound up with the ability to imagine the future.

11.2.1   Impression Reevaluation

Building on the approach developed in Klein et al. 2002, according to which the primary benefit of episodic memory is that it provides specific information that can be used to delimit the scope of the generalizations provided by semantic memory, Klein et al. (2009) argue that episodic memory may have a specifically social function. According to their impression-reevaluation hypothesis, episodic memory permits reevaluating conclusions drawn about other agents on the basis of past behavior; if we did not retain information about specific episodes but only summary judgments of the characters of those with whom we interact, we would be unable to reevaluate those judgments in light of new information. Building on this argument, Boyer (2009) points out that impression reevaluation might play a role in supporting epistemic vigilance (Sperber et al. 2010), since it enables the agent to revisit past occasions on which testimony was received in order to build up a track record for a given interlocutor (Cosmides and Tooby 2000; Hoffrage, Hertwig, and Gigerenzer 2000). As with the more general function of delimiting the scope of semantic generalizations, it is plausible that episodic memory might have this specifically social function, especially given our extensive dependence on testimony. However, like the more general explanation, this social explanation fails to take into account both the constructive character of episodic memory and its subjective dimension. Additionally, it raises the question of why episodic memory should have emerged in humans but not in other highly social species.

11.2.2 Other Social Factors

Skowronski and Sedikides have identified a number of additional social factors that may contribute to the adaptivity of episodic memory. They point out that being able to remember particular events should be of value to highly social agents involved in shifting alliances, since "optimal functioning in such an environment would seem to be facilitated if organisms were able to keep track of who had done what with whom (or to whom) at different specific times in the past" (2007, 509; cf. Sellers II and Schwartz 2013). Relatedly, they point to the value of being able to remember particular events—and hence to determine paternity—to members of a species that does not maintain sexual exclusivity. They likewise suggest that episodic memory might play a role in in self-enhancement (Sedikides and Strube 1997; cf. Newman and Lindsay 2009), since "development and maintenance of veridicality in [judgments that one has improved relative to the past] relies on the ability to remember what one was like at various points in the past" (2007, 509). Like impression reevaluation, these factors are past-oriented, and, like past-oriented explanations in general, they do not account for the subjective dimension of memory. Skowronski and Sedikides are aware of this limitation and argue that autonoetic consciousness may play a role in enabling the subject to locate events at specific points in time. On closer inspection, however, their argument says little about autonoesis as such. Instead, they point out that the sort of detailed experiential information (for example, sensory and affective detail) typically made available by episodic memory, in contrast to semantic memory, can enable the subject to locate an event in time. As we have seen, however, autonoesis is not necessary for the provision of such detail, and in principle need not accompany it.

11.3 Future-Oriented Explanations

The past-oriented and social explanations considered so far account for neither the simulational character of remembering, nor for its subjective dimension. An additional limitation of the social explanations is that they do not explain why conscious episodic memory should have developed in humans but not in other highly social species. Attempting to rectify the latter limitation, Osvath and Gärdenfors (2005) have developed a social explanation taking specifically human characteristics into account. Their explanation has the additional virtue of recognizing that episodic memory is intimately related to future-oriented mental time travel; it thus also begins to take the simulational character of remembering into account.

11.3.1 Niche Construction

Focusing on the emergence of anticipatory planning—as opposed to planning driven by immediate needs and drive states, which can also be observed in other primates (Gärdenfors 1995; Suddendorf and Corballis 1997)—Osvath and Gärdenfors argue that the "the cultural niche that was created by the use of Oldowan [pre-*Homo sapiens* hominins] tools, including transport of tools and carcasses, has led to a selection for anticipatory cognition, and in particular anticipatory planning" (2005, 1).[2] The key features of the relevant cultural niche included the manufacturing and use of simple tools, the transport of tools and animal carcasses, and the use of accumulation spots. Oldowan life was thus characterized by "an expansion in time and space"—for example, considerable time might elapse between creating and using a tool, and the source of raw materials for creating a tool might be separated by a considerable distance from the site at which the tool would eventually be used—and this meant that "there was energy to be saved and efficiency to be gained in this niche if anticipatory cognition could be used."

One virtue of this approach is that it does not abstract away from human culture. The idea is to treat niche construction, a process in which animals alter their environments in ways that may alter which traits are adaptive (Odling-Smee, Laland, and Feldman 2003), as an evolutionary process distinct from natural selection. Niche construction works via both genetic and ecological inheritance—that is, culture—and hominins are exceptionally culturally dependent. Explanations of the evolution of human capacities, therefore, must consider culture and not only natural ecological factors. A second virtue of Osvath and Gärdenfors' approach is that it accounts not only for past-oriented but also for future-oriented mental time travel. Indeed, given their approach, future-oriented mental time travel may have come first, in evolutionary terms, with past-oriented mental time travel then emerging as an exaptation; that is, the benefits in virtue of which the capacity for mental time travel was selected for may have derived primarily from mental time travel into the future, with mental time travel into the past emerging later. If so, this provides an important insight into why episodic memory should have a simulational character. However, the approach does not yet account for the subjective dimension of mental time travel. Granted that adaptive benefits are provided by a capacity for imagining, for example, a future occasion on which a presently available tool might be useful, it remains unclear what the characteristic phenomenology of mental time travel would contribute. The recognition that, though the tool is not now needed, it may be needed in the future would seem to be sufficient to inform the agent to pick up the tool now; what additional benefit is contributed by the subjective sense of mentally moving forward in time to the occasion on which it will be used?

11.3.2 Simulating the Future

The niche construction approach can be seen as part of a growing tendency to view the evolution of mental time travel, including episodic memory, in future-oriented terms. Klein (2013b), for example, argues that, while memory may be *of* the past, in the sense that it results from past experience, it is not in general *about* the past, in the sense that, while all forms of memory result from past experience, only episodic memory is subjectively oriented toward the past, with other forms of memory being oriented toward the immediate future (the "now and next"). Episodic memory would thus appear to be the one exception to the rule that memory is future-oriented (Klein 2015).³ In Tulving's terms, all other forms of memory are proscopic; only episodic memory is palinscopic (Tulving 1999). However, while episodic memory is indeed palinscopic, an adequate explanation of its evolution may nevertheless need to be future-oriented, in the sense that the primary benefits in virtue of which the capacity for mental time travel was selected for derive from mental time travel into the future. After all, one key advantage of the ability to mentally project oneself beyond the here and now is that "one can let one's hypotheses die instead of oneself" (Metcalfe and Kober 2005).

On De Brigard's (2014) view, for example, while the function of memory is to enable episodic counterfactual thinking, episodic counterfactual thinking may itself ultimately be in the service of simulation of future events. In general, there is growing consensus that episodic memory is adaptive due to its role in future-oriented mental time travel, since a capacity to simulate possible future episodes would contribute directly to adaptive behavior by enabling agents to plan and prepare (Schacter 2012). Allen and Fortin

(2013), for example, argue that the main function of episodic memory is to support memory-based predictions. In particular, they argue that episodic memory may contribute to the ability to make predictions by playing a role in a capacity to infer novel relationships, such as a novel path between two locations or an inferred social hierarchy.

The view that mental time travel is adaptive primarily because it enables the simulation of possible future episodes is plausible, but direct empirical evidence in favor of the view is limited at present. As Szpunar and Jing (2013) point out, little is actually known about the way in which people simulate possible future episodes when making decisions about the future. Beyond the lack of direct empirical evidence, caution is required when arguing for future-oriented explanations of the adaptivity of episodic memory. Suddendorf and Corballis, for instance, argue that "the crux of mental time travel lies in its role in enhancing biological fitness in the future, so that mental time travel into the past is subsidiary to our ability to imagine future scenarios" (2007, 302). The problem is the slide from the claim that the adaptivity of mental time travel must be due to its future effects (one kind of future-orientation) to the distinct claim that the adaptivity of mental time travel must be due to its ability to allow organisms to anticipate the future (a distinct kind of future-orientation). The former claim follows automatically from evolutionary theory—it is true of any capacity, not only memory (Nairne 2013)—but it does not imply the latter claim. Memory for past episodes could still be adaptive even if unaccompanied by a capacity to anticipate future episodes. To illustrate, consider the research on food-caching scrub jays discussed above: memory for what was cached when and where would presumably increase an organism's ability to survive by improving its ability to locate food in the future, independently of whether the organism were also capable of representing future episodes.

Despite the need for caution, it is likely that the capacity for mental time travel is adaptive at least in part in virtue of its contribution to planning and preparation. As Tulving remarks, future-oriented mental time travel made possible "a feat that had no precedence anywhere in nature: individuals intentionally, voluntarily, consciously taking action in response to something that did not exist in the physical world. As a consequence, humans were able to create a world to fit them, rather than live in one into which they had to fit" (2005, 22). However, even if we grant that the adaptive benefits of mental time travel derive in part from the ability to simulate possible future episodes, the precise role of its subjective dimension remains unclear. Just as it is possible to remember past episodes without undergoing the sort of phenomenal experience that characterizes human mental time travel into the past, it is possible to imagine future episodes without undergoing any special phenomenology. Thus, while the future-oriented explanations that have been considered so far do, by prioritizing future-oriented mental time travel, take the simulational character of episodic memory into account, they do not yet provide a full answer to the why question: what survival-relevant problem does conscious mental time travel solve that could not have been solved by mental time travel minus its conscious dimension?

11.3.3   Reducing Delay Discounting

One future-oriented approach that may provide a partial explanation of the subjective dimension is provided by Boyer, who hypothesizes that mental time travel may reduce delay discounting. The proposal is that mental time travel, including its subjective dimension, "provides a motivational 'brake' that counters natural dispositions toward opportunistic, short-termist, 'myopic' decision making" (Boyer 2008, 219). Mental time travel is characterized by the experience of emotions independent of the subject's current goals. Boyer argues that the mismatch between the emotions experienced in mental time travel and the subject's current goals may provide a clue to the function of the subjective dimension. Emotional content tends to counteract time discounting, the tendency to discount rewards and costs as they recede further into the future. For example, an inclination to betray an ally in order to secure a short-term benefit might be neutralized by the emotions involved in imagining the potential long-term consequences of such a betrayal. If we assume that, in order for the emotional content of simulated future episodes to have a motivational effect, the agent needs to feel as if the simulated episode were happening to him, Boyer's hypothesis identifies one possible evolutionary function of consciousness in mental time travel.

While the hypothesis is appealing, the relevant empirical evidence is mixed: though there is some evidence for the claim that mental time travel reduces delay discounting (Benoit, Gilbert, and Burgess 2011; Daniel, Stanton, and Epstein 2013; Peters and Büchel 2010), there is also contrary evidence (Craver et al. 2014; Kwan et al. 2012, 2013). At the theoretical level, while it is rational to counteract time discounting in some circumstances (e.g., in cooperation, where the rewards of altruistic behavior are typically received in the future), time discounting, as Boyer acknowledges, is in general rational, since the probability that a reward will be received diminishes as distance into the future increases. Similarly, we can in general do more to avoid penalties in the near future than in the far future (Maclaurin and Dyke 2002). Moreover, it is unclear whether the hypothesis can be extended to account for the involvement of autonoesis in forms of episodic imagination other than mental time travel into probable possible futures.[4]

11.4 Toward a Metacognitive Explanation

A survey of the available explanations of the evolution of episodic memory suggests that the capacity for mental time travel is adaptive in part because it provides agents with access to information about specific past events, a capacity that may have been particularly useful for a highly social species. The simulational character of memory may be accounted for by the fact that it is an exaptation, initially a by-product of the capacity to simulate possible future episodes, with certain features of the ancestral environment explaining why such a capacity is present in humans but not in other highly social species. However, while it is possible that autonoesis may play a role in reducing delay discounting, the subjective dimension of mental time travel remains largely unaccounted for—we still lack a satisfactory answer to the episodic version of the why question.

In the article in which he first introduced the concept of autonoesis, Tulving briefly suggested an intriguing answer to the question. One possibility

is that the adaptive value of episodic memory and autonoetic consciousness lies in the heightened subjective certainty with which organisms endowed with such memory and consciousness believe, and are willing to act upon, information retrieved from memory. ... By enhancing the perceived orderliness of an organism's universe, episodic memory and autonoetic consciousness lead to more decisive action in the present and more effective planning for the future. (Tulving 1985, 10)

More recently, Klein has advocated for a similar account, arguing that

autonoetic awareness of memory content ... may be the source of our confidence that our recollections track the past. Autonoesis ... automatically informs consciousness that the content of a recollection is true to its source ... unlike the offerings of other types of long-term memory, we do not have to infer (with the uncertainty that entails) that the recollected content of a current mental state is about the past; rather its pastness is directly given to awareness as a veridical representation of events that took place in one's life. In this way, autonoesis provides us with a direct and unmediated "sense or feeling of certainty" that occurrent mental content is an accurate portrayal of the past. (Klein 2013a, 257)

The view that autonoesis is responsible for producing a sense of subjective certainty suggests a metacognitive account of the adaptivity of conscious mental time travel. Just as cognition can be viewed as a means of coping with the uncertainty of the world, metacognition can be viewed as a means of coping with the uncertainty of the mind (Arango-Muñoz and Michaelian 2014; Proust 2013). Autonoesis, on this view, functions as a means of reducing uncertainty about whether or not an apparently remembered event actually occurred: by providing the agent with a sense that the remembered event belongs to his personal past, it provides him with a reason for accepting, and acting on, the retrieved content. In short, the suggestion is that autonoesis grounds a form of type 1 metacognition that renders it unnecessary for the agent to employ type 2 metacognition in order to determine whether to accept retrieved episodic memories.

While it is a step in the right direction, the view is unworkable in the form in which Tulving and Klein propose it. At best, it is incomplete, since it does not account for the role of chronesthesia. Setting this point aside, the suggestion that autonoesis directly gives rise to confidence that a remembered event actually occurred cannot be right, simply because autonoesis is also involved in a variety of other forms of episodic imagination. My sense that a simulated event belongs to me is no less strong when, for example, I simulate a counterfactual rather than an actual past episode. If autonoetic consciousness were to directly give rise to a sense of subjective certainty, I would be misled into believing that the counterfactual event had actually occurred. Of course, we are not usually misled in this way.

11.5 Consciousness, Metamemory, and Subjective Certainty

In response to these problems, it might be suggested that the combination of autonoesis (a sense that a simulated event belongs to me) and chronesthesia (a sense that the simulated event belongs to the past) might together give rise to subjective certainty that the event was part of my actual personal past. Since the combination of autonoesis and chronesthesia does not uniquely pick out events belonging to the actual personal past—episodic counterfactual thinking involves both forms of consciousness—this suggestion is not fully satisfactory, but it brings us closer to a satisfactory view.

As noted above, metacognition can be viewed as a means of coping with mental uncertainty. In the case of episodic memory, we can distinguish two kinds of uncertainty with which the agent must cope. First, he faces uncertainty about whether a given representation is accurate. Second, he faces uncertainty about the origin of the information it contains. Resolving the latter kind of uncertainty enables the agent to resolve the former with a relatively high degree of confidence. As we saw in part III, the agent faces two questions with respect to uncertainty about the experiential origin of a representation. First, he may be uncertain about whether the source of the representation lies primarily in experience (or another reliable source); this is the source problem. Second, he may be uncertain about whether the process that produced the representation was an instance of remembering or rather of another form of episodic imagination (i.e., whether the process was an attempt to simulate a past episode); this is the process problem.

11.5.1   Consciousness and Source Monitoring

Tulving and Klein can be read as suggesting that autonoesis, by giving rise to a sense of certainty that a given memory representation corresponds to past experience, plays a role in solving the source problem. Assume, for the moment, that autonoesis does indeed serve to indicate to the agent that a given representation originates in past experience. As Klein (2013a) emphasizes, the claim is merely that autonoesis functions as a criterion for the experiential origin of a representation, not that it is in fact a reliable criterion for experiential origin. Moreover, there is no necessary connection between the fact that a representation originates in experience and its accuracy: that a given representation originates in past experience does not imply that it is accurate with respect to past experience, and that a given representation does not originate in past experience does not imply that it is inaccurate with respect to past experience. On the whole, however, it is reasonable to assume that experiential origin is correlated sufficiently strongly with accuracy for the inference from experiential origin to accuracy to be reliable. So, if the agent gets himself—whether by relying on autonoesis or by relying on some other criterion—in a position to know that a given memory representation originates in experience, he thereby gets himself in a position to know (to reliably judge) that the representation is accurate with respect to the past episode. The suggestion is thus that autonoesis plays a role in enabling reliable source monitoring. Note that this is in contrast to the standard source-monitoring framework, which views source-monitoring criteria as being primarily content-based, rather than phenomenal.

Tulving and Klein may or may not mean to suggest that autonoesis also plays a role in process monitoring, but the suggestion is equally—in fact, more—plausible. As Tulving remarks, "when you remember an event, however vaguely, … you do not confuse it with perceiving, or imagining, or dreaming, or hallucinating, or having thoughts about what is or could be in the world" (2005, 15). The question raised by the process problem is: how do agents manage to avoid such confusion? According to the process-monitoring framework, autonoesis provides a partial answer, but only a partial answer, to this question. The involvement of autonoesis may thus be crucial to the reliability, and hence to the evolutionary adaptivity, of mental time travel and episodic imagination more generally. Cosmides and Tooby (2000) make a closely related point, arguing that planning and a number of other forms of human cognition require the ability to decouple the representations that they produce both from behavior and other representations. Consider planning. As Cosmides and Tooby argue, planning (which we can view as one form of future-oriented mental time travel), if it is to be adaptive, presupposes a capacity to decouple the plans that it produces—absent an ability to decouple, the agent would risk treating a planned sequence of actions as having already been performed (i.e., he would mistake an imagined sequence of actions for a remembered sequence), an error which would typically have maladaptive consequences. Along the same general lines, Perner (1993) refers to the need to "quarantine off" memories from representations of the current state of the world. In practice, this quarantining off or decoupling may not involve a sharp distinction between the current state of the world and remembered or imagined episodes (O'Connor and Aardema 2005). Setting aside this complication, the view developed here can be understood as claiming that we need to quarantine off memories not only from representations of the current state of the world but also from other products of episodic imagination: the products of different forms of episodic imagination need to be quarantined off from each other. As Boyer puts it, "a mind that is full of representations of imaginary situations may be in danger of mistaking them for the real thing. It would seem really maladaptive to assume that real bears are as approachable as Baloo in Kipling's *The Jungle Book*" (2009, 16).

Now, we have been assuming that autonoesis directly gives rise to a sense of subjective certainty that a representation corresponds to a past episode, but, as pointed out above, this cannot be right, simply because autonoesis is involved in forms of episodic construction other than memory. Might autonoesis nevertheless play a role as one of a larger set of source-monitoring criteria? This possibility is worth exploring, but, as the standard source-monitoring framework does a good job of explaining how agents solve the source problem without invoking phenomenal criteria such as autonoesis, the more conservative assumption is that the role of autonoesis is not to be found in solving the source problem.

11.5.2   Consciousness and Process Monitoring

As we saw in chapter 9, autonoesis is likewise insufficient, by itself, to explain how agents solve the process problem. The suggestion that it serves as one of a larger set of process-monitoring criteria, however, is more plausible. One key source-monitoring criterion is provided by information about the cognitive operations which originally gave rise to the stored representation. The idea is that representations stemming from experience typically contain little information about the cognitive operations which originally produced them, in contrast to representations stemming from imagination, which typically contain more information about the cognitive operations which produced them—when you remember an imagined episode, you typically also remember imagining it, whereas when you remember an experienced episode, you typically just remember the episode itself (and not the experiencing). Thus source monitoring may not need to rely on phenomenal criteria, in addition to content-based criteria—the content itself already contains information sufficient to ground reliable source judgments. The situation in process monitoring is different, since remembering and other forms of imagining, as ongoing processes, regularly produce representations that are indistinguishable on the basis of content alone. I remember taking the bus to Istanbul last month. I imagine taking the bus to Istanbul next month. I imagine someone else taking the bus to Istanbul, leaving at the same time and sitting in the same seat as me. The content of the simulated episodes might in principle be identical. Yet I do not mistake imagining an event that might occur next month for remembering an event that in fact occurred last month, and I do not mistake imagining an episode involving another agent for remembering an episode in which I was involved. Since content-based criteria cannot explain how I do this, it may be necessary to invoke phenomenal criteria.

Autonoesis, however, cannot do all the work, nor can autonoesis together with chronesthesia—there is a role for other criteria to play in process monitoring as well as in source monitoring. The survey of potential process-monitoring criteria undertaken in chapter 9, together with the descriptions of autonoesis and chronesthesia developed in chapter 10, suggests the following view of the contributions of various criteria.

- Autonoesis enables the agent to discriminate between self- and other-oriented forms of episodic imagination, but not between past- and future-oriented forms.
- Chronethesia, in turn, enables the agent to discriminate between past- and future-oriented forms of episodic imagination.
- Autonoesis and chronesthesia, even in combination, do not suffice to tell the agent what, exactly, he is simulating. The agent needs to discriminate between mental time travel into the actual past and mental time travel into counterfactual pasts, as well as between mental time travel into the (more or less probable) predicted future and mental time travel into inaccessible futures. Content-based and formal criteria enable him to do so.

11.5.3   Interactions between Source Monitoring and Process Monitoring

The challenge of answering the episodic version of the why question is accounting for the involvement of the subjective, conscious dimension of mental time travel. Past-oriented, social, and future-oriented explanations fail to do the trick. In contrast, the metamemory function performed by the conscious dimension provides an elegant explanation of its involvement. Given its simulational character, remembering would be unreliable and therefore maladaptive absent the subjective dimension, for agents would be unable to reliably distinguish among different forms of episodic imagination. If an episodic constructive process is classified as self-oriented, past-oriented, and actual rather than counterfactual, it is judged to be an instance of remembering—the agent has a feeling of remembering. This is the first step of the process that determines whether an agent accepts a representation produced by episodic simulation. In the second step, source monitoring, relying on content-based criteria, is applied to the produced representation. If the information contained in the representation is evaluated as originating in a reliable source, the agent endorses it, forming a memory belief. Figure 11.1 sums up the basic picture.

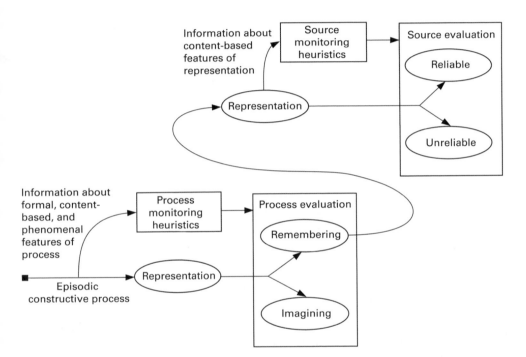

Figure 11.1
Interaction between source monitoring and process monitoring. Process monitoring precedes source monitoring, with source monitoring kicking in to determine the source of the given content if process monitoring classifies the relevant process as remembering.

Of course, the hypothesis that the evolutionary function of autonoesis and chronesthesia is metacognitive cannot be tested directly, and there is risk here of telling a "just so" story (Gould and Lewontin 1979). The hypothesis does, however, receive indirect support from evidence that impaired autonoesis or chronesthesia leads to metacognitive difficulties. In particular, the hypothesis predicts that, where autonoesis and chronesthesia are impaired, subjects should display an increased tendency to confuse past and future episodes, as well as to have difficulty determining whether a simulated episode concerns them or another agent. The well-known case of KC (Rosenbaum et al. 2005) is not directly relevant here, since KC lacked not only autonoesis but also the ability to retrieve past episodes (and the corresponding ability to imagine future episodes). But patient RB, for example, described by Klein and Nichols (2012), while lacking what they refer to as a sense of "ownership" for remembered episodes, was still able to remember episodes from his past. Falling back on semantic knowledge may enable such patients to compensate for impaired autonoesis, but it would be interesting to explore whether they have an increased tendency to confuse self and other in past (or future) episodes.

11.6   The Accuracy of Episodic Phenomenology

Dokic (2014) has defended a "two-tiered" account of episodic memory broadly similar to the overall account developed here, but there are important differences between the two accounts. Like the present account, Dokic's account posits the involvement of a metacognitive feeling of remembering in episodic memory. The account takes it for granted that episodic memories are "firsthand," in the sense that a genuine episodic memory does not essentially involve information deriving from a source (e.g., communication) other than the subject's own experience of the relevant episode, and it characterizes the feeling of remembering as a feeling that tells the subject that the relevant memory is firsthand. Dokic points out that, if his two-tiered account is right, a subject is in a position to learn not one but two things when he (accurately) remembers an episode. First, he learns about the episode itself. Second, he learns that his representation of the episode is firsthand—that is, it derives directly from his original experience of the episode.

The account developed here is in agreement with Dokic's account on the two-tiered character of episodic memory. But it differs from the latter with respect to both the first tier (i.e., the memory representation), and the second tier (i.e., the feeling of remembering). As far as the first tier is concerned, the simulation theory does not require that episodic memories be firsthand; indeed, episodic memory representations are usually at least in part second-hand and, in certain cases, may even be entirely second-hand.

As far as the second tier is concerned, whereas, on Dokic's view, the content of the feeling of remembering is something like [this representation originates in my experience of the episode it represents], on the present view, it is more plausible, given that the feeling plays a role in process monitoring (i.e., that its function is classifying the episodic constructive process, as opposed to determining the origin of the content delivered by the process) to view it as being something like [this representation is a representation of an event from my past].

These two differences interact. Suppose that we were to accept Dokic's account of the content of the feeling of remembering but that we were to accept the simulation theory account of remembering itself, so that remembering need not be (entirely) firsthand. Consider a case in which a subject remembers an episode from his personal past but in which part of the content of his representation of the episode derives not from his own experience but rather from other sources, for example, a case in which the content of the memory is influenced by conversations with other agents who experienced the event in question from various others points of view (e.g., Hirst and Echterhoff 2012). If the feeling of remembering refers to the agent's *experience* of the episode, the feeling will be inaccurate in such cases. If, on the other hand, it refers directly to *the episode itself*, the feeling will be accurate. Metacognitive feelings might play a role in reliable process monitoring despite being, strictly speaking, inaccurate. But given the additional complexity of the account developed here, on which source judgments are distinguished from process judgments, with the feeling of remembering playing a role in generating only the latter, there is little motivation for accepting Dokic's account of the content of the feeling of remembering.

11.7 The Necessity of Metamemory

A natural objection to the metacognitive account of the evolution of episodic memory concerns the very necessity of metamemory. On the approach developed here, the subjective dimension is integral to episodic memory because it serves a metacognitive function, enabling the agent to reduce uncertainty about whether he is remembering or imagining, in the service, ultimately, of reducing uncertainty about the accuracy of episodic representations. The suggestion is that autonoesis and chronesthesia play the role of what philosophers have termed "memory markers," criteria by means of which the agent can distinguish between remembering and imagining. According to the objection in question, the very search for memory markers is mistaken.

The objection is not new, but Hoerl, drawing on Urmson, has recently expressed it particularly clearly. The core idea is that the search for markers capable of distinguishing memory from imagination is motivated by a confusion between two senses of imagination. Suppose that I want to know whether I am genuinely remembering, as opposed to imagining. I might have either of two senses of imagination in mind: I might be asking about the accuracy of my apparent memory; or I might be asking whether I'm not "freely and creatively invent[ing], [making up], such and such, as a piece of imaginative fiction" (Urmson, 1967). With this distinction in mind, Hoerl suggests, we can readily see that the search for memory markers is pointless. On the one hand, if what is wanted are memory markers capable of dealing with uncertainty about accuracy, the search is hopeless, for "there is no specific mark internal to memory by which I can tell, on an individual occasion, whether I am recollecting accurately or inaccurately" (Hoerl 2014). On the other hand, if what is wanted are markers capable of distinguishing between remembering episodes and merely imagining them, there would seem to be no need for memory markers, since what enables one to know whether one remembering or imagining is simply knowing what one is trying to do—essentially, whether one *intends* to remember or imagine.

Both prongs of this objection ultimately fail. As far as the second prong goes, we saw in chapter 9 that the claim that the agent's intention suffices to tell him whether he is remembering or imagining is mistaken. As far as the first prong goes, while epistemologists might be interested, in the context of responding to Russell-style skepticism about memory knowledge, in the possibility of identifying markers capable of distinguishing remembering from imagining with perfect certainty—in which case the point that there are no perfectly reliable memory markers is important—if we are interested instead in explaining how agents manage, with imperfect reliability, to distinguish remembering from imagining in practice, the objection that memory markers are imperfectly reliable is irrelevant. Thus metamemory has a role to play in explaining the reliability of memory, and the hypothesis that autonoesis and chronesthesia have a metacognitive function is unaffected by the objection.

12 Conclusion

This book has had three main goals: first, to provide a general account of episodic remembering, as it occurs in real human beings, consistent with and shaped by the view of remembering as simulational mental time travel that has emerged in psychology in recent years; second, to provide a general account—again, based on the relevant psychology, including research on metamemory—of the factors ensuring the reliability of simulational remembering; and finally, to provide an account of the evolution of episodic memory, including the distinctive forms of consciousness which characterize it.

Part II was devoted to the first of these goals, arguing that viewing episodic remembering as a matter of constructive mental time travel requires us to abandon standard philosophical theories of remembering—the empiricist theory, the classical causal theory, and even an updated version of the causal theory meant to accommodate the constructive character of remembering—in favor of a more counterintuitive simulation theory. On the simulation theory, remembering is not, strictly speaking, distinct from imagining—remembering the past is a matter of imagining the past.

The simulation theory leads naturally to worries about the reliability of remembering. Responding to the second goal, part III developed an account of the reliability of remembering intended to assuage these worries. The fact that remembering has a simulational character does not imply that it is unreliable; given the nature of the heuristics governing simulational remembering, it will often produce accurate representations of past episodes. The simulational character of remembering does, however, introduce uncertainty about the accuracy of episodic representations; such uncertainty is reduced by source and process monitoring. Just as the simulation theory is counterintuitive, so is this explanation of the reliability of remembering. Intuitively, remembering seems to be simply a matter of preserving traces of past experiences; the reliability of such a preservative process is unmysterious. But given that remembering is a generative process which may produce representations containing little information stemming from the original experience of the relevant past episodes, a more roundabout explanation of its reliability is required.

One factor in this account is the subjective or conscious dimension of remembering, constituted by autonoesis and chronesthesia. The role of these forms of consciousness in enabling to the agent to reduce uncertainty about whether remembered events actually occurred plays a central role in the account of the evolution of human episodic memory developed in part IV. The available past-oriented, social, and future-oriented accounts may explain the evolution of animal episodic-like or what-when-where memory, but they do not fully explain the evolution of human episodic memory—conscious mental time travel. The conscious dimension of episodic simulation is necessary to enable remembering agents to discriminate between episodic constructive processes aimed at representing episodes from the personal past and episodic constructive processes aimed at other targets. Absent its conscious dimension, the constructive character of human episodic remembering would render it unreliable and hence maladaptive.

Even readers convinced by the broad outlines of the book's arguments may of course disagree with many of their details. But for those convinced by at least the broad outlines, the basic message of the book is meant to be reassuring. An anecdote may help to drive the point home. When I was a child in Canada, I drove with my family through part of the Northwest Territories. At some point, we stopped near a buffalo roll—an area where buffalo roll in the dirt—and my mother told me to stand in it while she took a picture. Naturally, I was frightened, imagining that a buffalo might appear at any moment, set about rolling, and thereby crush me. Or so I seem to remember. In reality, given my age at the time, and given that my parents repeated the amusing story to me a number of times afterwards, I can't be sure that much—or even any—of the content of my apparent memory of the episode actually originates in my experience, as opposed to the subsequent accounts provided by my parents and my own subsequent imaginings of the episode.[1] As von Leyden put it, memories are more like paintings than photographs, and the missing pieces of an episode may be filled in by information from other sources (von Leyden, 1961).

The point of the book is that, ultimately, it doesn't matter. My memory of the buffalo roll incident is just as much a memory as any other, regardless of how much of my original experience has been preserved. And it is likely to be reasonably accurate, again regardless of whether anything of the original experience has been preserved. Memory may be more like a painting than a photograph, but a painting can, after all, be quite accurate. Thus, while the overall account developed here may be counterintuitive, the fundamental message of the book is conservative. One's initial reaction to learning how memory works—to learning that it is not a matter of simply storing and retrieving information—may be to distrust one's memory. But evolution has equipped us with a system which is much more powerful and flexible than the simple storage model without thereby incurring a massive decrease in reliability. In short, though our intuitive picture of the way memory works may be inaccurate, our instinctive trust in our own memories is justified. Simulational memory functions, as it was meant to, to give us knowledge of the personal past.

Notes

•

Chapter 1

1. See, e.g., the debate over quasi-memory, where quasi-memory is a relation like memory, with the difference that one can quasi-remember experiences other than one's own (Burge, 2003; Parfit 1984; Shoemaker 1959).

2. Chapter 3 will argue that it is an oversimplification to view memory as storing dispositional beliefs, but, even on a more nuanced view, most of our beliefs are dependent on information stored in memory.

Chapter 2

1. For the sake of readability, the scare quotes are henceforth dropped.

2. Anderson's rational analysis of memory can perhaps be seen as one attempt to construct such a general theory, or at least it has sometimes been treated as such. If the claim that memory is not a natural kind is right, then, despite its merits, Anderson's theory is unlikely to be successful as an account of memory as a whole. If a more specific claim developed below—that many forms of nondeclarative memory are noncognitive—is right, in particular, then the theory, which conceives of memory in terms of managing "a huge database of millions of complex facts and experiences" (Anderson 1990, 42) and is stated in terms of search for and retrieval of stored representations, can apply at most to declarative memory, since these terms are inapplicable to noncognitive memory. Moreover, while it may be legitimate to attempt to develop a theory of declarative memory as a whole, the simulation theory defended here suggests that any theory that conceives of memory in terms of a database of stored records will fail to do justice to the constructive character of memory.

3. Admittedly, while the evidence strongly seems to favor the hypothesis, the consensus on the hypothesis is imperfect, and alternatives exist (e.g., Foster and Jelicic 1999; Gaffan 2002). Strictly speaking, the argument of this chapter supports only a

conditional claim: *if* the multiple memory systems hypothesis is right, *then* memory is not a natural kind.

4. The idea that natural kinds involve the stable clustering of properties brought about by underlying mechanisms is discussed further in chapter 3.

5. If nondeclarative remembering is not information processing, then the claim that the concept of a memory system is a concept of a system that requires a trilevel description becomes slightly misleading, for it now appears that there is a crucial ambiguity in the concept of a memory system. We can of course speak sensibly of nondeclarative systems. It is just that these are not memory systems in the sense in which the episodic and semantic systems are memory systems, since they do not require a description at the computational level.

6. Nevertheless, the difference between episodic and semantic memory should not be overstated. Recent work on personal semantic memory (Renoult et al. 2012), for example, may suggest that episodic and semantic memory are best viewed as being situated on a continuum, and the research on semantic contributions to mental time travel discussed in subsequent chapters can be interpreted as having similar implications. Semantic contributions are particularly apparent in memories of repeated or extended events; see the discussion in chapter 6 of the nature of the episodes with which episodic memory is concerned.

Chapter 3

1. Kornblith understands natural kinds according to Boyd's homeostatic property cluster theory, on which natural kinds are defined as mutually reinforcing clusters of properties, clusters such that the presence of some of the properties in them tends to bring about the presence of the remainder (Boyd 1999). This approach to natural kinds has the virtue of tolerating a certain amount of vagueness about the borders of natural kinds, but the details of the theory will not play a role in what follows.

2. It is worth noting that the track record of psychology in providing such hypothetical normative guidance is indisputably superior to that of epistemology. Weapon focus, for example, is real (Saunders 2009): the presence of weapons, under certain conditions, tends to impair eyewitness memory; if we are interested in knowing what happens in cases where weapons were involved, then, certain precautions are in order. The psychology of eyewitness memory more generally has provided a great deal of knowledge that is not only empirically well-grounded but that has had a real, beneficial impact on belief-forming processes used in high-stakes contexts, including criminal investigation (Ridley, Gabbert, and La Rooy 2012). Cases of this sort can easily be multiplied; for example, see Bishop and Trout (2005) on simple statistical prediction rules.

3. See, e.g., the cases discussed in chapter 7.

4. As chapter 8 will make clear, there are also important variations within individuals, since a given individual may apply more or less stringent metacognitive monitoring criteria on different occasions.

5. As is standard in epistemology, this glosses over complications around the relationship between degrees of belief and all-or-nothing belief (Huber and Schmidt-Petri 2009).

Chapter 4

1. In light of the remarks on factivity below, this should be read as "*S* had an experience as of *e*." The conditions discussed below should be read in an analogous manner.

2. This example, like most of the others used in this and the next two chapters, concerns memory for an entire episode. In practice, of course, there may be important differences among different components of a single episodic representation, both at the level of content (e.g., some components of a single representation may originate in the subject's experience of the relevant episode, while others do not) and at the level of phenomenology (e.g., the subject may endorse some components of a representation but not others). Focusing on memory for entire episodes simplifies the exposition of this part of the book considerably; the argument of part III will begin to take differences among different components of episodic representations into account.

3. For reasons given below, the initial, short-term memory representation should be distinguished not only from the agent's experience of the episode but also from the resulting long-term memory trace.

4. Note that the rejection of factivity should not be taken to imply that the *accuracy* of memories will not play an important role in the account of remembering. On the simulation theory, while it would be incorrect to say that a subject fails to *remember* because he does not satisfy the factivity condition, the accuracy of the subject's current representation nevertheless bears the entire weight of distinguishing between successful and unsuccessful remembering. If remembering is just imagining the past, the distinction between "genuine" and "merely apparent" memory collapses into that between accurately remembering (= imagining) the past and inaccurately remembering (= imagining) the past.

5. The same thing will go for the subsequent discussion of Martin and Deutscher's causal theory.

Chapter 5

1. Flage (1985) does make a case for reading Hume, in particular, as a causal theorist, but this is an unusual view (Traiger 1985).

2. Again, the focus here is not on interpreting the details of Martin and Deutscher's particular formulation of the causal theory, but rather on assessing the adequacy of a theory in its general spirit.

3. One worry that we need not deal with here is that the notion of a memory trace is incompatible with direct realism, as traces would function as intermediaries, analogous to sense-data, between the remembering agent and what he remembers. If the compromise between direct and indirect realism described above is workable, there need be no conflict between the involvement of traces in remembering and a form of direct realism sufficiently moderate to be plausible. For a much more thorough discussion of objections to traces, see Sutton 1998, to which this section is heavily indebted.

4. The distributed conception of traces also provides a response to a conceptual objection—voiced, for example, by Malcolm (1977) and Squires (1969)—according to which *retention* of a memory may occur without anything being *stored*; Malcolm offers the example of someone retaining his good looks without storing them. On a distributed conception of traces, the sense in which memory involves storage of information *is* a sense in which one could be said to store one's looks.

5. Their discussion of this condition is somewhat technical, turning on a distinction between a factor's being "operative for" and its being "operative in" the circumstance in which an event occurs, but the general upshot is sufficient for present purposes.

6. They discuss constructive and reconstructive processes in the context of schema theory, to which they object, largely on the ground that memory representations are richer and more detailed than the theory suggests. But even if we acknowledge that the theory critiqued by Alba and Hasher overexaggerates the extent to which memory is schematic, the concepts of selection, abstraction, interpretation, integration, and reconstruction remain available.

7. While it is natural to think of forgetting as a matter of passive loss of information, forgetting itself may amount to a constructive process. In retrieval-induced forgetting, recalling information from long-term memory results in forgetting of related information, thus potentially reshaping the representation of events available to the subject (Ciranni and Shimamura 1999).

8. An alternative argument for moderate generationism might appeal to the phenomenon of hypermnesia, in which the amount of information the subject is able to remember increases with repeated retrieval attempts (Erdelyi and Becker 1974; Roediger and Payne 1982).

Chapter 6

1. As we will see, the re-experiencing/pre-experiencing metaphor is in some respects inapt.

2. For a more detailed review of the relevant evidence, see Schacter et al. (2012), to which this section is indebted.

3. There are other approaches that could have been discussed here, such as Suddendorf and Corballis's evolutionary perspective (Suddendorf and Corballis 2007). As most current approaches agree on the essential point, a more comprehensive review would add little to the argument. Suddendorf and Corballis's approach, along with a number of other evolutionary perspectives, is discussed in detail in part IV.

4. The argument here does not depend on the details of the structure of the default network; for additional background, see Addis et al. 2007; Schacter et al. 2012; Szpunar et al. 2007.

5. The approach views the processes in question as adaptive in the sense that they are beneficial for the organism; no claim is made about adaptivity in the evolutionary sense. "Constructive process" will be used (as Schacter uses it) to refer to constructive processes within memory, such as the incorporation of testimonial information, discussed in the following chapter. "Episodic constructive process," in contrast, will be used to refer to forms of episodic imagination, including future-oriented mental time travel, episodic counterfactual thought, and remembering itself.

6. The importance of this capacity for generalization is illustrated by Borges's short story "Funes the Memorious," which recounts the case of a man capable of remembering every experience in perfect detail but (therefore) incapable of generalizing on the basis of experience.

7. Additional support for this view is provided by imaging evidence that the hippocampus is involved in imagining fictitious experiences (Hassabis et al. 2007b), imaging evidence that other structures may be responsible for the temporal aspects of past- and future-oriented mental time travel (Nyberg et al. 2010), with the hippocampus being primarily responsible for the process of scene construction (Andrews-Hanna et al. 2010), and evidence of impaired scene construction ability (Andelman et al. 2010) and impaired scene processing (Lee et al. 2012) in patients with hippocampal damage (Maguire and Mullally 2013).

8. Note, however, that, if the personal past is not defined in terms of experience, the theory leaves open the possibility that agents might remember nonexperienced episodes. This problem is discussed in section 6.9 below.

9. This purely formal characterization of the notion of an episode at work in episodic memory is meant to be provisional. The development of an adequate characterization of the notion is one important avenue for future research on episodic memory and episodic imagination more generally (Ezzyat and Davachi 2011, Cheng and Werning forthcoming).

10. See also Shanton 2012, on which the following summary draws.

11. Observer perspective memories are discussed in chapter 7.

12. Given that the researchers were trying to mislead him, however, he would not *know* that he had been lost in the mall; see chapter 7.

Chapter 7

1. The question of the epistemic status of beliefs resulting from the incorporation of accurate testimonial information should not be confused with the historically more prominent but only superficially similar question—discussed by Martin and Deutscher (1966), among others—of whether cases of "prompting," in which the agent must be provided with the to-be-remembered information before he is able to (apparently) remember it, are cases of genuine memory. There are two essential differences. First, incorporation does not refer to the same phenomenon as prompting. Incorporation refers to the integration of previously received testimonial information into the representation of an event output by retrieval. Prompting, in contrast, refers to the subject's reliance on testimonial information received at the time of retrieval. Second, discussions of prompting are typically about whether an agent who accepts a prompt can be said, strictly speaking, to remember; they thus belong to the metaphysics of memory. The present discussion, on the other hand, belongs to the epistemology of memory and concerns the epistemic status of beliefs resulting from incorporation. We could, of course, inquire into the epistemology of prompting, but that is not the focus of this chapter. Nor is the focus on the metaphysics of incorporation: given the simulation theory, we already know that incorporation is compatible with the occurrence of genuine remembering.

2. See Ayers and Reder 1998 for alternative explanations. One virtue of the source-monitoring explanation is that it has an easier time accounting for the reversed misinformation effect (discussed in section 7.8, below) than do other accounts, including Loftus's own overwriting account (Holliday and Hayes 2002). But, though the argument here will assume that the source-monitoring explanation is right, the exact nature of the mechanism responsible for the misinformation effect does not matter for the purposes of this chapter—for example, it is consistent with the argument that, due to reconsolidation, the receipt of the testimonial information results directly in the modification or replacement of stored experiential information, as in the overwriting account.

3. Partisans of at least some standard internalist conceptions of justification, incidentally, should come to a similar conclusion. According to a standard version of access internalism, the justificatory status of a belief is determined by how things stand with respect to it from the agent's point of view; i.e., by internally accessible factors. On such an approach, if there is to be a difference, in terms of justificatory status, between beliefs resulting from incorporation and other episodic memory beliefs, there must be an internally accessible difference between the bases for these beliefs. But, as far as internally accessible factors are concerned, incorporation cases

are normally indistinguishable from nonincorporation cases: the agent is not aware that he has incorporated testimonial information; nor, in most cases, could he become aware that he has incorporated testimonial information—from his point of view, the relevant testimonial information will typically be indistinguishable from experiential information.

4. The reflexive view does permit that helpful incorporation might give rise to true beliefs in certain unusual cases. Suppose that the agent sees the stop sign but encodes no memory for it or encodes a memory that is later lost. Suppose that he later incorporates the information that there was a stop sign. The resulting belief, with the content [I saw a stop sign at the scene], is true.

5. Note that this diagnosis of the appeal of the contamination view does not presuppose the epistemic theory of memory. According to the epistemic theory (e.g., Malcolm 1977; Munsat 1967; Ryle 1949), memory is retained knowledge. Taking the epistemic theory for granted, one might argue that memory is incompatible with helpful incorporation: helpful incorporation involves epistemic luck; knowledge is incompatible with epistemic luck; memory is retained knowledge; so memory is incompatible with helpful incorporation. As noted in chapter 3, a naturalistic approach rules out the epistemic theory, but it is worth emphasizing that the question here is whether helpful incorporation is compatible with *knowledge*, not whether it is compatible with *memory*. The two questions are distinct. The simulation theory of memory implies that beliefs resulting from incorporation are genuine memory beliefs, but this does not imply that the contamination view is false. The causal theory, in contrast, may imply that beliefs resulting from incorporation are not genuine memory beliefs, but this need not imply that they are epistemically defective.

6. The honesty bias is discussed in more detail below.

7. The truth bias is discussed in more detail below.

8. While the anti-luck condition has been influential, it is only one member of a larger family of proposed modal conditions on knowledge, including safety and sensitivity, among others (Comesana 2007). Given the subtle differences among these conditions, space does not permit a systematic exploration of their implications for the epistemic status of beliefs resulting from helpful incorporation. One prominent condition, defended by Sosa (2007), is discussed below, and what is said there goes for modal conditions in general: as they become increasingly demanding, they tend to imply that helpful incorporation is incompatible with knowledge, but that is better viewed as an indication that a condition is too demanding, rather than as evidence that incorporation is incompatible with knowledge.

9. Chapter 11 will argue that the episodic construction system may have been selected for as a means of providing agents with accurate representations of possible future events, with the capacity to remember past events being an exaptation. This

scenario is consistent with the argument of the present chapter, as the claim that memory is an exaptation does not imply that it does not tend to produce accurate representations of past events.

10. In a mirror image of this optimistic Reidian picture, Sperber et al. (2010) argue that, since dishonesty is often advantageous to communicators, it can be predicted to occur frequently—i.e., that we should predict that communicators are not honesty-biased. Moreover, since accepting dishonest testimony is normally disadvantageous, we can assume that hearers are not truth-biased but rather "epistemically vigilant"—i.e., on the alert for signs of deception. But if the strategy of dishonesty results in sufficiently infrequent dishonest testimony, we cannot infer that the default strategy must be one of vigilance toward deception; and, for general reasons, communication must be predominantly honest in order for it to have evolved (Searcy and Nowicki 2005). See Michaelian 2013 and Sperber 2013 for further discussion.

Chapter 8

1. Some researchers use the term "metacognition" more broadly, to refer simply to any thinking about thinking. See Proust (2010) for an overview.

2. The source problem arises because we are bound to rely on imperfect information sources. While it is natural to think of information sources as being imperfect to the extent that they produce inaccurate representations, a source is also imperfect to the extent that it *fails* to produce accurate representations. Hence memory, in particular, is imperfect not only in that retrieval sometimes produces inaccurate representations, but also in that attempts to retrieve the answer to a question are not always successful. This second type of imperfection gives rise to a distinct "selection problem": selecting one's information sources so that one receives the information one needs. It is likely that, just as a capacity for metacognition is crucial to explaining how agents solve the endorsement problem, metacognition will turn out to be crucial to explaining how agents solve the selection problem. Though the argument here focuses on retrospective evaluation, metacognitive monitoring also includes prospective evaluation (i.e., prediction of whether one's cognitive resources are sufficient for performing a given task; Proust 2013). Just as retrospective evaluation helps to explain how agents solve the endorsement problem, prospective evaluation may play a role in explaining how agents solve the selection problem. In the case of memory, an agent's feeling of knowing (Koriat 2000), perhaps along with other epistemic feelings (Arango-Muñoz and Michaelian 2014; Dokic 2014), might enable him to determine whether continued efforts to retrieve a given item from memory are likely to be successful, or whether he should instead abandon the attempt, perhaps to consult another source of information (Arango-Muñoz 2013; Michaelian 2014, Michaelian and Arango-Muñoz forthcoming).

3. This description of two-level processes assumes that it is possible for a system to entertain a representation without endorsing it; i.e., without representing it as true or accurate. Some have argued that representations are always initially endorsed, with rejection being a later, optional step (Gilbert et al. 1990, 1993). The argument here assumes for convenience that information can be represented without being endorsed, but the assumption is not necessary for the argument: those who sub-scribe to something like Gilbert's view (which can be challenged; see Hasson et al. 2005; Richter et al. 2009; Sperber et al. 2010) can treat the outputs of the informa-tion producer as beliefs which are later ratified (in which case they persist) or not (in which case they do not) by the endorsement mechanism. See the discussion below of modeling two-level processes as belief-dependent processes. An analogous point holds with respect to views on which imagination and belief are continuous (Liao and Doggett 2014; Schellenberg 2013; Sinhababu 2013).

4. At least as far as reliability is concerned; an endorsement mechanism might still be necessary for achieving an appropriate balance of reliability, power, and speed. See section 8.4 below.

5. Metacognitive mechanisms capable of initiating new processes might in principle play a role in enabling agents to solve the selection problem.

6. On the distinction between type 1 and type 2 processing, see Evans and Stanov-ich 2013; Frankish 2010; Thompson 2009; Thompson et al. 2013.

7. The emphasis in this section on attaining an acceptable balance of reliability, power, and speed is influenced by Lepock's version of virtue epistemology (2007; 2014). We might also wonder about the role of metamemory in enabling agents to avoid epistemic luck. As we will see, agents do have a genuine sensitivity to the ori-gins of remembered information, and metacognitive monitoring thus tends to mini-mize the role of luck in memory belief formation. The question of luck thus comes up primarily in cases—such as those discussed in chapter 7—in which the agent forms a true belief despite the inability of metamemory to accurately determine the origins of remembered information.

8. A similar but less flexible negotiation of the trade-off between reliability and power can be achieved by employing a much more sophisticated automatic endorse-ment policy, but this will involve a sacrifice in the speed of automatic monitoring.

9. See Mitchell and Johnson (2009) for a recent review of evidence in support of the framework.

Chapter 9

1. Another example may be provided by discovery misattribution (Dougal and Schooler 2007), in which the experience of solving a problem is confused with remembering, in a sort of inversion of cryptomnesia.

2. Similarly, there may be important differences between attempting to simulate another's experience and attempting to imagine the experience that one would have were one in another's place (Batson 2008; Wirling 2014).

3. Or, in some cases, reinterpreted—the discussion to follow will not be particularly concerned with textual faithfulness.

4. This section and the next two draw on Bernecker's survey of theories of memory markers (Bernecker 2008) but differ from the latter on many points. Klein (2014) comes to similar conclusions about a number of the criteria canvassed here.

5. The flexibility criterion might be taken to concern not remembered content but rather the extent to which the remembering subject is free to manipulate the generated representation. In this case, it is subject to the limitations noted for the spontaneity criterion discussed below.

6. More recently, Plantinga has described a feeling of pastness as playing an important role: "What is more important than the accompanying sensuous imagery is a sort of sense of *pastness*; a memory comes as of something past. ...A memory *comes* as about the past, or about something past (a past event, perhaps) in something like the way in which a belief about Sam comes as a belief about Sam. It has a sort of *past tinged* feel about it" (1993, 59).

7. The feeling of familiarity at issue here is distinct from the feeling of familiarity associated with semantic memory—as when subjects, asked to make remember/ know judgments, say, on the basis of a feeling of familiarity, that they *know* that an item was presented, as opposed to *remembering* its presentation (Rajaram 1993). The feeling of familiarity at issue in the context of process monitoring is a feeling that the internally constructed episode is familiar, as opposed to a feeling that an externally available item is familiar.

Chapter 10

1. On the emergence of the earliest forms of learning and memory, see Ginsburg and Jablonka 2007a, 2007b.

2. Since we have limited information about episodic memory in nonavian reptiles, they concede that current evidence is insufficient to determine whether episodic memory emerged before mammals and reptiles diverged, or whether the presence of analogous forms of episodic memory in mammals and birds is a result of convergent evolution.

3. In order to see the necessity of distinguishing between these two forms of subjective time, consider a scenario described by Dainton:

You wake up one day and are puzzled to discover that whereas you can venture only the haziest speculations as to what you were doing yesterday, or at any points in your past, you find yourself quite certain about exactly what you will be doing for the rest of the day, and for much of the remainder of your life. You still have what seem to be memories about your own experiences but, as you soon realize, the events you now "remember" have yet to occur. As the days and weeks pass, you learn that these future-oriented "memories" are just as reliable as their past-oriented counterparts: what you "remember" happening does happen. Despite this difference, the character of your experience remains essentially the same: the direction of immanent flow remains future-directed; you find your phenomenal present sliding forwards towards future events that you know will occur. Since phenomenal flow is an intrinsic feature of experience, its direction is independent of that of memory. (Dainton 2010, 116)

Essentially, what Dainton describes here is a scenario (similar to that described by the White Queen) in which the subject's mental time travel into the future somehow takes on the characteristics of mental time travel into the past. As he points out, this would leave the subject's sense of the temporal structure of his ongoing experience unaffected.

4. The notion of re-experiencing is also problematic to the extent that it suggests a simple repetition of an earlier experience. Given the constructive character of episodic memory, including the possibility of remembering events that one did not actually experience, episodic remembering should not be viewed as literal re-experiencing.

Chapter 11

1. Past-oriented explanations assume that memory's adaptivity presupposes its global reliability. While there are cases in which inaccurate memories can have adaptive benefits, these appear to be special cases (Fernández 2015) and therefore do not pose a problem for the assumption.

2. The relevant period is pre-1.6 million years ago (Plummer 2004). The explanation takes it for granted that anticipatory cognition was in place by the emergence of the Acheulean culture, which followed the Oldowan culture (Savage-Rumbaugh 1994). This is consistent with Mithen's argument that the sort of full-blown creative imagination necessary for art and science emerged only with *Homo sapiens* about 200,000 years ago (Mithen 2007).

3. If the simulation theory is right, of course, episodic memory may be *about* the past without necessarily being *of* the past.

4. Boyer might argue that the subjective dimension of, for example, simulation of inaccessible futures is a by-product of the motivational function of subjective awareness in simulation of probable possible futures. Even if this is right, however, the hypothesis accounts at most for autonoesis—consciousness of self—and leaves chronesthesia—consciousness of time—unexplained.

Chapter 12

1. For a less rustic example, consider Dokic's memory of a flight on the Concorde when he was three years old, which derives from being told about the episode by his parents when he was six years old (Dokic 2014).

References

Addis, D. R., A. T. Wong, and D. L. Schacter. 2007. Remembering the past and imagining the future: Common and distinct neural substrates during event construction and elaboration. *Neuropsychologia* 45 (7): 1363–1377.

Addis, D. R., L. Pan, M.-A. Vu, N. Laiser, and D. L. Schacter. 2009. Constructive episodic simulation of the future and the past: Distinct subsystems of a core brain network mediate imagining and remembering. *Neuropsychologia* 47 (11): 2222–2238.

Addis, D. R., R. P. Roberts, and D. L. Schacter. 2011. Age-related neural changes in autobiographical remembering and imagining. *Neuropsychologia* 49 (13): 3656–3669.

Adler, J. 2013. Epistemological problems of testimony. In E. N. Zalta (ed.), *The Stanford Encyclopedia of Philosophy* (Fall 2013 ed.). http://plato.stanford.edu/archives/spr2013/entries/testimony-_episprob/.

Ahlstrom-Vij, K. 2013. In defense of veritistic value monism. *Pacific Philosophical Quarterly* 94 (1): 19–40.

Alba, J. W., and L. Hasher. 1983. Is memory schematic? *Psychological Bulletin* 93 (2): 203–231.

Alea, N., and S. Bluck. 2003. Why are you telling me that? A conceptual model of the social function of autobiographical memory. *Memory* 11 (2): 165–178.

Allen, T. A., and N. J. Fortin. 2013. The evolution of episodic memory. *Proceedings of the National Academy of Sciences of the United States of America* 110 (Supplement 2): 10379–10386.

Alston, W. 1971. Varieties of privileged access. *American Philosophical Quarterly* 8 (3): 223–241.

Alston, W. P. 1978. Meta-ethics and meta-epistemology. In *Values and Morals*, ed. A. I. Goldman and J. Kim, 275–297. Springer.

Alston, W. P. 1986. Epistemic circularity. *Philosophy and Phenomenological Research* 47 (1): 1–30.

Alston, W. P. 1993. Epistemic desiderata. *Philosophy and Phenomenological Research* 53 (3): 527–551.

Anastasio, T. J., K. A. Ehrenberger, P. Watson, and W. Zhang. 2012. *Individual and Collective Memory Consolidation: Analogous Processes on Different Levels.* Cambridge, MA: MIT Press.

Andelman, F., D. Hoofien, I. Goldberg, O. Aizenstein, and M. Y. Neufeld. 2010. Bilateral hippocampal lesion and a selective impairment of the ability for mental time travel. *Neurocase* 16 (5): 426–435.

Anderson, J. R. 1990. *The Adaptive Character of Thought.* Hillsdale, NJ: Erlbaum.

Anderson, J. R., and R. Milson. 1989. Human memory: An adaptive perspective. *Psychological Review* 96 (4): 703–719.

Anderson, M. L. 2010. Neural reuse: A fundamental organizational principle of the brain. *Behavioral and Brain Sciences* 33 (04): 245–266.

Andrews-Hanna, J. R., J. S. Reidler, J. Sepulcre, R. Poulin, and R. L. Buckner. 2010. Functional-anatomic fractionation of the brain's default network. *Neuron* 65 (4): 550–562.

Arango-Muñoz, S. 2011. Two levels of metacognition. *Philosophia* 39 (1): 71–82.

Arango-Muñoz, S. 2013. Scaffolded memory and metacognitive feelings. *Review of Philosophy and Psychology* 4 (1): 135–152.

Arango-Muñoz, S. 2014. The nature of epistemic feelings. *Philosophical Psychology* 27 (2): 193–211.

Arango-Muñoz, S., and K. Michaelian. 2014. Epistemic feelings, epistemic emotions: Review and introduction to the focus section. *Philosophical Inquiries* 2 (1): 97–122.

Arnold, K., K. McDermott, and K. Szpunar. 2011. Imagining the near and far future: The role of location familiarity. *Memory & Cognition* 39 (6): 954–967.

Atance, C. M., and D. K. O'Neill. 2001. Episodic future thinking. *Trends in Cognitive Sciences* 5 (12): 533–539.

Atance, C. M., and D. K. O'Neill. 2005. The emergence of episodic future thinking in humans. *Learning and Motivation* 36 (2): 126–144.

Audi, R. 1995. Memorial justification. *Philosophical Topics* 23:31–45.

Audi, R. 2002. The sources of knowledge. In *Oxford Handbook of Epistemology,* ed. P. Moser, 71–94. Oxford: Oxford University Press.

Augustine, S. (398). *Confessions.* Translation by A. C. Outler available at http://www.georgetown.edu/faculty/jod/augustine/conf.pdf.

Ayer, A. J. 1956. *The Problem of Knowledge.* London: Macmillan.

Ayers, M., and L. Reder. 1998. A theoretical review of the misinformation effect: Predictions from an activation-based memory model. *Psychonomic Bulletin & Review* 5 (1): 1–21.

Babb, S. J., and J. D. Crystal. 2006. Episodic-like memory in the rat. *Current Biology* 16 (13): 1317–1321.

Baddeley, A. 2012. Working memory: Theories, models, and controversies. *Annual Review of Psychology* 63 (1): 1–29.

Bahrick, H. P., L. K. Hall, and S. A. Berger. 1996. Accuracy and distortion in memory for high school grades. *Psychological Science* 7 (5): 265–271.

Baird, B., J. Smallwood, and J. W. Schooler. 2011. Back to the future: Autobiographical planning and the functionality of mind-wandering. *Consciousness and Cognition* 20 (4): 1604–1611.

Bartlett, F. C. 1932. *Remembering: A Study in Experimental and Social Psychology*. Cambridge: Cambridge University Press.

Batson, C. D. 2008. Two forms of perspective taking: Imagining how another feels and imagining how you would feel. In *Handbook of Imagination and Mental Simulation*, ed. K. D. Markman, W. M. P. Klein and J. A. Suhr, 268–279. New York: Psychology Press.

Becker, K. 2013. Why reliabilism does not permit easy knowledge. *Synthese* 190 (17): 3751–3775.

Benoit, R. G., S. J. Gilbert, and P. W. Burgess. 2011. A neural mechanism mediating the impact of episodic prospection on farsighted decisions. *Journal of Neuroscience* 31 (18): 6771–6779.

Bergson, H. 1896. *Matière et mémoire: Essai sur la relation du corps a l'esprit*. Paris: Félix Alcan.

Bernecker, S. 2007. Remembering without knowing. *Australasian Journal of Philosophy* 85 (1): 137–156.

Bernecker, S. 2008. *The Metaphysics of Memory*. Springer.

Bernecker, S. 2010. *Memory: A Philosophical Study*. Oxford: Oxford University Press.

Berntsen, D. 2009. *Involuntary Autobiographical Memories: An Introduction to the Unbidden Past*. Cambridge: Cambridge University Press.

Berntsen, D., and A. Bohn. 2010. Remembering and forecasting: The relation. *Memory & Cognition* 38 (3): 265–278.

Berntsen, D., and A. S. Jacobsen. 2008. Involuntary (spontaneous) mental time travel into the past and future. *Consciousness and Cognition* 17 (4): 1093–1104.

Bishop, M. A., and J. D. Trout. 2005. *Epistemology and the Psychology of Human Judgment*. Oxford: Oxford University Press.

Bloch, D. 2007. *Aristotle on Memory and Recollection: Text, Translation, Interpretation, and Reception in Western Scholasticism*. Leiden: Brill.

Bok, S. 2011. *Lying: Moral Choice in Public and Private Life*. New York: Random House.

Boyd, R. 1999. Homeostasis, species, and higher taxa. In *Species: New Interdisciplinary Essays*, ed. R. A. Wilson, 141–185. Cambridge, MA: MIT Press.

Boyer, P. 2008. Evolutionary economics of mental time travel? *Trends in Cognitive Sciences* 12 (6): 219–224.

Boyer, P. 2009. What are memories for? Functions of recall in cognition and culture. In *Memory in Mind and Culture*, ed. P. Boyer and J. V. Wertsch, 1–26. Cambridge: Cambridge University Press.

Brainerd, C., and V. Reyna. 2002. Fuzzy-trace theory and false memory. *Current Directions in Psychological Science* 11 (5): 164–169.

Brainerd, C. J., and V. F. Reyna. 2005. *The Science of False Memory*. Oxford: Oxford University Press.

Brewer, W. F. 1996. What is recollective memory? In *Remembering Our Past: Studies in Autobiographical Memory*, ed. D. C. Rubin, 19–66. Cambridge: Cambridge University Press.

Broad, C. 1925. *The Mind and its Place in Nature*. New York: The Humanities Press.

Brook, A. 2009. Introduction: Philosophy in and philosophy of cognitive science. *Topics in Cognitive Science* 1 (2): 216–230.

Brown, A. S., and D. R. Murphy. 1989. Cryptomnesia: Delineating inadvertent plagiarism. *Journal of Experimental Psychology: Learning, Memory, and Cognition* 15 (3): 432–442.

Buckner, R., and D. Carroll. 2007. Self-projection and the brain. *Trends in Cognitive Sciences* 11 (2): 49–57.

Buckner, R. L., J. R. Andrews-Hanna, and D. L. Schacter. 2008. The brain's default network: Anatomy, function, and relevance to disease. *Annals of the New York Academy of Sciences* 1124 (1): 1–38.

Burge, T. 1993. Content preservation. *Philosophical Review* 102 (4): 457–488.

Burge, T. 2003. Memory and persons. *Philosophical Review* 112 (3): 289–337.

Burnham, W. H. 1888. Memory, historically and experimentally considered. I. An historical sketch of the older conceptions of memory. *American Journal of Psychology* 2 (1): 39–90.

Byrne, A. 2010. Recollection, perception, imagination. *Philosophical Studies* 148 (1): 15–26.

Byrne, R. 2007. *The Rational Imagination*. Cambridge, MA: MIT Press.

Caruso, E. M. 2010. When the future feels worse than the past: A temporal inconsistency in moral judgment. *Journal of Experimental Psychology. General* 139 (4): 610–624.

Caruso, E. M., D. T. Gilbert, and T. D. Wilson. 2008. A wrinkle in time. *Psychological Science* 19 (8): 796–801.

Cheke, L. G., and N. S. Clayton. 2010. Mental time travel in animals. *Wiley Interdisciplinary Reviews: Cognitive Science* 1 (6): 915–930.

Cheng, S., and M. Werning. Forthcoming. What is episodic memory if it is a natural kind? *Synthese*.

Churchland, P. S. 1986. *Neurophilosophy: Toward a Unified Science of the Mind/Brain*. Cambridge, MA: MIT Press.

Ciaramelli, E., S. Ghetti, M. Frattarelli, and E. Làdavas. 2006. When true memory availability promotes false memory: Evidence from confabulating patients. *Neuropsychologia* 44 (10): 1866–1877.

Ciranni, M. A., and A. P. Shimamura. 1999. Retrieval-induced forgetting in episodic memory. *Journal of Experimental Psychology: Learning, Memory, and Cognition* 25 (6): 1403–1414.

Clayton, N. S., and A. Dickinson. 1998. Episodic-like memory during cache recovery by scrub jays. *Nature* 395 (6699): 272–274.

Coady, C. A. J. 1992. *Testimony: A Philosophical Study*. Oxford: Oxford University Press.

Cohen, N., and L. Squire. 1980. Preserved learning and retention of pattern-analyzing skill in amnesia: Dissociation of knowing how and knowing that. *Science* 210 (4466): 207–210.

Comesana, J. 2007. Knowledge and subjunctive conditionals. *Philosophy Compass* 2 (6): 781–791.

Conee, E., and R. Feldman. 1998. The generality problem for reliabilism. *Philosophical Studies* 89 (1): 1–29.

Conway, M. A. 2005. Memory and the self. *Journal of Memory and Language* 53 (4): 594–628.

Corballis, M. C. 2011. *The Recursive Mind: The Origins of Human Language, Thought, and Civilization*. Princeton, NJ: Princeton University Press.

Corballis, M. C. 2013. Mental time travel: A case for evolutionary continuity. *Trends in Cognitive Sciences* 17 (1): 5–6.

Cosentino, E. 2011. Self in time and language. *Consciousness and Cognition* 20 (3): 777–783.

Cosmides, L., and J. Tooby. 2000. Consider the source: The evolution of adaptations for decoupling and metarepresentation. In *Metarepresentations: A Multidisciplinary Perspective*, ed. D. Sperber, 53–115. Oxford: Oxford University Press.

Craver, C. F., F. Cova, L. Green, J. Myerson, R. S. Rosenbaum, D. Kwan, and S. Bourgeois-Gironde. 2014. An Allais paradox without mental time travel. *Hippocampus* 24 (11): 1375–1380.

Crawley, R., and M. Eacott. 2006. Memories of early childhood: Qualities of the experience of recollection. *Memory & Cognition* 34 (2): 287–294.

Crystal, J. D. 2010. Episodic-like memory in animals. *Behavioural Brain Research* 215 (2): 235–243.

Currie, G., and I. Ravenscroft. 2002. *Recreative Minds: Imagination in Philosophy and Psychology*. Oxford: Oxford University Press.

Dainton, B. 2010. *Time and Space*. 2nd ed. Durham: Acumen.

Dalla Barba, G. 1993. Different patterns of confabulation. *Cortex* 29 (4): 567–581.

Dalla Barba, G. 2001. Beyond the memory-trace paradox and the fallacy of the homunculus: A hypothesis concerning the relationship between memory, consciousness and temporality. *Journal of Consciousness Studies* 8 (3): 51–78.

Dalla Barba, G., and M.-F. Boissé. 2009. Temporal consciousness and confabulation: Is the medial temporal lobe "temporal"? *Cognitive Neuropsychiatry* 15 (1–3): 95–117.

Dalla Barba, G., J. Y. Cappelletti, M. Signorini, and G. Denes. 1997. Confabulation: Remembering "another" past, planning "another" future. *Neurocase* 3 (6): 425–436.

Dalla Barba, G., and V. La Corte. 2013. The hippocampus, a time machine that makes errors. *Trends in Cognitive Sciences* 17 (3): 102–104.

Dalla Barba, G., M. C. Mantovan, E. Ferruzza, and G. Denes. 1997. Remembering and knowing the past: A case study of isolated retrograde amnesia. *Cortex* 33 (1): 143–154.

Daniel, T. O., C. M. Stanton, and L. H. Epstein. 2013. The future is now: Comparing the effect of episodic future thinking on impulsivity in lean and obese individuals. *Appetite* 71:120–125.

D'Argembeau, A., O. Renaud, and M. Van der Linden. 2011. Frequency, characteristics and functions of future-oriented thoughts in daily life. *Applied Cognitive Psychology* 25 (1): 96–103.

D'Argembeau, A., and M. Van der Linden. 2004. Phenomenal characteristics associated with projecting oneself back into the past and forward into the future: Influence of valence and temporal distance. *Consciousness and Cognition* 13 (4): 844–858.

D'Argembeau, A., and M. Van der Linden. 2006. Individual differences in the phenomenology of mental time travel: The effect of vivid visual imagery and emotion regulation strategies. *Consciousness and Cognition* 15 (2): 342–350.

D'Argembeau, A., and M. Van der Linden. 2012. Predicting the phenomenology of episodic future thoughts. *Consciousness and Cognition* 21 (3): 1198–1206.

Daw, N. D., Y. Niv, and P. Dayan. 2005. Uncertainty-based competition between prefrontal and dorsolateral striatal systems for behavioral control. *Nature Neuroscience* 8 (12): 1704–1711.

De Brigard, F. 2014a. Is memory for remembering? Recollection as a form of episodic hypothetical thinking. *Synthese* 191 (2): 155–185.

De Brigard, F. 2014b. The nature of memory traces. *Philosophy Compass* 9 (6): 402–414.

De Brigard, F., D. Addis, J. Ford, D. Schacter, and K. Giovanello. 2013. Remembering what could have happened: Neural correlates of episodic counterfactual thinking. *Neuropsychologia* 51 (12): 2401–2414.

De Brigard, F., and K. S. Giovanello. 2012. Influence of outcome valence in the subjective experience of episodic past, future, and counterfactual thinking. *Consciousness and Cognition* 21 (3): 1085–1096.

De Brigard, F., K. K. Szpunar, and D. L. Schacter. 2013. Coming to grips with the past: Effect of repeated simulation on the perceived plausibility of episodic counterfactual thoughts. *Psychological Science* 24 (7): 1329–1334.

De Sousa, R. 2008. Epistemic feelings. In *Epistemology and Emotions*, ed. U. Doğuoğlu and D. Kuenzle, 185–204. Aldershot: Ashgate.

De Vito, S., N. Gamboz, and M. A. Brandimonte. 2012. What differentiates episodic future thinking from complex scene imagery? *Consciousness and Cognition* 21 (2): 813–823.

Debus, D. 2008. Experiencing the past: A relational account of recollective memory. *Dialectica* 62 (4): 405–432.

Debus, D. 2014. "Mental time travel": Remembering the past, imagining the future, and the particularity of events. *Review of Philosophy and Psychology* 5 (3): 333–350.

Deese, J. 1959. On the prediction of occurrence of particular verbal intrusions in immediate recall. *Journal of Experimental Psychology* 58 (1): 17–22.

Dennett, D. 1987. *The Intentional Stance*. Cambridge, MA: MIT Press.

DePaul, M. 2001. Value monism in epistemology. In *Knowledge, Truth, and Duty: Essays on Epistemic Justification, Responsibility, and Virtue*, ed. M. Steup, 170–186. Oxford: Oxford University Press.

DePaulo, B. M., D. A. Kashy, S. E. Kirkendol, M. M. Wyer, and J. A. Epstein. 1996. Lying in everyday life. *Journal of Personality and Social Psychology* 70 (5): 979–995.

Dokic, J. 2001. Is memory purely preservative? In *Time and Memory: Issues in Philosophy and Psychology*, ed. C. Hoerl and T. McCormack, 213–232. Oxford: Oxford University Press.

Dokic, J. 2012. Seeds of self-knowledge: Noetic feelings and metacognition. In *Foundations of Metacognition*, ed. M. Beran, J. Brandl, J. Perner and J. Proust, 302–321. Oxford: Oxford University Press.

Dokic, J. 2014a. Feeling the past: A two-tiered account of episodic memory. *Review of Philosophy and Psychology* 5 (3): 413–426.

Dokic, J. 2014b. Feelings of (un)certainty and margins for error. *Philosophical Inquiries* 2 (1): 123–144.

Dougal, S., and J. W. Schooler. 2007. Discovery misattribution: When solving is confused with remembering. *Journal of Experimental Psychology. General* 136 (4): 577–592.

Draaisma, D. 2000. *Metaphors of Memory: A History of Ideas about the Mind*. Cambridge, MA: Cambridge University Press.

Droege, P. 2013. Memory and consciousness. *Philosophia Scientiæ* 17 (2): 171–193.

Dudai, Y. 2004. The neurobiology of consolidations, or, how stable is the engram? *Annual Review of Psychology* 55 (1): 51–86.

Dummett, M. 1994. Memory and testimony. In *Knowing from Words: Western and Indian Philosophical Analysis of Understanding and Testimony*, ed. B. K. Matilal and A. Chakrabarty, 251–272. Springer.

Dunlosky, J., and J. Metcalfe. 2008. *Metacognition*. Los Angeles, CA: Sage.

Eacott, M. J., and A. Easton. 2012. Remembering the past and thinking about the future: Is it really about time? *Learning and Motivation* 43 (4): 200–208.

Earle, W. 1956. Memory. *Review of Metaphysics* 10:3–27.

Ebbinghaus, H. 1885. *Über das Gedächtnis*. Leipzig: Duncker und Humblot.

Eichenbaum, H. 2010. Memory systems. *Wiley Interdisciplinary Reviews: Cognitive Science* 1 (4): 478–490.

Eichenbaum, H., N. J. Fortin, C. Ergorul, S. P. Wright, and K. L. Agster. 2005. Episodic recollection in animals: "If it walks like a duck and quacks like a duck …" *Learning and Motivation* 36 (2): 190–207.

Erdelyi, M. H., and J. Becker. 1974. Hypermnesia for pictures: Incremental memory for pictures but not words in multiple recall trials. *Cognitive Psychology* 6 (1): 159–171.

Evans, J. S. B. T., and K. E. Stanovich. 2013. Dual-process theories of higher cognition: Advancing the debate. *Perspectives on Psychological Science* 8 (3): 223–241.

Ezzyat, Y., and L. Davachi. 2011. What constitutes an episode in episodic memory? *Psychological Science* 22 (2): 243–252.

Feeney, M., W. Roberts, and D. Sherry. 2009. Memory for what, where, and when in the black-capped chickadee (*poecile atricapillus*). *Animal Cognition* 12 (6): 767–777.

Feeney, M. C., and W. A. Roberts. 2012. Comparative mental time travel: Is there a cognitive divide between humans and animals in episodic memory and planning? In *The Oxford Handbook of Comparative Evolutionary Psychology*, ed. J. Vonk and T. K. Shackelford, 236–260. Oxford: Oxford University Press.

Feest, U. 2011. Remembering (short-term) memory: Oscillations of an epistemic thing. *Erkenntnis* 75 (3): 391–411.

Feldman, R. 1985. Reliability and justification. *Monist* 68 (2): 159–174.

Fernández, J. 2006. The intentionality of memory. *Australasian Journal of Philosophy* 84 (1): 39–57.

Fernández, J. 2008. Memory and time. *Philosophical Studies* 141 (3): 333–356.

Fernández, J. 2015. What are the benefits of memory distortion? *Consciousness and Cognition* 33 (0): 536–547.

Fernández, J. Forthcoming. Epistemic generation in memory. *Philosophy and Phenomenological Research*.

Finnbogadóttir, H., and D. Berntsen. 2013. Involuntary future projections are as frequent as involuntary memories, but more positive. *Consciousness and Cognition* 22 (1): 272–280.

Fischhoff, B., and R. Beyth. 1975. "I knew it would happen": Remembered probabilities of once-future things. *Organizational Behavior and Human Performance* 13 (1): 1–16.

Flage, D. E. 1985. Hume on memory and causation. *Hume Studies* 10: 168–188.

Foster, J. K., and M. Jelicic, eds. 1999. *Memory: Systems, Process, or Function*. Oxford: Oxford University Press.

Frankish, K. 2010. Dual-process and dual-system theories of reasoning. *Philosophy Compass* 5 (10): 914–926.

Fricker, E. 1994. Against gullibility. In *Knowing from Words: Western and Indian Philosophical Analysis of Understanding and Testimony*, ed. B. K. Matilal and A. Chakrabarti, 125–161. Springer.

Fricker, E. 1995. Telling and trusting: Reductionism and anti-reductionism in the epistemology of testimony. *Mind* 104 (414): 393–411.

Fricker, E. 2006. Second-hand knowledge. *Philosophy and Phenomenological Research* 73 (3): 592–618.

Furlong, E. 1951. *A Study in Memory: A Philosophical Essay.* London: Thomas Nelson.

Furlong, E. J. 1948. Memory. *Mind* 57 (225): 16–44.

Furlong, E. J. 1953. Memory and the argument from illusion. *Proceedings of the Aristotelian Society* 54:131–144.

Gabbert, F., A. Memon, and D. Wright. 2007. I saw it for longer than you: The relationship between perceived encoding duration and memory conformity. *Acta Psychologica* 124 (3): 319–331.

Gaesser, B., D. C. Sacchetti, D. R. R. Addis, and D. L. Schacter. 2011. Characterizing age-related changes in remembering the past and imagining the future. *Psychology and Aging* 26 (1): 80–84.

Gaffan, D. 2002. Against memory systems. *Philosophical Transactions of the Royal Society of London. Series B, Biological Sciences* 357 (1424): 1111–1121.

Gallagher, S. 2000. Philosophical conceptions of the self: Implications for cognitive science. *Trends in Cognitive Sciences* 4 (1): 14–21.

Gallo, D. A. 2010. False memories and fantastic beliefs: 15 years of the DRM illusion. *Memory & Cognition* 38 (7): 833–848.

Gamboz, N., M. A. Brandimonte, and S. De Vito. 2010. The role of past in the simulation of autobiographical future episodes. *Experimental Psychology* 57 (6): 419–428.

Gärdenfors, P. 1995. Cued and detached representations in animal cognition. *Behavioural Processes* 35 (13): 263–273.

Gardiner, J. M. 2001. Episodic memory and autonoetic consciousness: A first-person approach. *Philosophical Transactions of the Royal Society of London. Series B, Biological Sciences* 356 (1413): 1351–1361.

Garry, M., C. Manning, E. Loftus, and S. Sherman. 1996. Imagination inflation: Imagining a childhood event inflates confidence that it occurred. *Psychonomic Bulletin & Review* 3 (2): 208–214.

Gelfert, A. 2014. *A Critical Introduction to Testimony.* London: Bloomsbury.

Gennaro, R. J. 1992. Consciousness, self-consciousness and episodic memory. *Philosophical Psychology* 5 (4): 333–347.

Geraerts, E., J. W. Schooler, H. Merckelbach, M. Jelicic, B. J. A. Hauer, and Z. Ambadar. 2007. The reality of recovered memories: Corroborating continuous and discontinuous memories of childhood sexual abuse. *Psychological Science* 18 (7): 564–568.

Gilbert, D. T., D. S. Krull, and P. S. Malone. 1990. Unbelieving the unbelievable: Some problems in the rejection of false information. *Journal of Personality and Social Psychology* 59 (4): 601–613.

Gilbert, D. T., R. W. Tafarodi, and P. S. Malone. 1993. You can't not believe everything you read. *Journal of Personality and Social Psychology* 65 (2): 221–233.

Gilbert, D. T., and T. D. Wilson. 2007. Prospection: Experiencing the future. *Science* 317 (5843): 1351–1354.

Ginsburg, S., and E. Jablonka. 2007a. The transition to experiencing I: Limited learning and limited experiencing. *Biological Theory* 2 (3): 218–230.

Ginsburg, S., and E. Jablonka. 2007b. The transition to experiencing II: The evolution of associative learning based on feelings. *Biological Theory* 2 (3): 231–243.

Goff, L., and H. Roediger. 1998. Imagination inflation for action events: Repeated imaginings lead to illusory recollections. *Memory & Cognition* 26 (1): 20–33.

Goldman, A. I. 1986. *Epistemology and Cognition*. Cambridge, MA: Harvard University Press.

Goldman, A. I. 1992. *Liaisons: Philosophy Meets the Cognitive and Social Sciences*. Cambridge, MA: MIT Press.

Goldman, A. I. 2006. *Simulating Minds: The Philosophy, Psychology, and Neuroscience of Mindreading*. Oxford: Oxford University Press.

Goldman, A. I. 2012. *Reliabilism and Contemporary Epistemology: Essays*. Oxford: Oxford University Press.

Gopnik, A. 1997. *Words, Thoughts, and Theories*. Cambridge, MA: MIT Press.

Gould, S. J., and R. C. Lewontin. 1979. The spandrels of San Marco and the Panglossian paradigm: A critique of the adaptationist programme. *Proceedings of the Royal Society of London. Series B, Biological Sciences* 205 (1161): 581–598.

Green, A. 2014. Evaluating distributed cognition. *Synthese* 91 (1): 79–95.

Griffiths, D., A. Dickinson, and N. Clayton. 1999. Episodic memory: What can animals remember about their past? *Trends in Cognitive Sciences* 3 (2): 74–80.

Grysman, A., J. Prabhakar, S. M. Anglin, and J. A. Hudson. 2013. The time travelling self: Comparing self and other in narratives of past and future events. *Consciousness and Cognition* 22 (3): 742–755.

Hamilton, A. 2003. "Scottish commonsense" about memory. *Australasian Journal of Philosophy* 81 (2): 229–245.

Hamlyn, D. W. 1970. *The Theory of Knowledge*. Garden City, NY: Anchor.

Harris, C. B., A. S. Rasmussen, and D. Berntsen. 2014. The functions of autobiographical memory: An integrative approach. *Memory* 22 (5): 559–581.

Hassabis, D., D. Kumaran, and E. A. Maguire. 2007a. Using imagination to understand the neural basis of episodic memory. *Journal of Neuroscience* 27 (52): 14365–14374.

Hassabis, D., D. Kumaran, S. D. Vann, and E. A. Maguire. 2007b. Patients with hippocampal amnesia cannot imagine new experiences. *Proceedings of the National Academy of Sciences of the United States of America* 104 (5): 1726–1731.

Hassabis, D., and E. Maguire. 2007. Deconstructing episodic memory with construction. *Trends in Cognitive Sciences* 11 (7): 299–306.

Hassabis, D., and E. A. Maguire. 2009. The construction system of the brain. *Philosophical Transactions of the Royal Society of London. Series B, Biological Sciences* 364 (1521): 1263–1271.

Hasson, U., J. P. Simmons, and A. Todorov. 2005. Believe it or not: On the possibility of suspending belief. *Psychological Science* 16 (7): 566–571.

Hazlett, A. 2010. The myth of factive verbs. *Philosophy and Phenomenological Research* 80 (3): 497–522.

Hesslow, G. 2012. The current status of the simulation theory of cognition. *Brain Research* 1428 (0): 71–79.

Hetherington, S. 1999. Knowing failably. *Journal of Philosophy* 96 (11): 565–587.

Hirst, W., and G. Echterhoff. 2012. Remembering in conversations: The social sharing and reshaping of memories. *Annual Review of Psychology* 63 (1): 55–79.

Hoerl, C. 2008. On being stuck in time. *Phenomenology and the Cognitive Sciences* 7 (4): 485–500.

Hoerl, C. 2014. Remembering events and remembering looks. *Review of Philosophy and Psychology* 5 (3): 351–372.

Hoerl, C., and T. McCormack. 2001. The child in time: Temporal concepts and self-consciousness in the development of episodic memory. In *The Self in Time: Developmental Perspectives*, ed. K. Lemmon and C. Moore, 203–227. Mahway, NJ: Lawrence Erlbaum.

Hoffman, M. L., M. J. Beran, and D. A. Washburn. 2009. Memory for what, where, and when information in rhesus monkeys (*macaca mulatta*). *Journal of Experimental Psychology. Animal Behavior Processes* 35 (2): 143.

Hoffrage, U., R. Hertwig, and G. Gigerenzer. 2000. Hindsight bias: A by-product of knowledge updating? *Journal of Experimental Psychology: Learning, Memory, and Cognition* 26 (3): 566.

Holland, A. 1974. Retained knowledge. *Mind* 83 (331): 355–371.

Holland, R. F. 1954. The empiricist theory of memory. *Mind* 63 (252): 464–486.

Holliday, R. E., and B. K. Hayes. 2002. Automatic and intentional processes in children's recognition memory: The reversed misinformation effect. *Applied Cognitive Psychology* 16 (1): 1–16.

Hopkins, R. 2014. Episodic memory as representing the past to oneself. *Review of Philosophy and Psychology* 5 (3): 313–331.

Hopkins, R. forthcoming. Imagining the past: On the nature of episodic memory. In *Memory and Imagination*, ed. F. Macpherson and F. Dorsch. Oxford: Oxford University Press.

Horvath, J. forthcoming. Conceptual analysis and natural kinds: The case of knowledge.

Howe, M. L., and M. L. Courage. 1993. On resolving the enigma of infantile amnesia. *Psychological Bulletin* 113 (2): 305.

Huber, F., and C. Schmidt-Petri, eds. 2009. *Degrees of Belief.* Springer.

Hume, D. 1739. *A Treatise of Human Nature.* London: John Noon.

Husserl, E. 1990. *On the phenomenology of the consciousness of internal time (1893–1917).* Trans. J. B. Brough. Dordrecht: Kluwer.

Hyman, I. E., T. H. Husband, and F. J. Billings. 1995. False memories of childhood experiences. *Applied Cognitive Psychology* 9 (3): 181–197.

Hyman, I. E., Jr., and J. Pentland. 1996. The role of mental imagery in the creation of false childhood memories. *Journal of Memory and Language* 35 (2): 101–117.

Intraub, H. 2010. Rethinking scene perception: A multisource model. In *Psychology of Learning and Motivation*, ed. B. Ross, 231–264. Academic Press.

Intraub, H., R. S. Bender, and J. A. Mangels. 1992. Looking at pictures but remembering scenes. *Journal of Experimental Psychology: Learning, Memory, and Cognition* 18:180–191.

Ismael, J. 2011. Decision and the open future. In *The Future of the Philosophy of Time*, ed. A. Bardon, 149–168. London: Routledge.

James, W. 1890. *The Principles of Psychology.* London: Macmillan.

Johnson, M., and C. Raye. 1981. Reality monitoring. *Psychological Review* 88 (1): 67–85.

Johnson, M. K. 1997. Source monitoring and memory distortion. *Philosophical Transactions of the Royal Society of London. Series B, Biological Sciences* 352 (1362): 1733–1745.

Johnson, M. K., S. Hashtroudi, and D. S. Lindsay. 1993. Source monitoring. *Psychological Bulletin* 114 (1): 3–28.

Johnson, M. K., and C. L. Raye. 2000. Cognitive and brain mechanisms of false memories and beliefs. In *Memory, Brain, and Belief*, ed. D. L. Schacter and E. Scarry, 35–86. Cambridge, MA: Harvard University Press.

Kandel, E. R., and C. Pittenger. 1999. The past, the future and the biology of memory storage. *Philosophical Transactions of the Royal Society of London. Series B, Biological Sciences* 354 (1392): 2027–2052.

Kelly, T. 2003. Epistemic rationality as instrumental rationality: A critique. *Philosophy and Phenomenological Research* 66 (3): 612–640.

Kim, J. J., and M. G. Baxter. 2001. Multiple brain-memory systems: The whole does not equal the sum of its parts. *Trends in Neurosciences* 24 (6): 324–330.

Kind, A. 2013. The heterogeneity of the imagination. *Erkenntnis* 78 (1): 141–159.

Kirsh, D. 1992. When is information explicitly represented? In *Vancouver Studies in Cognitive Science*, 340–365. Oxford: Oxford University Press.

Klein, S. B. 2013a. The complex act of projecting oneself into the future. *Wiley Interdisciplinary Reviews: Cognitive Science* 4 (1): 63–79.

Klein, S. B. 2013b. Looking ahead: Memory and subjective temporality. *Journal of Applied Research in Memory and Cognition* 2 (4): 254–258.

Klein, S. B. 2013c. The temporal orientation of memory: It's time for a change of direction. *Journal of Applied Research in Memory and Cognition* 2 (4): 222–234.

Klein, S. B. 2014. Autonoesis and belief in a personal past: An evolutionary theory of episodic memory indices. *Review of Philosophy and Psychology* 5 (3): 427–447.

Klein, S. B. 2015. What memory is. *Wiley Interdisciplinary Reviews: Cognitive Science* 6 (1): 1–38.

Klein, S. B., L. Cosmides, C. E. Gangi, B. Jackson, J. Tooby, and K. A. Costabile. 2009. Evolution and episodic memory: An analysis and demonstration of a social function of episodic recollection. *Social Cognition* 27 (2): 283–319.

Klein, S. B., L. Cosmides, J. Tooby, and S. Chance. 2002. Decisions and the evolution of memory: Multiple systems, multiple functions. *Psychological Review* 109 (2): 306.

Klein, S. B., J. Loftus, and J. F. Kihlstrom. 2002. Memory and temporal experience: The effects of episodic memory loss on an amnesic patient's ability to remember the past and imagine the future. *Social Cognition* 20 (5): 353–379.

Klein, S. B., and S. Nichols. 2012. Memory and the sense of personal identity. *Mind* 121 (483): 677–702.

Knobe, J. 2015. Philosophers are doing something different now: Quantitative data. *Cognition* 135 (0): 36–38.

Koriat, A. 2000. The feeling of knowing: Some metatheoretical implications for consciousness and control. *Consciousness and Cognition* 9 (2): 149–171.

Koriat, A., and S. Adiv. 2012. Confidence in one's social beliefs: Implications for belief justification. *Consciousness and Cognition* 21 (4): 1599–1616.

Koriat, A., and M. Goldsmith. 1996. Memory metaphors and the real-life/laboratory controversy: Correspondence versus storehouse conceptions of memory. *Behavioral and Brain Sciences* 19 (02): 167–188.

Koriat, A., M. Goldsmith, and A. Pansky. 2000. Toward a psychology of memory accuracy. *Annual Review of Psychology* 51:481–537.

Kornblith, H. 1995. *Inductive Inference and its Natural Ground: An Essay in Naturalistic Epistemology.* Cambridge, MA: MIT Press.

Kornblith, H. 2003. *Knowledge and its Place in Nature.* Oxford: Oxford University Press.

Kumar, V. 2014. "Knowledge" as a natural kind term. *Synthese* 191 (3): 439–457.

Kwan, D., C. F. Craver, L. Green, J. Myerson, P. Boyer, and R. S. Rosenbaum. 2012. Future decision-making without episodic mental time travel. *Hippocampus* 22 (6): 1215–1219.

Kwan, D., C. F. Craver, L. Green, J. Myerson, and R. S. Rosenbaum. 2013. Dissociations in future thinking following hippocampal damage: Evidence from discounting and time perspective in episodic amnesia. *Journal of Experimental Psychology. General* 142 (4): 1355–1369.

Lackey, J. 2005. Memory as a generative epistemic source. *Philosophy and Phenomenological Research* 70 (3): 636–658.

Lackey, J. 2007a. Why memory really is a generative epistemic source: A reply to Senor. *Philosophy and Phenomenological Research* 74 (1): 209–219.

Lackey, J. 2007b. Why we don't deserve credit for everything we know. *Synthese* 158 (3): 345–361.

Lackey, J. 2008. *Learning from Words: Testimony as a Source of Knowledge.* Oxford: Oxford University Press.

Lashley, K. S. 1950. In search of the engram. *Symposia of the Society for Experimental Biology* 4:454–482.

Latus, A. 2000. Moral and epistemic luck. *Journal of Philosophical Research* 25:149–172.

Lee, A. C., L.-K. Yeung, and M. D. Barense. 2012. The hippocampus and visual perception. *Frontiers in Human Neuroscience* 6: 91.

Lepock, C. 2007. *Metacognition and intellectual virtue*. Ph. D. thesis, University of Alberta.

Lepock, C. 2014. Metacognition and intellectual virtue. In *Virtue Epistemology Naturalized: Bridges between Virtue Epistemology and Philosophy of Science*, ed. A. Fairweather. Springer.

Levine, B., S. E. Black, R. Cabeza, M. Sinden, A. R. Mcintosh, J. P. Toth, E. Tulving, and D. T. Stuss. 1998. Episodic memory and the self in a case of isolated retrograde amnesia. *Brain* 121 (10): 1951–1973.

Levine, L. J. 1997. Reconstructing memory for emotions. *Journal of Experimental Psychology. General* 126 (2): 165–177.

Levine, T. R., R. K. Kim, and L. M. Hamel. 2010. People lie for a reason: Three experiments documenting the principle of veracity. *Communication Research Reports* 27 (4): 271–285.

Levine, T. R., R. K. Kim, H. S. Park, and M. Hughes. 2006. Deception detection accuracy is a predictable linear function of message veracity base-rate: A formal test of Park and Levine's probability model. *Communication Monographs* 73 (3): 243–260.

Levine, T. R., H. S. Park, and S. A. McCornack. 1999. Accuracy in detecting truths and lies: Documenting the "veracity effect." *Communication Monographs* 66 (2): 125–144.

Liao, S., and T. Doggett. 2014. The imagination box. *Journal of Philosophy* 111 (5): 259–275.

Liao, S., and A. Sandberg. 2008. The normativity of memory modification. *Neuroethics* 1 (2): 85–99.

Lindsay, D. 1994. Memory source monitoring and eyewitness testimony. In D. Ross, J. Read, and M. Toglia (ed.), *Adult Eyewitness Testimony: Current Trends and Developments*. Cambridge: Cambridge University Press.

Lindsay, D. S., and J. D. Read. 2005. The recovered memories controversy: Where do we go from here? In *Recovered Memories: Seeking the Middle Ground*, ed. G. M. Davies and T. Dalgleish, 69–93. Chichester: Wiley.

Lindsay, S., and M. Johnson. 1989. The reversed eyewitness suggestibility effect. *Bulletin of the Psychonomic Society* 27 (2): 111–113.

Locke, D. 1971. *Memory*. London: Macmillan.

Locke, J. 1689. *An Essay Concerning Human Understanding*. London: Printed by Eliz. Holt for Thomas Basset.

Loftus, E. 1996. *Eyewitness Testimony*. 2nd ed. Cambridge, MA: Harvard University Press.

Loftus, E. F. 1993. The reality of repressed memories. *American Psychologist* 48 (5): 518–537.

Loftus, E. F. 2005. Planting misinformation in the human mind: A 30-year investigation of the malleability of memory. *Learning & Memory* 12 (4): 361–366.

Lorenzini, C. A., E. Baldi, C. Bucherelli, B. Sacchetti, and G. Tassoni. 1999. Neural topography and chronology of memory consolidation: A review of functional inactivation findings. *Neurobiology of Learning and Memory* 71 (1): 1–18.

Loussouarn, A., D. Gabriel, and J. Proust. 2011. Exploring the informational sources of metaperception: The case of change blindness blindness. *Consciousness and Cognition* 20 (4): 1489–1501.

Maclaurin, J., and H. Dyke. 2002. "Thank goodness that's over": The evolutionary story. *Ratio* 15 (3): 276–292.

Maffie, J. 1990. Naturalism and the normativity of epistemology. *Philosophical Studies* 59 (3): 333–349.

Maguire, E. A., and S. L. Mullally. 2013. The hippocampus: A manifesto for change. *Journal of Experimental Psychology. General* 142 (4): 1180–1189.

Malcolm, N. 1963. *Knowledge and Certainty*. Englewood Cliffs, NJ: Prentice-Hall.

Malcolm, N. 1977. *Memory and Mind*. Ithaca, NY: Cornell University Press.

Mangan, B. 2001. Sensation's ghost: The non-sensory "fringe" of consciousness. *Psyche* 7 (18).

Manning, L., D. Cassel, and J.-C. Cassel. 2013. St. Augustine's reflections on memory and time and the current concept of subjective time in mental time travel. *Behavioral Science* 3 (2): 232–243.

Manns, J. R., and H. Eichenbaum. 2006. Evolution of declarative memory. *Hippocampus* 16 (9): 795–808.

Markowitsch, H. J., and A. Staniloiu. 2011. Memory, autonoetic consciousness, and the self. *Consciousness and Cognition* 20 (1): 16–39.

Markowitsch, H. J., and A. Staniloiu. 2013. The impairment of recollection in functional amnesic states. *Cortex* 49 (6): 1494–1510.

Markowitsch, H. J., and H. Welzer. 2010. *The Development of Autobiographical Memory*. Hove: Psychology Press.

Marr, D. 1982. *Vision*. San Francisco, CA: W.H. Freeman.

Marsh, R. L., J. D. Landau, and J. L. Hicks. 1997. Contributions of inadequate source monitoring to unconscious plagiarism during idea generation. *Journal of Experimental Psychology: Learning, Memory, and Cognition* 23 (4): 886–897.

Martin, C. B., and M. Deutscher. 1966. Remembering. *Philosophical Review* 75: 161–196.

Martin, M. G. F. 2001. Out of the past: Episodic recall as retained acquaintance. In *Time and Memory: Issues in Philosophy and Psychology*, ed. C. Hoerl and T. McCormack, 257–284. Oxford: Oxford University Press.

Martin-Ordas, G., C. M. Atance, and A. Louw. 2012. The role of episodic and semantic memory in episodic foresight. *Learning and Motivation* 43 (4): 209–219.

Martin-Ordas, G., D. Haun, F. Colmenares, and J. Call. 2010. Keeping track of time: evidence for episodic-like memory in great apes. *Animal Cognition* 13 (2): 331–340.

Mascaro, O., and D. Sperber. 2009. The moral, epistemic, and mindreading components of children's vigilance towards deception. *Cognition* 112 (3): 367–380.

Mason, M. F., M. I. Norton, J. D. van Horn, D. M. Wegner, S. T. Grafton, and C. N. Macrae. 2007. Wandering minds: The default network and stimulus-independent thought. *Science* 315 (5810): 393–395.

Matthen, M. 2010. Is memory preservation? *Philosophical Studies* 148 (1): 3–14.

Mazzoni, G., A. Scoboria, and L. Harvey. 2010. Nonbelieved memories. *Psychological Science* 21 (9): 1334–1340.

McClelland, J. L. 1995. Constructive memory and memory distortions: A parallel-distributed processing approach. In *Memory Distortion: How Minds, Brains, and Societies Reconstruct the Past*, ed. D. L. Schacter, 69–90. Cambridge, MA: Harvard University Press.

McClelland, J. L., B. L. McNaughton, and R. C. O'Reilly. 1995. Why there are complementary learning systems in the hippocampus and neocortex: Insights from the successes and failures of connectionist models of learning and memory. *Psychological Review* 102 (3): 419–457.

McCormack, T. 2001. Attributing episodic memory to animals and children. In *Time and Memory: Issues in Philosophy and Psychology*, ed. C. Hoerl and T. McCormack, 285–314. Oxford: Oxford University Press.

McCormack, T., and C. Hoerl. 1999. Memory and temporal perspective: The role of temporal frameworks in memory development. *Developmental Review* 19 (1): 154–182.

McDonald, R. J., B. D. Devan, and N. S. Hong. 2004. Multiple memory systems: The power of interactions. *Neurobiology of Learning and Memory* 82 (3): 333–346.

McDonough, I. M., and D. A. Gallo. 2010. Separating past and future autobiographical events in memory: Evidence for a reality monitoring asymmetry. *Memory & Cognition* 38 (1): 3–12.

McDonough, J. K. 2002. Hume's account of memory. *British Journal for the History of Philosophy* 10 (1): 71–87.

McKay, R. T., and D. C. Dennett. 2009. The evolution of misbelief. *Behavioral and Brain Sciences* 32 (06): 493–510.

Mcnamara, T. P., and V. A. Diwadkar. 1997. Symmetry and asymmetry of human spatial memory. *Cognitive Psychology* 34 (2): 160–190.

McTaggart, J. E. 1908. The unreality of time. *Mind* 17 (68): 457–474.

Meade, M. L., and H. L. Roediger. 2002. Explorations in the social contagion of memory. *Memory & Cognition* 30 (7): 995–1009.

Merleau-Ponty, M. 1945. *Phénoménologie de la perception*. Paris: Librairie Gallimard.

Merritt, D. J., D. Casasanto, and E. M. Brannon. 2010. Do monkeys think in metaphors? Representations of space and time in monkeys and humans. *Cognition* 117 (2): 191–202.

Metcalfe, J., and H. Kober. 2005. Self-reflective consciousness and the projectable self. In *The Missing Link in Cognition: Origins of Self-Reflective Consciousness*, ed. H. S. Terrace and J. Metcalfe, 57–83. Oxford: Oxford University Press.

Michaelian, K. 2008. Testimony as a natural kind. *Episteme* 5 (2): 180–202.

Michaelian, K. 2010. In defence of gullibility: The epistemology of testimony and the psychology of deception detection. *Synthese* 176 (3): 399–427.

Michaelian, K. 2012a. Is external memory memory? Biological memory and extended mind. *Consciousness and Cognition* 21 (3): 1154–1165.

Michaelian, K. 2012b. (Social) metacognition and (self-)trust. *Review of Philosophy and Psychology* 3 (4): 481–514.

Michaelian, K. 2013. The evolution of testimony: Receiver vigilance, speaker honesty, and the reliability of communication. *Episteme* 10 (1): 37–59.

Michaelian, K. 2014. JFGI: From distributed cognition to distributed reliabilism. *Philosophical Issues* 24:313–345.

Michaelian, K., and S. Arango-Muñoz. Forthcoming. Collaborative memory knowledge: A distributed reliabilist perspective. In *Collaborative Remembering: How Remembering with Others Influences Memory*, ed. M. Meade, A. Barnier, P. V. Bergen, C. Harris and J. Sutton. Oxford: Oxford University Press.

Miles, L. K., K. Karpinska, J. Lumsden, and C. N. Macrae. 2010. The meandering mind: Vection and mental time travel. *PLoS One* 5 (5): e10825.

Mill, J. 1869. *Analysis of the Phenomena of the Human Mind.* London: Longmans, Green, Reader and Dyer.

Millikan, R. G. 1984. *Language, Thought, and Other Biological Categories: New Foundations for Realism.* Cambridge, MA: MIT Press.

Mitchell, K. J., and M. K. Johnson. 2000. Source monitoring: Attributing mental experiences. In *Oxford Handbook of Memory*, ed. E. Tulving and F. I. M. Craik, 175–195. Oxford: Oxford University Press.

Mitchell, K. J., and M. K. Johnson. 2009. Source monitoring 15 years later: What have we learned from fMRI about the neural mechanisms of source memory? *Psychological Bulletin* 135 (4): 638–677.

Mithen, S. 2007. Seven steps in the evolution of the human imagination. *Proceedings of the British Academy* 147:3–29.

Moulton, S. T., and S. M. Kosslyn. 2009. Imagining predictions: Mental imagery as mental emulation. *Philosophical Transactions of the Royal Society of London. Series B, Biological Sciences* 364 (1521): 1273–1280.

Moyal-Sharrock, D. 2009. Wittgenstein and the memory debate. *New Ideas in Psychology* 27 (2): 213–227.

Mullally, S. L., H. Intraub, and E. A. Maguire. 2012. Attenuated boundary extension produces a paradoxical memory advantage in amnesic patients. *Current Biology* 22 (4): 261–268.

Mullally, S. L., and E. A. Maguire. 2014. Memory, imagination, and predicting the future: A common brain mechanism? *Neuroscientist* 20 (3): 220–234.

Munsat, S. 1967. *The Concept of Memory.* New York: Random House.

Nairne, J. S. 2013. Fitness-relevance and the temporal orientation of memory. *Journal of Applied Research in Memory and Cognition* 2 (4): 235–236.

Nairne, J. S., and J. N. Pandeirada. 2008. Adaptive memory: Remembering with a stone-age brain. *Current Directions in Psychological Science* 17 (4): 239–243.

Naqshbandi, M., and W. A. Roberts. 2006. Anticipation of future events in squirrel monkeys (*saimiri sciureus*) and rats (*rattus norvegicus*): Tests of the Bischof-Kohler hypothesis. *Journal of Comparative Psychology* 120 (4): 345–357.

Neisser, U. 1981. John Dean's memory: A case study. *Cognition* 9 (1): 1–22.

Nelson, T. O., and L. Narens. 1990. Metamemory: A theoretical framework and new findings. In *The Psychology of Learning and Motivation: Advances in Research and Theory*, vol. 26, ed. G. Bower, 125–173. New York: Academic Press.

Newen, A., and A. Bartels. 2007. Animal minds and the possession of concepts. *Philosophical Psychology* 20 (3): 283–308.

Newman, E. J., and D. S. Lindsay. 2009. False memories: What the hell are they for? *Applied Cognitive Psychology* 23 (8): 1105–1121.

Nichols, S., and S. P. Stich. 2003. *Mindreading: An Integrated Account of Pretence, Self-Awareness, and Understanding Other Minds*. Oxford: Oxford University Press.

Nigro, G., and U. Neisser. 1983. Point of view in personal memories. *Cognitive Psychology* 15 (4): 467–482.

Northoff, G., and J. Panksepp. 2008. The trans-species concept of self and the subcortical-cortical midline system. *Trends in Cognitive Sciences* 12 (7): 259–264.

Noxon, J. 1976. Remembering and imagining the past. In *Hume: A Re-evaluation*, ed. D. W. Livingston and J. T. King, 270–295. New York: Fordham University Press.

Nyberg, L., A. S. N. Kim, R. Habib, B. Levine, and E. Tulving. 2010. Consciousness of subjective time in the brain. *Proceedings of the National Academy of Sciences of the United States of America* 107 (51): 22356–22359.

O'Connor, K. P., and F. Aardema. 2005. The imagination: Cognitive, pre-cognitive, and meta-cognitive aspects. *Consciousness and Cognition* 14 (2): 233–256.

Odling-Smee, F. J., K. N. Laland, and M. W. Feldman. 2003. *Niche Construction: The Neglected Process in Evolution*. Princeton, NJ: Princeton University Press.

Okuda, J., T. Fujii, H. Ohtake, T. Tsukiura, K. Tanji, K. Suzuki, R. Kawashima, H. Fukuda, M. Itoh, and A. Yamadori. 2003. Thinking of the future and past: The roles of the frontal pole and the medial temporal lobes. *NeuroImage* 19 (4): 1369–1380.

Ost, J., and A. Costall. 2002. Misremembering Bartlett: A study in serial reproduction. *British Journal of Psychology* 93 (2): 243–255.

Osvath, M., and P. Gärdenfors. 2005. *Oldowan culture and the evolution of anticipatory cognition. Technical Report LUCS 122*. Lund University Cognitive Science.

Otgaar, H., A. Scoboria, and G. Mazzoni. 2014. On the existence and implications of nonbelieved memories. *Current Directions in Psychological Science* 23 (5): 349–354.

Owens, D. 2002. *Reason without Freedom: The Problem of Epistemic Normativity*. London: Routledge.

Panksepp, J. 1998. *Affective Neuroscience: The Foundations of Human and Animal Emotions*. Oxford: Oxford University Press.

Parfit, D. 1984. *Reasons and Persons*. Oxford: Oxford University Press.

Park, H. S., and T. Levine. 2001. A probability model of accuracy in deception detection experiments. *Communication Monographs* 68 (2): 201–210.

Paxton, R., and R. R. Hampton. 2009. Tests of planning and the Bischof-Köhler hypothesis in rhesus monkeys (*macaca mulatta*). *Behavioural Processes* 80 (3): 238–246.

Payne, D. G., J. S. Neuschatz, J. M. Lampinen, and S. J. Lynn. 1997. Compelling memory illusions: The qualitative characteristics of false memories. *Current Directions in Psychological Science* 6 (3): 56–60.

Pears, D. 1990. *Hume's System: An Examination of the First Book of his Treatise.* Oxford: Oxford University Press.

Perner, J. 1993. *Understanding the Representational Mind.* Cambridge, MA: MIT Press.

Perner, J., and T. Ruffman. 1995. Episodic memory and autonoetic consciousness: Developmental evidence and a theory of childhood amnesia. *Journal of Experimental Child Psychology* 59 (3): 516–548.

Pernu, T. 2009. Is knowledge a natural kind? *Philosophical Studies* 142 (3): 371–386.

Perrin, D. 2011. Une défense de l'approche simulationniste du souvenir épisodique. *Dialogue: Canadian Philosophical Review/Revue canadienne de philosophie* 50 (1), 39–76.

Perrin, D., and S. Rousset. 2014. The episodicity of memory. *Review of Philosophy and Psychology* 5 (3): 291–312.

Perry, J. 1985. Self-knowledge and self-representation. In Proceedings of the 9th International Joint Conference on Artificial Intelligence, vol. 2: 85: 1238–1242.

Perry, J. 2002. *Identity, Personal Identity, and the Self.* Indianapolis, IN: Hackett.

Peters, J., and C. Büchel. 2010. Episodic future thinking reduces reward delay discounting through an enhancement of prefrontal-mediotemporal interactions. *Neuron* 66 (1): 138–148.

Phelps, E. A., and T. Sharot. 2008. How (and why) emotion enhances the subjective sense of recollection. *Current Directions in Psychological Science* 17 (2): 147–152.

Pillemer, D. 2003. Directive functions of autobiographical memory: The guiding power of the specific episode. *Memory* 11 (2): 193–202.

Piolino, P., B. Desgranges, D. Clarys, B. Guillery-Girard, L. Taconnat, M. Isingrini, and F. Eustache. 2006. Autobiographical memory, autonoetic consciousness, and self-perspective in aging. *Psychology and Aging* 21 (3): 510–525.

Plantinga, A. 1993. *Warrant and Proper Function.* Oxford: Oxford University Press.

Plummer, T. 2004. Flaked stones and old bones: Biological and cultural evolution at the dawn of technology. *American Journal of Physical Anthropology* 125 (S39): 118–164.

Poldrack, R. A., J. Clark, E. J. Pare-Blagoev, D. Shohamy, J. C. Moyano, C. Myers, and M. A. Gluck. 2001. Interactive memory systems in the human brain. *Nature* 414 (6863): 546–550.

Poldrack, R. A., and M. G. Packard. 2003. Competition among multiple memory systems: Converging evidence from animal and human brain studies. *Neuropsychologia* 41 (3): 245–251.

Pollock, J. L. 1984. Reliability and justified belief. *Canadian Journal of Philosophy* 14 (1): 103–114.

Pritchard, D. 2005. *Epistemic Luck.* Oxford: Oxford University Press.

Pritchard, D. 2010. Cognitive ability and the extended cognition thesis. *Synthese* 175 (1), 133–151.

Proust, J. 2007. Metacognition and metarepresentation: Is a self-directed theory of mind a precondition for metacognition? *Synthese* 159 (2): 271–295.

Proust, J. 2010. Metacognition. *Philosophy Compass* 5 (11): 989–998.

Proust, J. 2013. *The Philosophy of Metacognition: Mental Agency and Self-Awareness.* Oxford: Oxford University Press.

Quine, W. V. O. 1969. Natural kinds. In *Essays in Honor of Carl G. Hempel*, ed. N. Rescher, 5–23. Springer.

Quine, W. V. O. 1986. Reply to Morton White. In *The Philosophy of W. V. Quine*, ed. L. Hahn and P. Schilpp, 663–665. La Salle, IL: Open Court.

Quine, W. V. O. 1994. Epistemology naturalized. In *Naturalizing Epistemology*, ed. H. Kornblith, 16–32. Cambridge, MA: MIT Press.

Rajaram, S. 1993. Remembering and knowing: Two means of access to the personal past. *Memory & Cognition* 21 (1): 89–102.

Rajaram, S. 2011. Collaboration both hurts and helps memory: A cognitive perspective. *Current Directions in Psychological Science* 20 (2): 76–81.

Rathbone, C. J., M. A. Conway, and C. J. A. Moulin. 2011. Remembering and imagining: The role of the self. *Consciousness and Cognition* 20 (4): 1175–1182.

Rattenborg, N., and D. Martinez-Gonzalez. 2011. A bird-brain view of episodic memory. *Behavioural Brain Research* 222 (1): 236–245.

Reber, R., N. Schwarz, and P. Winkielman. 2004. Processing fluency and aesthetic pleasure: Is beauty in the perceiver's processing experience? *Personality and Social Psychology Review* 8 (4): 364–382.

Reber, R., and C. Unkelbach. 2010. The epistemic status of processing fluency as source for judgments of truth. *Review of Philosophy and Psychology* 1 (4): 563–581.

Recanati, F. 2007. *Perspectival Thought: A Plea for (Moderate) Relativism*. Oxford: Oxford University Press.

Redshaw, J. 2014. Does metarepresentation make human mental time travel unique? *Wiley Interdisciplinary Reviews: Cognitive Science* 5 (5): 519–531.

Regis, M. 2013. *Daydreams and the Function of Fantasy*. Houndmills: Palgrave Macmillan.

Reid, T. 1764. *An Inquiry into the Human Mind*. Dublin: Printed for Alexander Ewing.

Reid, T. 1785. *Essays on the Intellectual Powers of Man*. Edinburgh: Printed for John Bell.

Renoult, L., P. S. Davidson, D. J. Palombo, M. Moscovitch, and B. Levine. 2012. Personal semantics: At the crossroads of semantic and episodic memory. *Trends in Cognitive Sciences* 16 (11): 550–558.

Rhodes, G. 1997. *Superportraits: Caricatures and Recognition*. Hove: Psychology Press.

Rice, H. J. 2010. Seeing where we're at: A review of visual perspective and memory retrieval. In *The Act of Remembering: Toward an Understanding of How We Recall the Past*, ed. J. H. Mace, 228–258. Chichester: Wiley.

Rice, H. J., and D. C. Rubin. 2009. I can see it both ways: First- and third-person visual perspectives at retrieval. *Consciousness and Cognition* 18 (4): 877–890.

Richter, T., S. Schroeder, and B. Wöhrmann. 2009. You don't have to believe everything you read: Background knowledge permits fast and efficient validation of information. *Journal of Personality and Social Psychology* 96 (3): 538.

Ridley, A. M., F. Gabbert, and D. J. La Rooy, eds. 2012. *Suggestibility in Legal Contexts: Psychological Research and Forensic Implications*. Hoboken, NJ: Wiley.

Ristau, C. A. 2013. Cognitive ethology. *Wiley Interdisciplinary Reviews: Cognitive Science* 4 (5): 493–509.

Roberts, W. A. 2007. Mental time travel: Animals anticipate the future. *Current Biology* 17 (11): R418–R420.

Roberts, W. A., and M. C. Feeney. 2009. The comparative study of mental time travel. *Trends in Cognitive Sciences* 13 (6): 271–277.

Robin, F. 2010. Imagery and memory illusions. *Phenomenology and the Cognitive Sciences* 9 (2): 253–262.

Roediger, H. L. 1996. Memory illusions. *Journal of Memory and Language* 35:76–100.

Roediger, H. L., and K. B. McDermott. 1995. Creating false memories: Remembering words not presented in lists. *Journal of Experimental Psychology: Learning, Memory, and Cognition* 21 (4): 803–814.

Roediger, H. L., M. L. Meade, and E. T. Bergman. 2001. Social contagion of memory. *Psychonomic Bulletin & Review* 8 (2): 365–371.

Roediger, H. L., and D. G. Payne. 1982. Hypermnesia: The role of repeated testing. *Journal of Experimental Psychology: Learning, Memory, and Cognition* 8 (1): 66–72.

Romero, K., and M. Moscovitch. 2012. Episodic memory and event construction in aging and amnesia. *Journal of Memory and Language* 67 (2): 270–284.

Rosen, D. A. 1975. An argument for the logical notion of a memory trace. *Philosophy of Science* 42 (1): 1–10.

Rosenbaum, R. S., S. Köhler, D. L. Schacter, M. Moscovitch, R. Westmacott, S. E. Black, F. Gao, and E. Tulving. 2005. The case of KC: Contributions of a memory-impaired person to memory theory. *Neuropsychologia* 43 (7): 989–1021.

Rowlands, M. 2009. Memory. In *Routledge Companion to Philosophy of Psychology*, ed. P. Calvo and J. Symons, 336–345. London: Routledge.

Rubin, D. C. 1999. *Remembering Our Past: Studies in Autobiographical Memory*. Cambridge: Cambridge University Press.

Russell, B. 1912. *The Problems of Philosophy*. New York: H. Holt and Co.

Russell, B. 1921. *The Analysis of Mind*. London: George Allen & Unwin.

Russell, B. 1948. *Human Knowledge: Its Scope and Limits*. London: Allen & Unwin.

Russell, J., D. Alexis, and N. Clayton. 2010. Episodic future thinking in 3- to 5-year-old children: The ability to think of what will be needed from a different point of view. *Cognition* 114 (1): 56–71.

Ryle, G. 1949. *The Concept of Mind*. Chicago: University Press.

Sara, S. J. 2000. Retrieval and reconsolidation: Toward a neurobiology of remembering. *Learning & Memory* 7 (2): 73–84.

Saunders, J. 2009. Memory impairment in the weapon focus effect. *Memory & Cognition* 37 (3): 326–335.

Savage-Rumbaugh, E. S. 1994. Hominid evolution: Looking to modern apes for clues. In *Hominid Culture in Primate Perspective*, ed. D. Quiatt and J. Itani, 7–49. Niwot, CO: University Press of Colorado.

Schacter, D. L. 1995. Memory distortion: History and current status. In *Memory Distortion: How Minds, Brains, and Societies Reconstruct the Past*, ed. D. L. Schacter, 1–43. Cambridge, MA: Harvard University Press.

Schacter, D. L. 1996. *Searching for Memory: The Brain, the Mind, and the Past*. New York: Basic Books.

Schacter, D. L. 2012. Adaptive constructive processes and the future of memory. *American Psychologist* 67 (8): 603.

Schacter, D. L. 2013. Memory: Sins and virtues. *Annals of the New York Academy of Sciences* 1303 (1): 56–60.

Schacter, D. L., and D. R. Addis. 2007a. The cognitive neuroscience of constructive memory: Remembering the past and imagining the future. *Philosophical Transactions of the Royal Society of London. Series B, Biological Sciences* 362 (1481): 773–786.

Schacter, D. L., and D. R. Addis. 2007b. Constructive memory: The ghosts of past and future. *Nature* 445 (7123): 27.

Schacter, D. L., D. R. Addis, and R. L. Buckner. 2007. Remembering the past to imagine the future: The prospective brain. *Nature Reviews. Neuroscience* 8 (9): 657–661.

Schacter, D. L., D. R. Addis, and R. L. Buckner. 2008. Episodic simulation of future events: Concepts, data, and applications. *Annals of the New York Academy of Sciences* 1124 (1): 39–60.

Schacter, D. L., D. R. Addis, D. Hassabis, V. C. Martin, R. N. Spreng, and K. K. Szpunar. 2012. The future of memory: Remembering, imagining, and the brain. *Neuron* 76 (4): 677–694.

Schacter, D. L., R. G. Benoit, F. De Brigard, and K. K. Szpunar. 2015. Episodic future thinking and episodic counterfactual thinking: Intersections between memory and decisions. *Neurobiology of Learning and Memory* 117 (0): 14–21.

Schacter, D. L., and R. L. Buckner. 1998. Priming and the brain. *Neuron* 20 (2): 185–195.

Schacter, D. L., S. A. Guerin, and P. L. St Jacques. 2011. Memory distortion: An adaptive perspective. *Trends in Cognitive Sciences* 15 (10): 467–474.

Schacter, D. L., K. A. Norman, and W. Koutstaal. 1998. The cognitive neuroscience of constructive memory. *Annual Review of Psychology* 49 (1): 289–318.

Schacter, D. L., and E. Tulving. 1994. What are the memory systems of 1994? In *Memory Systems*, ed. D. L. Schacter and E. Tulving, 1–38. Cambridge, MA: MIT Press.

Schacter, D. L., A. D. Wagner, and R. L. Buckner. 2000. Memory systems of 1999. In *Oxford Handbook of Memory*, ed. E. Tulving and F. Craik, 627–643. Oxford: Oxford University Press.

Schank, R. C. 1999. *Dynamic Memory Revisited*. Cambridge: Cambridge University Press.

Schellenberg, S. 2013. Belief and desire in imagination and immersion. *Journal of Philosophy* 110 (9): 497–517.

Schwartz, B. L., M. L. Howe, M. P. Toglia, and H. Otgaar, eds. 2014. *What is Adaptive about Adaptive Memory?* Oxford: Oxford University Press.

Searcy, W., and S. Nowicki. 2005. *The Evolution of Animal Communication: Reliability and Deception in Signalling Systems.* Princeton, NJ: Princeton University Press.

Searle, J. R. 1983. *Intentionality: An Essay in the Philosophy of Mind.* Cambridge: Cambridge University Press.

Sedikides, C., and M. J. Strube. 1997. Self-evaluation: To thine own self be good, to thine own self be sure, to thine own self be true, and to thine own self be better. *Advances in Experimental Social Psychology* 29:209–269.

Sellers, P. D., II, and B. L. Schwartz. 2013. Episodic-like animals, functional faces, and a defense of accuracy. *Journal of Applied Research in Memory and Cognition* 2 (4): 243–245.

Senor, T. D. 2007. Preserving preservationism: A reply to Lackey. *Philosophy and Phenomenological Research* 74 (1): 199–208.

Senor, T. D. 2013. Epistemological problems of memory. In E. N. Zalta (ed.), *The Stanford Encyclopedia of Philosophy* (Fall 2013 ed.). http://plato.stanford.edu/archives/fall2013/entries/memory-_episprob/.

Serota, K. B., T. R. Levine, and F. J. Boster. 2010. The prevalence of lying in America: Three studies of self-reported lies. *Human Communication Research* 36 (1): 2–25.

Shanton, K. 2011. Memory, knowledge, and epistemic competence. *Review of Philosophy and Psychology* 2 (1): 89–104.

Shanton, K. 2012. A simulation theory of episodic memory. Unpublished manuscript.

Shanton, K., and A. Goldman. 2010. Simulation theory. *WIREs Cognitive Science* 1 (4): 527–538.

Sharot, T., M. R. Delgado, and E. A. Phelps. 2004. How emotion enhances the feeling of remembering. *Nature Neuroscience* 7 (12): 1376–1380.

Sharot, T., M. Verfaellie, and A. P. Yonelinas. 2007. How emotion strengthens the recollective experience: A time-dependent hippocampal process. *PLoS One* 2 (10): e1068.

Sherry, D. F., and D. L. Schacter. 1987. The evolution of multiple memory systems. *Psychological Review* 94 (4): 439.

Shoemaker, S. S. 1959. Personal identity and memory. *Journal of Philosophy* 56 (22): 868–882.

Siegel, H. 1996. Naturalism and the abandonment of normativity. In *The Philosophy of Psychology*, ed. W. O'Donohue and R. F. Kitchener, 4–18. London: Sage.

Simeon, D., and J. Abugel. 2006. *Feeling Unreal: Depersonalization Disorder and the Loss of the Self*. Oxford: Oxford University Press.

Sinhababu, N. 2013. Distinguishing belief and imagination. *Pacific Philosophical Quarterly* 94 (2): 152–165.

Skowronski, J. J., and C. Sedikides. 2007. Temporal knowledge and autobiographical memory: An evolutionary perspective. In *Oxford Handbook of Evolutionary Psychology*, ed. R. Dunbar and L. Barrett, 505–517. Oxford: Oxford University Press.

Smallwood, J., L. Nind, and R. C. O'Connor. 2009. When is your head at? An exploration of the factors associated with the temporal focus of the wandering mind. *Consciousness and Cognition* 18 (1): 118–125.

Smallwood, J., and J. W. Schooler. 2006. The restless mind. *Psychological Bulletin* 132 (6): 946–958.

Smallwood, J., and J. W. Schooler. 2015. The science of mind wandering: Empirically navigating the stream of consciousness. *Annual Review of Psychology* 66 (1): 487–518.

Smolensky, P. 1988. On the proper treatment of connectionism. *Behavioral and Brain Sciences* 11 (1): 1–74.

Sosa, E. 2007. *A Virtue Epistemology*. Vol. I. Apt Belief and Reflective Knowledge. Oxford: Oxford University Press.

Sperber, D. 2013. Speakers are honest because hearers are vigilant: Reply to Kourken Michaelian. *Episteme* 10:61–71.

Sperber, D., F. Clément, C. Heintz, O. Mascaro, H. Mercier, G. Origgi, and D. Wilson. 2010. Epistemic vigilance. *Mind & Language* 25 (4): 359–393.

Sperber, D., and D. Wilson. 1995. *Relevance: Communication and Cognition*. Oxford: Blackwell.

Spiers, H. J., and E. A. Maguire. 2006. Thoughts, behaviour, and brain dynamics during navigation in the real world. *NeuroImage* 31 (4): 1826–1840.

Spreng, R. N., and B. Levine. 2006. The temporal distribution of past and future autobiographical events across the lifespan. *Memory & Cognition* 34 (8): 1644–1651.

Squire, L. R. 2004. Memory systems of the brain: A brief history and current perspective. *Neurobiology of Learning and Memory* 82 (3): 171–177.

Squire, L. R. 2009. Memory and brain systems: 1969–2009. *Journal of Neuroscience* 29 (41): 12711–12716.

Squires, R. 1969. Memory unchained. *Philosophical Review* 78 (2): 178–196.

Statman, D. 1991. Moral and epistemic luck. *Ratio* 4 (2): 146–156.

Stern, D. G. 1991. Models of memory: Wittgenstein and cognitive science. *Philosophical Psychology* 4 (2): 203–218.

Stocker, K. 2012. The time machine in our mind. *Cognitive Science* 36 (3): 385–420.

Stone, C. B., A. J. Barnier, J. Sutton, and W. Hirst. 2009. Building consensus about the past: Schema consistency and convergence in socially shared retrieval-induced forgetting. *Memory* 18 (2): 170–184.

Suddendorf, T. 2010. Episodic memory versus episodic foresight: Similarities and differences. *Wiley Interdisciplinary Reviews: Cognitive Science* 1 (1): 99–107.

Suddendorf, T., and M. C. Corballis. 1997. Mental time travel and the evolution of the human mind. *Genetic, Social, and General Psychology Monographs* 123 (2): 133–167.

Suddendorf, T., and M. C. Corballis. 2007. The evolution of foresight: What is mental time travel, and is it unique to humans? *Behavioral and Brain Sciences* 30 (3): 299–312.

Sutton, J. 1998. *Philosophy and Memory Traces: Descartes to Connectionism*. Cambridge: Cambridge University Press.

Sutton, J. 2010. Observer perspective and acentred memory: Some puzzles about point of view in personal memory. *Philosophical Studies* 148 (1): 27–37.

Sutton, J. 2012. Memory. In E. N. Zalta (ed.), *Stanford Encyclopedia of Philosophy* (Winter 2012 ed.). http://plato.stanford.edu/archives/win2012/entries/memory/.

Sutton, R. S., and A. G. Barto. 1998. *Reinforcement Learning*. MIT Press.

Szabó Gendler, T. 2010. *Intuition, Imagination, and Philosophical Methodology*. Oxford: Oxford University Press.

Szpunar, K., and E. Tulving. 2011. Varieties of future experience. In *Predictions in the Brain: Using our Past to Generate a Future*, ed. M. Bar, 3–12. Oxford: Oxford University Press.

Szpunar, K. K. 2010. Episodic future thought: An emerging concept. *Perspectives on Psychological Science* 5 (2): 142–162.

Szpunar, K. K. 2011. On subjective time. *Cortex* 47 (3): 409–411.

Szpunar, K. K., and H. G. Jing. 2013. Memory-mediated simulations of the future: What are the advantages and pitfalls? *Journal of Applied Research in Memory and Cognition* 2 (4): 240–242.

Szpunar, K. K., and K. B. McDermott. 2008. Episodic future thought: Remembering the past to imagine the future. In *Handbook of Imagination and Mental Simulation*, ed. K. D. Markman, W. M. P. Klein, and J. A. Suhr, 119–129. New York: Psychology Press.

Szpunar, K. K., R. N. Spreng, and D. L. Schacter. 2014. A taxonomy of prospection: Introducing an organizational framework for future-oriented cognition. *Proceedings of the National Academy of Sciences of the United States of America* 111 (52): 18414–18421.

Szpunar, K. K., J. M. Watson, and K. B. McDermott. 2007. Neural substrates of envisioning the future. *Proceedings of the National Academy of Sciences of the United States of America* 104 (2): 642–647.

Templer, V. L., and R. R. Hampton. 2013. Episodic memory in nonhuman animals. *Current Biology* 23 (17): R801–R806.

Thompson, V. A. 2009. Dual process theories: A metacognitive perspective. In *In Two Minds: Dual Processes and Beyond*, ed. J. S. B. T. Evans and K. Frankish, 171–195. Oxford University Press.

Thompson, V. A., J. A. Turner, G. Pennycook, L. J. Ball, H. Brack, Y. Ophir, and R. Ackerman. 2013. The role of answer fluency and perceptual fluency as metacognitive cues for initiating analytic thinking. *Cognition* 128 (2): 237–251.

Traiger, S. 1985. Flage on Hume's account of memory. *Human Studies* 11 (2): 166–172.

Trope, Y., and N. Liberman. 2003. Temporal construal. *Psychological Review* 110 (3): 403–421.

Tulving, E. 1972. Episodic and semantic memory. In *Organization of Memory*, ed. E. Tulving and W. Donaldson, 381–402. New York: Academic Press.

Tulving, E. 1983. *Elements of Episodic Memory*. Oxford: Clarendon Press.

Tulving, E. 1984a. Multiple learning and memory systems. In *Psychology in the 1990s*, ed. K. M. J. Lagerspetz and P. Niemi, 163–184. Amsterdam: Elsevier.

Tulving, E. 1984b. Relations among components and processes of memory. *Behavioral and Brain Sciences* 7:257–268.

Tulving, E. 1985. Memory and consciousness. *Canadian Psychology* 26 (1): 1–12.

Tulving, E. 1999. On the uniqueness of episodic memory. In *Cognitive Neuroscience of Memory*, ed. L.-G. Nilsson and H. J. Markowitsch, 11–42. Seattle: Hogrefe & Huber Publishers.

Tulving, E. 2000. Concepts of memory. In *Oxford Handbook of Memory*, ed. E. Tulving and F. I. M. Craik, 33–43. Oxford: Oxford University Press.

Tulving, E. 2001. Origin of autonoesis in episodic memory. In *The Nature of Remembering: Essays in Honor of Robert G. Crowder*, ed. H. L. Roediger, III, J. S. Nairne, I. Neath and A. M. Surprenant, 17–34. Washington, DC: American Psychological Association.

Tulving, E. 2002a. Chronesthesia: Conscious awareness of subjective time. In *Principles of Frontal Lobe Function*, ed. R. T. Knight, 311–325. Oxford: Oxford University Press.

Tulving, E. 2002b. Episodic memory: From mind to brain. *Annual Review of Psychology* 53 (1): 1–25.

Tulving, E. 2005. Episodic memory and autonoesis: Uniquely human? In *The Missing Link in Cognition: Origins of Self-reflective Consciousness*, ed. H. S. Terrace and J. Metcalfe, 3–56. Oxford: Oxford University Press.

Tulving, E. 2007. Are there 256 different kinds of memory? In *The Foundations of Remembering: Essays in Honor of Henry L. Roediger, III*, ed. J. S. Nairne, 39–52. New York: Psychology Press.

Tulving, E., and H. J. Markowitsch. 1998. Episodic and declarative memory: Role of the hippocampus. *Hippocampus* 8 (3): 198–204.

Tversky, A., and D. Kahneman. 1971. Belief in the law of small numbers. *Psychological Bulletin* 76 (2): 105.

Unkelbach, C. 2007. Reversing the truth effect: Learning the interpretation of processing fluency in judgments of truth. *Journal of Experimental Psychology: Learning, Memory, and Cognition* 33 (1): 219–230.

Urmson, J. O. 1967. Memory and imagination. *Mind* 76 (301): 83–91.

Vaesen, K. 2011. Knowledge without credit, exhibit 4: Extended cognition. *Synthese* 181 (3): 515–529.

Van Boven, L., and L. Ashworth. 2007. Looking forward, looking back: Anticipation is more evocative than retrospection. *Journal of Experimental Psychology. General* 136 (2): 289–300.

Van Boven, L., J. Kane, and A. P. McGraw. 2008. Temporally asymmetric constraints on mental simulation: Retrospection is more constrained than prospection. In *Handbook of Imagination and Mental Simulation*, ed. K. D. Markman, W. M. P. Klein and J. A. Suhr, 131–147. New York: Psychology Press.

Van Hoeck, N., N. Ma, L. Ampe, K. Baetens, M. Vandekerckhove, and F. van Overwalle. 2013. Counterfactual thinking: An fMRI study on changing the past for a better future. *Social Cognitive and Affective Neuroscience* 8 (5): 556–564.

Van Hoeck, N., N. Ma, F. Van Overwalle, and M. Vandekerckhove. 2010. Counterfactual thinking and the episodic system. *Behavioural Neurology* 23 (4): 225–227.

Vandekerckhove, M. 2009. Memory, autonoetic consciousness and the self: Consciousness as a continuum of stages. *Self and Identity* 8 (1): 4–23.

Vandekerckhove, M., and J. Panksepp. 2009. The flow of anoetic to noetic and autonoetic consciousness: A vision of unknowing (anoetic) and knowing (noetic) consciousness in the remembrance of things past and imagined futures. *Consciousness and Cognition* 18 (4): 1018–1028.

Vandekerckhove, M., and J. Panksepp. 2011. A neurocognitive theory of higher mental emergence: From anoetic affective experiences to noetic knowledge and autonoetic awareness. *Neuroscience and Biobehavioral Reviews* 35 (9): 2017–2025.

Verschuere, B., A. Spruyt, E. H. Meijer, and H. Otgaar. 2011. The ease of lying. *Consciousness and Cognition* 20 (3): 908–911.

Vetter, P., and A. Newen. 2014. Varieties of cognitive penetration in visual perception. *Consciousness and Cognition* 27 (0): 62–75.

Von Leyden, W. 1961. *Remembering: A Philosophical Problem*. London: Duckworth.

Vrij, A. 2008. *Detecting Lies and Deceit: Pitfalls and Opportunities*. 2nd ed. Hoboken, NJ: Wiley.

Weiskrantz, L. 1990. Problems of learning and memory: One or multiple memory systems? *Philosophical Transactions of the Royal Society of London. Series B, Biological Sciences* 329 (1253): 99–108.

Wheeler, M. A., D. T. Stuss, and E. Tulving. 1997. Toward a theory of episodic memory: The frontal lobes and autonoetic consciousness. *Psychological Bulletin* 121 (3): 331.

Wilkins, J. S. 2011. Philosophically speaking, how many species concepts are there? *Zootaxa* 2765:58–60.

Williamson, T., and J. Stanley. 2001. Knowing how. *Journal of Philosophy* 98:411–444.

Wirling, Y. 2014. Imagining oneself being someone else: The role of the self in the shoes of another. *Journal of Consciousness Studies* 21 (9–10): 205–225.

Wittgenstein, L. 2005. *Philosophical Grammar*. Berkeley, CA: University of California Press.

Zagzebski, L. 1994. The inescapability of Gettier problems. *Philosophical Quarterly* 44 (174): 65–73.

Zaragoza, M. S., and S. M. Lane. 1994. Source misattributions and the suggestibility of eyewitness memory. *Journal of Experimental Psychology: Learning, Memory, and Cognition* 20 (4): 934–945.

Zaragoza, M. S., and K. J. Mitchell. 1996. Repeated exposure to suggestion and the creation of false memories. *Psychological Science* 7 (5): 294–300.

Zemach, E. M. 1968. A definition of memory. *Mind* 77 (308): 526–536.

Zemach, E. M. 1983. Memory: What it is, and what it cannot possibly be. *Philosophy and Phenomenological Research* 44 (1): 31–44.

Zentall, T. R. 2006. Mental time travel in animals: A challenging question. *Behavioural Processes* 72 (2): 173–183.

Index